Surfing
California

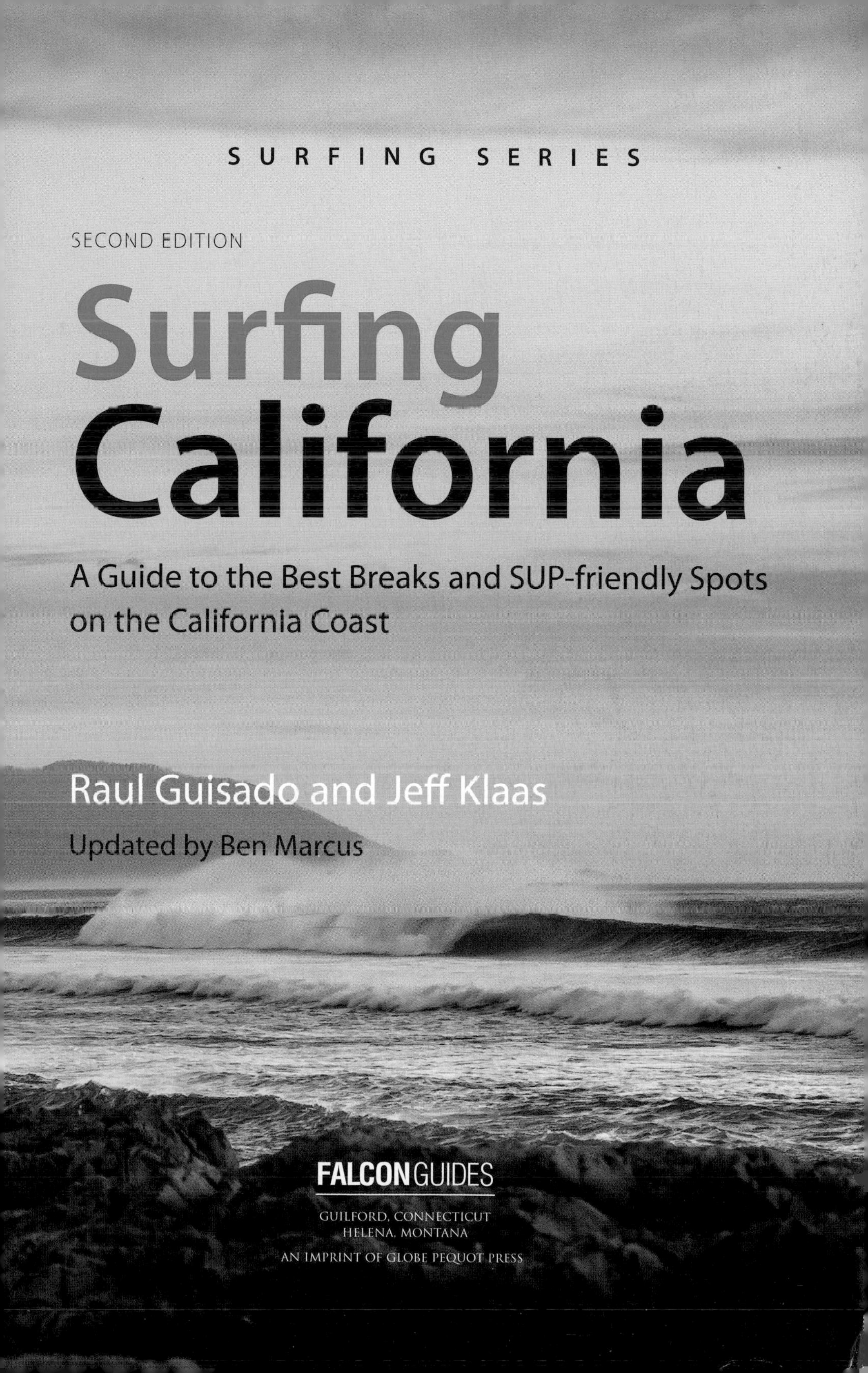

SURFING SERIES

SECOND EDITION

Surfing
California

A Guide to the Best Breaks and SUP-friendly Spots
on the California Coast

Raul Guisado and Jeff Klaas

Updated by Ben Marcus

FALCONGUIDES

GUILFORD, CONNECTICUT
HELENA, MONTANA
AN IMPRINT OF GLOBE PEQUOT PRESS

FALCONGUIDES®

Text design: Sheryl Kober
Page layout: Casey Shain
Maps by Melissa Baker © Morris Book Publishing, LLC

Library of Congress Cataloging-in-Publication Data is available on file.

ISBN 978-0-7627-8164-5

Printed in the United States of America
10 9 8 7 6 5 4 3 2 1

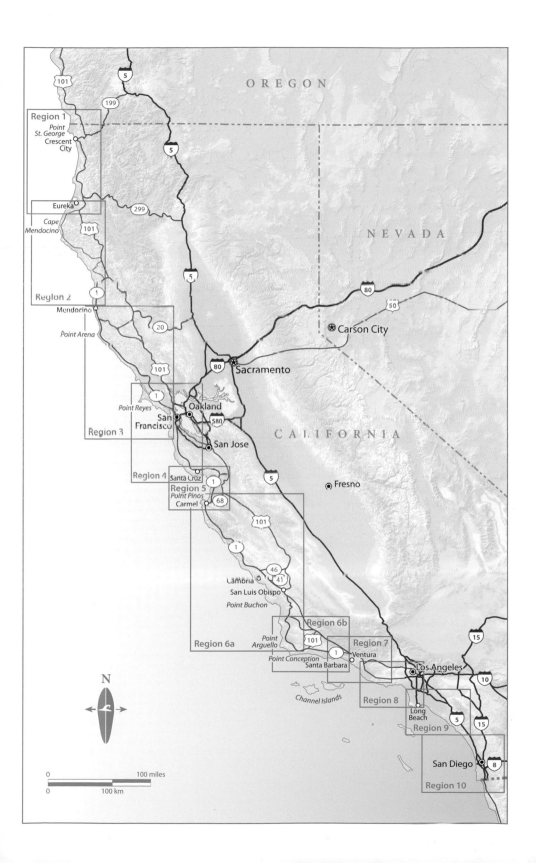

Contents

Introduction

Our goal in writing this book is to provide surfers with an accurate and helpful travel guide to the numerous breaks on the coast of California. Although the sport has become extremely popular on the West Coast, you don't need to take a two-week vacation, spend your life's savings, and travel thousands of miles to find good surf with no one around. There are still isolated spots that rarely get surfed right here in beautiful California. The perception is that the Golden State's coast is overdeveloped and overpopulated, with few worthwhile surf spots that aren't filled with people. To the contrary: California is a huge state with an abundance of pristine coastline. Once you get away from the major coastal cities, there are quality, empty breaks just waiting to be explored and enjoyed.

The History of Surfing in California

Surfing is a magical sport dating back to before AD 1500, when it's believed that royalty in the Sandwich Isles surfed on wooden boards as long as 18 feet and weighing as much as 150 pounds. In 1778 Captain Cook reported finding Hawaiian natives surfing. In the 1800s, however, the white settlers of Hawaii considered surfing heathen; the sport was nearly extinct by the end of the century. From 1903 to 1908 the Waikiki area of Oahu was the center of surfing for the few still enjoying the sport, and the revival of surfing began during this time.

The sport arrived in California in 1907. Surfer George Freeth, of Hawaiian and Irish heritage, was brought from Waikiki to Redondo Beach to surf as a publicity stunt promoting the opening of the Redondo–Los Angeles railroad. Freeth stayed in California where he used his water skills to lay down the foundation for the LA lifeguard services and is credited with teaching the first Californians to ride waves.

In 1915 Duke Kahanamoku gave a surfing exhibition while in Australia for a swimming competition. He also impressed spectators in California, New York, and New Jersey. Duke went on to make movies in Hollywood and is considered the father of modern surfing.

In the 1920s surfing became very popular in Southern California in part due to the lighter boards produced by Tom Blake. In 1935 Blake put a small fin on the rear of a surfboard, making it more maneuverable. And in 1946 Preston "Pete" Peterson built a fiberglass-and-foam surfboard.

In the 1950s board manufacturing became completely commercialized and surfing morphed from a pastime to a multimillion-dollar industry. In 1952 Jack O'Neill sold the first wet suit in Northern California, prolonging surf sessions at cold-water

California dream days. Two local blokes, who apparently have had enough of a good thing, turn their backs and walk casually away from firing, October Santa Ana southern hemi barrels on the south side of Huntington Pier.   Chris Sardelis

breaks considerably. And in 1953 Southern Californians Dave Velzy and Hap Jacobs began making the only commercially available balsa boards.

Hobie Alter and Gordon Clark created the first foam surfboard blanks in 1958. These blanks were easily shaped and accelerated surfboard design into the 1960s. In that decade surf movies flourished, as did surfing. California was considered the sport's capital, and boards were being made smaller and lighter.

The years from the 1970s until now have seen numerous innovations in surfing equipment, style, and competitions. The sport that originated and was enjoyed more than 500 years ago by Polynesian royalty has now become established, with surfers found all over the globe. And California is recognized for having some of the best and most consistent breaks anywhere on earth.

How Waves Are Formed

Unsurprisingly, the most common source of waves is wind action in the open ocean. Earthquakes and volcanic eruptions beneath the ocean can cause seismic sea waves, but these are rare occurrences. Storms in the open ocean, on the other hand, are quite common, and they result in variations in air pressure to force gusty winds upon the ocean's surface. If the wind is strong and steady enough, it will form chop over a large area, which is referred to as a "sea." As these wind waves are blown downwind, they become longer, smoother, and more organized, taking the form of what is known as a "swell." A swell is what we recognize as the marching lines of energy that travel across the open ocean. Swells can travel for thousands of miles without losing much energy at all until they hit the shallow water on our shores to form a breaking wave.

California's surf is a result of north, northwest, west, southwest, south, and wind swells. North and northwest swells are produced by storms in the North Pacific in the winter months and are the largest and most powerful. West swells are created by storms in the West Pacific and are most common in fall and spring. South and southwest swells are generated by storms in the South Pacific in our summer months and can also result in strong and good-size waves.

Wind swell is a term used to refer to less consistent and usually smaller waves that are produced by storms or strong winds within a couple of hundred miles of our coast. Waves generated by the wind may range in height from less than an inch to as much as 60 feet. The size of ocean waves is determined by wind velocity, the size of the area affected by the wind, and the length of time the wind blows. Big surf is made by large, long-lasting storms with strong winds far out at sea. Surf forecasters today can precisely determine when large waves will hit a particular spot on the coast by using weather data and computer models.

Wave Parts

The highest part of a wave is called the crest or peak. The lowest part is called the trough or pit. The front of the wave is called the face, while the back is generally referred to as simply the back. The "curl" is the part of the wave that's breaking. The "lip" is a term used to describe the very tip of a cresting wave that curls or plunges down. The "wall" is a general term used to refer to the area of the face that has yet to break. A "section" is a portion or an area of a wave. The "pocket" is the section of the wall just ahead of the curl; it's usually the steepest part of the wave and the most desirable place to surf. The "shoulder," or "flats," is the less steep section of the wave face away from the breaking part.

Wave Measurement

Some folks measure waves from the face of the wave, while others, especially in Hawaii, measure from the back. Waves are dynamic and change in width, height, and shape as they approach shore. To complicate things further, wave size differs depending on the angle of the observer.

Regardless of your choice of measurement while in the water, it's important to understand how it's done in surf predictions. Satellites, ocean buoys, vessel reports, and meteorological data have become very accurate at predicting surf. These surf reports usually describe what direction the swell is traveling, the time interval between waves, and the wave height. Wave height is determined by measuring the vertical distance between the crest and trough. Wavelength is the distance between two successive wave crests.

Wave Shape

Wave shape can vary drastically from day to day at the same spot. Swell size, speed, and direction; tides; currents; curve and shape of the shore; and kelp and wind conditions affect shape. Every surf spot has a unique set of variables that affect wave shape.

Areas with long, gradual rises from deep to shallow water usually result in what's known as a peeling wave. A peeling wave breaks easily down the face or front side of the wave, spilling or toppling over. It appears to crumble or peel along its length and is generally the most forgiving type of wave.

Breaks with a more abrupt change from deep to shallow water usually result in what's called a tubing wave. A tubing wave breaks from top to bottom as the swell peaks more quickly and pitches the crest down the wave face. This type of wave creates a hollow tube or barrel section. The term hollow is used to describe this concave and steep wave-face shape. The term "sucky" is also used to describe wave conditions that are hollow and breaking in shallow water. And when waves break all at once along their entire face, they are referred to as closed out.

Tides

Tides are related to the moon's cycles and occur in all bodies of water, but they're most prominent along the coast. In most places the tide rises and falls twice a day. The maximum and minimum levels of the rise and fall are called high and low tide, respectively. It takes roughly 6 hours for rising water to reach high tide and approximately another 6 to reach low tide again. This sequence is called the tidal cycle and is repeated every 12 hours, 25 minutes. The amount of change in the water level during the cycle is known as the tidal range. During the first and last quarter of the moon's cycle, called a neap tide, there is minimal difference between high and low tides. When there's a full or new moon cycle, known as a spring tide, there's a bigger difference between high and low tides.

Most surf shops provide a book listing the times that high and low tide will occur each day for the entire year. This can help you plan your surfing sessions, as changes in water depth at the points where waves break can significantly alter the shape of the wave. For example, if the tide is too high and a significant swell isn't on the way, the waves are likely to be small and have little power. When the tide is too low, on the other hand, waves may close out with a large swell. A spot that has a lot of kelp might also be difficult to surf at lower tides, because less water results in the kelp being thicker at the surface.

Wind Conditions

The direction the wind is blowing can greatly affect wave shape. In the morning or evening, there tends to be little or no wind, and the surf is more likely to be glassy. This refers to the incredibly smooth appearance of the water.

An onshore wind is one that blows from the ocean and is usually the least favorable direction. Strong onshore winds often result in blown-out surf—waves that have been made bumpy or flattened by the wind. This type of surf is also referred to as mush.

A side-shore wind blows across the swell. Although it's better than an onshore wind, it can also lead to deteriorating conditions.

An offshore wind blows from the shore into the surf and can enhance wave shape. An offshore wind helps hold up the incoming waves, giving them cleaner faces to ride.

Types of Breaks

Surf spots are also called breaks, referring to an area where surfable waves form. Wave energy will break differently depending on the tide, the swell direction, and—just as important—the characteristics of the shore bottom.

Beach breaks are areas where waves are breaking very close to shore. Often such breaks are very steep and hollow and are difficult to surf.

Sand breaks are areas where waves break over a sandbar. These breaks can be altered, because sand shifts and can look very different from time to time. Sand breaks are usually found relatively close to shore.

Reef breaks are areas where waves break over a coral or rocky reef. Coral reef breaks tend to occur in shallow water and can create some of the most spectacular barrels in the world. The majority of the famous island breaks in the world are coral reef breaks. California's rock reef breaks can also be incredible.

Point breaks are areas where waves break at a part of the shore that extends outward. These breaks tend to be larger and more consistent than other breaks because they're the first areas of shallow water that the swell hits. Often a swell will wrap around a point.

Outside breaks are areas of somewhat shallow water where waves break farther from shore. These breaks can create some of the largest and most powerful waves. Because the water is deeper than inside breaks, outside breaks usually require a deeper groundswell for waves to form.

"Lefts" are waves that break from the peak to the surfer's left. "Rights" are waves that break from the peak to the surfer's right.

The 10 Commandments of SUP Etiquette

Since the time this surf guide was first published in 2005, the California coast has been witness to a sharp rise in the use of standup paddleboards—also known as SUP. To many surfers, the emergence of standup paddleboarding has been alarming as beginner and experienced SUPistas have further complicated the already complex equation of etiquette in crowded lineups.

At worst, a beginning SUP surfer can be like a bull in a china shop. Where beginning surfers are usually timid and stay off to the side and out of trouble, beginning standup paddlers will often wobble into the middle of an already grumpy pack. The line of sight from standing on a SUP, combined with the paddling speed, gives even a beginning standup paddler a huge advantage over traditional paddlers. A beginning standup paddler riding waves can be very dangerous, as the boards are big, thick, and heavy, like rolling logs when loose on a wave.

Beginning SUP riders often don't know the etiquette of surfing and will shatter the vibe of a lineup by taking too many waves, dropping in on other surfers, or wiping out and taking out nearby surfers.

Beginners are dangerous, but there are also SUP riders who use standup paddleboards unfairly, as a tool for domination. A SUP under the wrong feet is also an undefeatable tool for catching waves. Being a wave hog on a SUP is the easiest thing in the world, and there are standup paddlers out there who aren't afraid to use their advantage to snag every wave in sight—and that has been causing unrest.

The California coast offers a wide variety of opportunities for people to have a lot of fun on a standup paddleboard, not just in the surf zone, but also lakes, harbors, rivers, and other waterways. Any body of water is fair game to a SUP, and SUP can make even the most mundane body of water a lot more fun.

This surf guide has been updated to include SUP opportunities from Oregon to Mexico—places that a lot of standup paddlers have been wanting to check off their "SUPit lists." So while this book encourages standup paddlers to get out there and stroke their way to fun, it also implores them to behave themselves when they are in the surf zone.

By following the commandments described below, a standup paddler can help everyone get along in the surf, and not add to the continued chaos as this new species of surfer enters already crowded lineups.

1. Use SUP to find waves to yourself. Standup paddleboards can turn a crummy, 2-foot day into the challenge of a lifetime. Just about any wave is fun on a SUP, so try to find waves that have been discarded or overlooked by other surfers. Use the SUP to stay away from other surfers, and everyone will be happy.

2. Paddling into a crowded lineup on a SUP can be intimidating: People either look away in fear or give you stinkeye. To them, you are a threat to their fun. Instead, share a wave and make a friend. If you are in a crowded lineup, you can make yourself more welcome by using your SUP advantages to help others get waves. You can see what's coming better than traditional surfers, so tell surfers that sets are coming, where waves are shifting. Help surfers get better waves, and they will love you.

3. Don't be a wave hog. On a paddleboard it's easy to catch any wave you want, but resist the temptation to grab every wave you can. Your advantage over other surfers is complete, so be kind: Don't take the first wave of a set. Don't take two waves in the same set. Use the SUP to catch inside waves. Sit outside, wait for a set to clear out the crowd, and then go.

4. You are responsible for everyone inside of you. When taking off on a SUP, you can usually see everything that is going on between you and the beach. You need to be situationally aware of people paddling out, potential drop-ins—everything. Even if you know what you're doing, if someone else does something stupid in front of you, you both are going to pay. And because you are a SUP rider, you will be blamed. When in doubt, don't go.

5. Never, ever drop in on another surfer while riding a SUP. This is the worst offense. You have a huge advantage over other surfers, so be wise with it. Wait your turn. Let others go, then take the waves they can't see coming.

6. Keep mobile. Standup paddleboards give you a range that prone paddlers would never consider. Thinking in terms of Santa Cruz, on a SUP you can launch at Capitola and surf your way up the coast, spending a little time at Trees, then Private's, then Inside Sharks, then Shark Cove. Maybe snag one or two waves at the Hook if it's not too packed, then paddle up to Pleasure Point and spend a little time catching waves at Insides, then Second Peak, First Peak, etc. That's the way to do it. Don't spend too much time at any one spot.

7. Pro surfer and writer/director Sam George offers a few more tips. He says, "Don't learn to paddle in the surf line. Until you can paddle and balance comfortably enough to perform a tail spin-around 'jibe' turn, stick to flat water."

8. George says: "Control your board and paddle at all times. Meaning: Don't bail your board while surfing, nor paddling out. If you absolutely have to bail off your board

paddling out, look around and behind you before doing so. If there are other surfers in the way, grab your rails and take the pounding."

9. "After riding a wave never paddle straight back out through the lineup. Take a wider course and take your time," George says.

10. And lastly, George recommends: "Never stand looming over conventional surfers. Give everyone a bit of space. And sit down to chat."

How to Use This Guide

For your convenience, all the surf spots in this book—both featured spots and secondary spots—are arranged in geographical order from north to south. We've divided the state into ten regions that take you from surf spots in the north near Crescent City to spots in the south near San Diego.

Each section of the book begins with a regional introduction followed by a regional map, a discussion of the surf by season, and average air and water temperatures by month.

The featured surf spots are indicated by boldface type in the table of contents and on the regional maps. They are given full write-ups within the interior of each section. These write-ups contain driving directions, detailed information, and surf descriptions, as well as surfer ratings for novice, intermediate, and advanced surfers. The featured spots also include brief listings of nearby surf shops, places to stay, and places to eat.

The secondary surf spots are indicated by regular type in the table of contents and on the regional maps. Throughout the book they are boxed and include thumbnail photos. These secondary spot listings contain short descriptions and useful facts.

To drive to many of the surf destinations included in this book, you will travel primarily along US Highway 101, California Highway 1, and Interstates 5 and 405. For the purposes of this book, US Highway 101 will appear in the driving directions simply as "US 101." California Highway 1—also known as the "Pacific Coast Highway," "Cabrillo Highway," "El Camino Real," and the "Coast Highway" in local areas—will appear simply as "CA 1" in driving directions. However, local street names for these routes have been retained in the addresses for surf shops, places to stay, and places to eat. In this book Interstate 5 will appear as "I-5," Interstate 405 as "I-405."

Finally, you will find a map legend at the end of the introduction explaining the symbols used on the maps in this book. Elevations shown are for land elevation, not for the depth of the water.

We hope you find this travel guide helpful and informative. Any surfer who has the opportunity to visit the endless miles of amazing coastline and excellent surf spots in California is truly fortunate. Travel safely, and may all your surf sessions be enjoyable!

Map Legend

15	Interstate Highway
101	US Highway
299	State Highway
	Local Road
	International Border
	State Border
	River or Creek
	Body of Water
	Campground
	Capital
	City
	Mountain Peak
	Point of Interest
	State Park
	Surfing Location
	Town

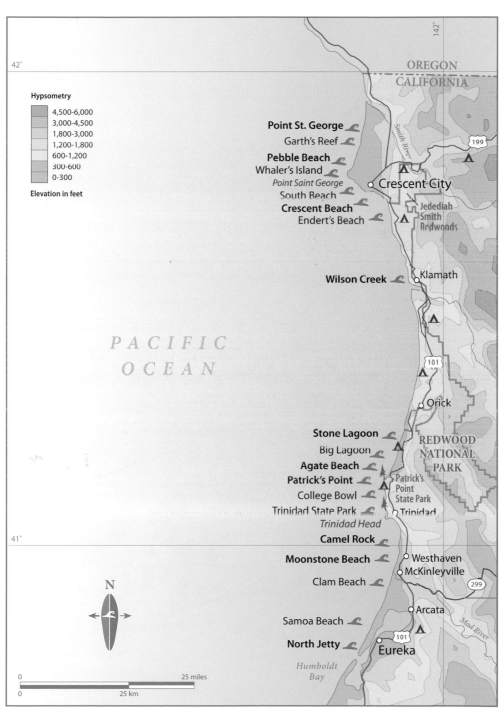

42°

OREGON
CALIFORNIA

Hypsometry

4,500-6,000
3,000-4,500
1,800-3,000
1,200-1,800
600-1,200
300-600
0-300

Elevation in feet

Point St. George
Garth's Reef
Pebble Beach
Whaler's Island
Point Saint George
South Beach
Crescent Beach
Endert's Beach

Smith River

199

Crescent City

Jedediah
Smith
Redwoods

Wilson Creek

Klamath

PACIFIC
OCEAN

101

Orick

Stone Lagoon
Big Lagoon
Agate Beach
Patrick's Point
College Bowl
Trinidad State Park
Trinidad Head

REDWOOD
NATIONAL
PARK

Patrick's
Point
State Park

Trinidad

41°

Camel Rock
Moonstone Beach
Clam Beach

Westhaven
McKinleyville

299

Samoa Beach

Arcata

Mad River

N

North Jetty

101

Eureka

*Humboldt
Bay*

0 ———————————————————— 25 miles
0 ———————————————————— 25 km

Region 1 (Crescent City to Eureka)

REGION 1: CRESCENT CITY TO EUREKA

It's hard to believe this green, lush, underpopulated rural California is in the same state as dry, dusty, overpopulated southern California. This part of the California coast is not stereotypical California. It's also referred to as the Redwood Coast due to the groves of 300-foot-tall redwood trees found here. This region is home to numerous state parks as well as the Redwood National Park, making it one of the most picturesque and undeveloped sections of coast in the state.

The weather and scenery feel and look more like Oregon than California. The trees are mossy, and the frequent rain keeps the hillsides lush and green. If you're fond of the climate and mellow vibe of the Pacific Northwest, you'll feel right at home in this part of California. And if you haven't spent much time in this area of the United States, it's a great place to experience. If you have the right attitude and enjoy exploring coastline without crowds, you'll have a great time.

There are long stretches of beach between the Oregon state line and Crescent City, and sheer cliffs line the coast from Crescent City all the way down to the Prairie Creek Redwoods State Park. As you travel south from the old-growth redwoods down to Arcata, you'll find miles of lagoons, lineups surrounded by large boulders, endless sand dunes, and cows grazing in ocean-view pastures. Pacific storms can be relentless and harsh in this northernmost region of California, and they can last for weeks. As a result, the weather can be unpredictable and not very welcoming at certain times of the year.

Overall Surf Description

The surf along the Redwood Coast can be temperamental. An entire month can go by in which the reef breaks are funky, the sandbars shifty, and the big-wave spots 20 feet and junky. If you're motivated and adventurous, however, the Redwood Coast is definitely worth visiting. To increase your odds of having an enjoyable surf trip to northernmost California, you'll need to bring some patience, endurance, strength, rain gear, a thick wet suit, and an arsenal of boards. There are some great spots up here if you know where to look and aren't a fair-weather surfer. The Redwood Coast definitely isn't for everyone, but the people are friendly, the views are incredible, and you might possibly enjoy some of the best waves of your life—all by yourself!

Double barrel over-under, somewhere along the Humboldt coast
Chris Burkard

Fall Surf

Fall is generally the best season for good swell and weather to get together. Water temperatures are usually bearable, the wind dies down, and the sun can be seen on most days. This is a good time of year to experience glassy waves all day with clean, organized, longer interval swell.

Winter Surf

Winter can be challenging up here. You're bound to encounter huge swell, heavy rain, and strong winds. Unfortunately, the days when the surf is poor tend to out-number the days when it's good. If you're looking for surf several times overhead, winter is the season to head north. However, these months can be the worst for fun-size surf. The majority of winter surfing in this region is done at a few spots that can handle the size. The spots that face northwest are the best, as south-southeast winds prevail December through March.

Spring Surf

Spring tends to be windy, sunny, and cold. North winds of 40 to 50 knots are not rare. The surf gets big in spring, but there's also usually less swell activity from the Gulf of Alaska. The south-facing spots are best this time of year.

Summer Surf

Summer definitely isn't the best season to visit this section of coast. The surf tends to be small and junky due to onshore winds. The water is still relatively cold, and the skies are foggy.

Average Temperatures for Region (Crescent City to Eureka)		
	Air (Crescent City)	Water (Crescent City)
Jan	55	50
Feb	56	51
Mar	57	51
Apr	58	52
May	61	53
June	63	55
July	65	57
Aug	66	59
Sept	66	57
Oct	64	54
Nov	56	53
Dec	55	51

Point Saint George

This is a rocky shelf, reef, and point break that produces numerous quality peaks.

Best tide: Low

Best swell direction: Any

Best wave size: Chest to head high

Bottom: Rock

Type of break: Right and left reef

Skill level: Intermediate to advanced

Best boards: Shortboard, funshape

Best season: Winter

Crowds: Not crowded

Water quality: Clean

Hazards: Sharks

Fees and permits: None

Finding the Break

From Crescent City: Go north on US 101. Turn left onto Northcrest Drive, then left again onto Washington Boulevard. Point Saint George is at the end of Washington Boulevard roughly 2 miles from Northcrest Drive. Park at the end of Washington Boulevard, and follow the dirt path down to the beach. GPS: N41 46.732 / W124 15.201

Surf Description

Point Saint George is one of the best breaks in the area. You can find waves here even when nearby spots are virtually flat. This point is positioned to capture swell from any direction and can be especially good in the winter months when northwest swells roll into town. The reef at Point Saint George can deliver fast, large, and well-shaped surf. The rides can be long, and the waves can get hollow at lower tides.

Point Saint George is one of those surf spots that can be relaxing and invigorating at the same time. The area is beautiful and feels far removed from nearby Crescent City. As you walk down the dirt trail from where you park, you'll get the sense that very few people ever visit this beach. The area is pristine and undeveloped. The only sounds you're likely to hear

This is a great break to score waves all by yourself. And there is a nice hostel close to the beach.

Point Saint George sticks out into the Pacific Ocean and is exposed to a lot of swell, a lot of wind, and a lot of weather so it has ever-changing moods. This is Point Saint George showing a sunnier disposition on a spring day, before the northwest winds started to howl.   Chris Burkard

are those of the pounding surf and perhaps a few birds chirping on the hillside. And even if it's not raining when you visit, you'll quickly find evidence of how much rain this place receives. The ground will probably be saturated with water, and even in summer the plants and shrubs will appear healthy and green. The serenity of the area coupled with the quality of this break are sure to lead to a memorable surf session.

If you look out to sea on a clear day, you can see a lighthouse far in the distance. This is the St. George Reef Lighthouse, located a few miles from shore. It was built in response to a terrible accident a century and a half ago. In July 1865 a coastal steamer named *Brother Jonathan* sank on this offshore reef and more than 150 lives were lost.

The St. George Reef Lighthouse has been called America's most expensive lighthouse. Construction began in 1882; the light took ten years and over $700,000 to build. It's built on a rock that's a mere 17 feet above sea level. Imagine the punishment

SUPDATE: DEL NORTE COUNTY

There is a lot of water up here in farthest Northern California: water falling from the sky, condensed water in the form of fog, water flowing from the mountains from cute creeks to mighty rivers. Lakes, lagoons, harbors, and, of course, the mighty Pacific. All that water in various forms make Del Norte SUP heaven. If you have ever wanted to shoot a river on a SUP, the Smith is the perfect river for that. Most of the time it's a gentle flow with not-too-hairy rapids, and it's also a beautiful little river all the way down to the lagoon, which empties into the ocean. The Klamath River is also a fun place to go SUP touring—from the mouth and lagoon, upriver as far as you want to go. People in NorCal are generally pretty friendly, but they will not suffer fools who come blundering into their surf spots on SUPs and shatter the vibe. Point Saint George and Garth's Reef would be fun on a SUP, but there are miles and miles of empty beaches up here that an adventurous standup paddleboarder can get to and get some with no one knowing they were ever there. Crescent City Harbor is infamous for being a tsunami magnet, but it's also fun for cruising around on a SUP, saying "what's up" to the fishermen and maybe buying some crab or salmon in season. Just outside of Crescent City Harbor, there's about 3.5 miles of beach break from Crescent City South Beach to Endert's Beach. Surely you can find a wave to yourself along there. And if you really, really want some solitude, try a 20-mile downwinder from Crescent City down to the Klamath River mouth.

this building has taken from winter storms and wave action over the years! It was constructed from hundreds of large granite blocks that were brought to the reef by steamer. The lighthouse was in operation until 1975, and four keepers were killed over the years while on duty there. A not-for-profit organization has launched an effort to preserve the St. George Reef Lighthouse and, with it, a part of this area's history.

Other Information

Local Surf Shops: South Beach Outfitters, 128 Anchor Way, Crescent City; (707) 464-2963; southbeachoutfitters.com. Rhyn Noll Surf Shop, 275 L St. #A, Crescent City; (707) 465-4400.

Chris Burkard

Garth's Reef is a right point break just north of Crescent City off US 101. There's an outer rock reef here that generates a thick wave that re-forms and breaks over a shallow rock shelf. This break can capture swell from any direction but works best at low tide when it's chest to head high. You're likely to find the best surf at Garth's Reef during winter.

Places to Stay: Oceanfront Lodge, 100 A St., Crescent City; (707) 465-5400. Crescent Beach Motel, 1455 US 101 S., Crescent City; (707) 464-5436. Mill Creek Campground, call for directions; (707) 464-6101 or (800) 444-7275.

Places to Eat: Jefferson State Brewery, 400 Front St., Crescent City; (707) 464-1139. Beachcomber Restaurant, 1400 US 101 S., Crescent City; (707) 464-2205. Taco Man, 530 L St., Crescent City; (707) 464-3013. 101 Hawaiian BBQ (legendary surfer Greg "Da Bull" Noll's favorite), 1270 Front St. #C, Crescent City.

Pebble Beach

This is a fun and consistent beach break that can produce left and right barrels.

Best tides: Low to medium
Best swell direction: Any
Best wave size: Waist to head high
Bottom: Sand and rock
Type of break: Left and right beach break
Skill level: Intermediate to advanced
Best board: Short
Best season: Winter
Crowds: Not crowded
Water quality: Clean
Hazards: Sharks, floating logs at high tide
Fees and permits: None

A clean, green day at Pebble Beach in the northlands.   Chris Burkard

Finding the Break

From Crescent City: Take US 101 north. Turn left onto Front Street to Pebble Beach Drive. Follow Pebble Beach Drive north along the coast and look for the sign for Pebble Beach. Park along the side of Pebble Beach Drive and walk a few steps to the beach. GPS: N41 45.101 / W124 12.786

Surf Description

Pebble Beach is a mostly west-facing beach protected by some small rock outcroppings. The waves here are generally thin and friendly, with easy takeoffs. In a strong swell the waves can be fast and the tube rides plentiful. At higher tides Pebble Beach cannot be surfed. At lower tides, however, this can be a fun and relatively safe place to ride some medium-size waves.

The weather in this region can be fickle. Dense fog, strong winds, and heavy rain are all common in this part of California. The air and water temperatures are generally both on the colder side. You're technically in California, but Oregon weather has a strong influence here. Still, if you can brave the conditions, you'll more than likely be rewarded by getting to surf a quality break with very few other surfers around. In fact, if it wasn't for the invention of a little thing called the wet suit, it's unlikely that many surfers would venture out into these waters at all.

Surfing originated in the warm waters of the South Pacific where staying warm isn't a concern. And in the early days, California surfing was more or less limited to the southern part of the state, where the water is still relatively warm. However, as surfers began exploring the breaks in the northern half of the state, they began looking for ways to handle the frigid waters. Some would dance around fires before sessions. Others would surf with wool sweaters or even the bulky and cumbersome scuba suits of the time. Overall, if you surfed in

This is a great beach to hang out on when the weather is nice.

cold water back then, you probably surfed for a relatively short period of time, and you surfed conservatively so as to spend as little time as possible in the water.

Then along came a window salesman from San Francisco who began experimenting with various materials that would allow surfers to prolong sessions in colder water. One day while traveling on a DC-3 passenger plane, he noticed a strange rubberlike material that lined the aisles. The substance was neoprene, and the window salesman was Jack O'Neill. In 1952 O'Neill opened San Francisco's first surf shop and began selling wet suits. Since then wet suits have undergone various modifications to improve durability, mobility, warmth, and performance. You can find wet suits of varying thicknesses, styles, and colors. And there are now numerous manufacturers attempting to improve upon the original innovation. But those of us who surf in cold water owe our relative comfort to the man who started it all, Jack O'Neill.

Chris Burkard

Above, Whaler's Island is located just south of Pebble Beach. This is a good place to surf during a big swell when all the nearby spots are closed out. The best peak is a right near the island. The waves here peel over a shallow rock ledge and are best at lower tides. Whaler's Island isn't a very consistent break, but it just might be your only option under certain conditions.

Right, South Beach is just south of the jetty in Crescent City. This is a beach break with several peaks. It's positioned to catch south swells and works best when it's waist to chest high. South Beach is most fun in the summer and fall but can also produce some small winter surf. Rhyn Noll hosts an annual long-boarding contest on this beach the first weekend in October.

Nikki Brooks

Other Information

Local Surf Shops: South Beach Outfitters, 128 Anchor Way, Crescent City; (707) 464-2963; southbeachoutfitters.com. Rhyn Noll Surf Shop, 275 L St. #A, Crescent City; (707) 465-4400.

Places to Stay: Oceanfront Lodge, 100 A St., Crescent City; (707) 465-5400. Crescent Beach Motel, 1455 US 101 S., Crescent City; (707) 464-5436. Mill Creek Campground, call for directions; (707) 464-6101 or (800) 444-7275.

Places to Eat: Jefferson State Brewery, 400 Front St., Crescent City; (707) 464-1139. Beachcomber Restaurant, 1400 US 101 S., Crescent City; (707) 464-2205. Taco Man, 530 L St., Crescent City; (707) 464-3013. 101 Hawaiian BBQ (legendary surfer Greg "Da Bull" Noll's favorite), 1270 Front St. #C, Crescent City.

Crescent Beach

This is a long stretch of sandy beach with numerous right and left peaks.

Best tides: Medium to high
Best swell direction: Any
Best wave size: Waist to chest high
Bottom: Sand
Type of break: Left and right beach break
Skill level: Intermediate
Best boards: Shortboard, funshape, longboard
Best season: Fall
Crowds: Not crowded
Water quality: Clean
Hazards: Sharks
Fees and permits: None

Finding the Break

From Crescent City: Head south on US 101. Turn right onto Endert's Beach Road; it's marked by a sign for Crescent Beach. Follow Endert's Beach Road for about a mile and make your first right toward the picnic area. Park at the end of the road and walk a few steps to the beach. GPS: N41 43.624 / W124 09.135

Surf Description

Crescent Beach is a large beach just south of Crescent City. Due to the size of this beach, it can work with virtually any swell direction. However, being wide open also leaves the waves here very exposed to the wind. When the conditions are right, there are numerous peaks to surf along this beach. And if the weather cooperates, Crescent Beach can be a nice place to hang out. There's plenty of parking and very easy access to the sand, making this a great beach for family outings.

Crescent Beach is adjacent to South Beach, where Rhyn Noll holds an annual longboard contest. Rhyn is the son of Greg Noll, also known as Da Bull, a well-known big-wave surfer who now lives in Crescent City. Greg Noll was born in San Diego in 1937. When he was 3, his family moved to Manhattan Beach, where he learned how to build boards from famous shaper Dave Velzy. Velzy taught him how to shape shorter, lighter, and more maneuverable balsa boards.

South Beach, Crescent City, on a decent day. Not too much wind, good sandbars, and not a tsunami in sight.   Chris Burkard

Noll became a Los Angeles County lifeguard and was one of the premier Malibu surfers of the 1950s. In high school he began making surf trips to Hawaii, where he enjoyed the challenge of surfing big waves. And in 1957 Greg was one of the first to surf Waimea Bay. Seven years later, in 1964, he surfed Third Reef Pipeline on a huge day and solidified himself as an elite big-wave surfer. He made surfing history when he rode what is said to have been the biggest wave you can paddle into at Makaha in 1969. After that monstrous wave Greg Noll quit surfing and moved to Alaska. He disappeared from the surfing scene and entered the world of commercial fishing. As the longboard became popular again, however, Noll returned to shaping.

This is one of the longest stretches of beach in the area.

Lucia Griggi

Endert's Beach is a medium-size beach surrounded by large boulders that is home to several right and left outside peaks. It's located just south of Crescent City at the end of Endert's Beach Road. From the parking lot at the end of the road, it's roughly a 0.5-mile walk down to the beach on a dirt path. Endert's Beach is a little more protected from the north and northwest winds common in this region. As a result, it's a good place to check out when Crescent Beach is blown out.

Greg Noll was involved in the surf films of the late 1950s, started a surfboard factory with Miki Dora in Hermosa Beach, and even started a surf clothing company in San Clemente. He has organized surfing events around the globe and still shapes a few boards every year out of old-growth redwood. Noll was winner of the Surf Industry Manufacturers Association (SIMA) Waterman of the Year award in 1999 and was honored on the Surfing Walk of Fame in Huntington Beach. You can learn more about Greg Noll and his contributions to the sport of surfing in his biography, *Da Bull: Life Over the Edge* (North Atlantic Books, 1989).

Other Information

Local Surf Shops: South Beach Outfitters, 128 Anchor Way, Crescent City; (707) 464-2963; southbeachoutfitters.com. Rhyn Noll Surf Shop, 275 L St. #A, Crescent City; (707) 465-4400.

Places to Stay: Oceanfront Lodge, 100 A St., Crescent City; (707) 465-5400. Crescent Beach Motel, 1455 US 101 S., Crescent City; (707) 464-5436. Mill Creek Campground, call for directions; (707) 464-6101 or (800) 444-7275.

Places to Eat: Jefferson State Brewery, 400 Front St., Crescent City; (707) 464-1139. Beachcomber Restaurant, 1400 US 101 S., Crescent City; (707) 464-2205. Taco Man, 530 L St., Crescent City; (707) 464-3013. 101 Hawaiian BBQ (Da Bull's favorite), 1270 Front St. #C, Crescent City.

Wilson Creek

This is a small beach with a fun and sheltered beach break.

Best tide: Medium
Best swell direction: Southwest, west
Best wave size: Waist to chest high
Bottom: Sand and rock
Type of break: Left and right beach break
Skill level: Intermediate
Best boards: Shortboard, funshape, longboard
Best season: Spring
Crowds: Not crowded
Water quality: Clean
Hazards: Sharks
Fees and permits: None

Finding the Break

From Crescent City: Head south on US 101 for about 11 miles. Look for a small parking lot on the beach side of 101 and a sign for Wilson Creek. Park in the small lot on the side of the highway and walk a few feet to the beach. GPS: N 41 36.191 / W124 06.025

Surf Description

Wilson Creek can be a fun little break. Because it's a creek break, the waves here are influenced by the amount of water coming down from the hills. The sandbars are most developed in early spring, which results in better wave shape at this time of year. Wilson Creek is also more protected from north and northwest winds, which makes it a good spot when the breaks closer to Crescent City are blown out.

Great white sharks like the water temperatures in this region of California, so it's possible that they could be patrolling these waters. There haven't been any reported shark attacks at Wilson Creek. However, two reported great-white attacks occurred a

The setup at Wilson Creek, with the surf spot, the US 101 bridge, and a choice youth hostel in view. californiacoastline.org

few miles south of Wilson Creek at the mouth of the Klamath River. One attack was on August 11, 1988; the other, on August 18, 1992. Both involved surfers.

Although shark attacks are very rare, there are several ways you can minimize your risk. First, since sharks tend to attack solitary individuals, avoid surfing alone. In addition to preventing attacks, the buddy system has saved the lives of a high percentage of shark-attack victims. Second, avoid surfing too far from shore. The farther from shore you wait for waves, the more susceptible you are to an attack and the longer it takes to get to safety. It's also a good idea to avoid surfing at twilight hours, when sharks are most active, or in murky waters, where they have a sensory advantage.

This is a great break to score waves all by yourself. And there is a nice hostel close to the beach.

And since sharks can sense blood from great distances, don't get in the water if you're bleeding from an open wound or are menstruating. Next, avoid wearing anything too shiny, such as jewelry; the reflected light could resemble the scales of a fish. And breaks that are populated with shark bait such as large groups of seals are definitely more likely to be teeming with sharks. River and creek mouths, like the breaks at the mouths of the Klamath River and Wilson Creek, or areas with a high concentration of sewage, are also known to be favored shark-feeding spots. Breaks that are located near steep drop-offs feature increased odds of sharks lurking nearby as well. Lastly, take extra precaution in August and September—the months in which shark attacks are most common in California.

Again, your odds of being attacked by a shark while surfing are extremely low. But they are out there, and we are easy targets. Following the tips listed above just might decrease your chance of experiencing a shark encounter of your own.

Other Information

Local Surf Shops: South Beach Outfitters, 128 Anchor Way, Crescent City; (707) 464-2963; southbeachoutfitters.com. Rhyn Noll Surf Shop, 275 L St. #A, Crescent City; (707) 465-4400.

Places to Stay: Oceanfront Lodge, 100 A St., Crescent City; (707) 465-5400. Crescent Beach Motel, 1455 US 101 S., Crescent City; (707) 464-5436. Mill Creek Campground, call for directions; (707) 464-6101 or (800) 444-7275. Redwood National Park Hostel, 14480 US 101, Klamath; (707) 482-8265.

Places to Eat: Jefferson State Brewery, 400 Front St., Crescent City; (707) 464-1139. Beachcomber Restaurant, 1400 US 101 S., Crescent City; (707) 464-2205. Taco Man, 530 L St., Crescent City; (707) 464-3013. 101 Hawaiian BBQ (Da Bull's favorite), 1270 Front St. #C, Crescent City.

Stone Lagoon

This is a long beach with multiple right and left peaks that break outside a lagoon.

Best tide: Medium
Best swell direction: Northwest, west
Best wave size: Waist high to slightly overhead
Bottom: Sand
Type of break: Right and left beach break
Skill level: Intermediate to advanced
Best boards: Shortboard, funshape
Best season: Winter
Crowds: Not crowded
Water quality: Clean
Hazards: Sharks, rip currents
Fees and permits: None

Finding the Break

From Crescent City: Head south on US 101. Stone Lagoon is between the towns of Orick and Trinidad. Look for the sign for Stone Lagoon and turn right onto the small paved road that leads to the beach. Park at the end of the road and walk a few steps to the beach. GPS: N41 15.520 / W124 05.933

Surf Description

Stone Lagoon is a picturesque beach that protects a tranquil lagoon. When you first drive down the narrow road that leads to the beach, you'll be able to tell if the waves are breaking. The coastline here faces northwest, making this a great place to capture winter swell. There are several well-shaped right and left peaks along this sandy peninsula that can be surfed. The beach break here can get big and the waves fast with the right conditions. The sand drops off significantly from the beach toward the various breaks, making the size of the waves at Stone Lagoon somewhat deceiving from a distance. Because of the consistent wave action that has developed this drop-off, rip currents can be strong and shore poundings severe when a large winter swell rolls through. Stone Lagoon isn't very close to the major towns of Crescent City to the north and Eureka to the south, making it a somewhat isolated spot. As a result, even when the waves are epic, there's a good chance you'll be surfing by yourself.

There are several lagoons in this area known collectively as the Humboldt Lagoons. If you have the time, this is a unique, serene, and beautiful area to explore. About

As seen from about a mile away along US 101: a crumbly peak along a mile of beach in front of Stone Lagoon.

a hundred years ago, one of the lagoons, aptly named Dry Lagoon, was drained by farmers. They attempted to grow a variety of different crops here, but none ended up worthwhile. Around the same time, several dairy ranches sprang up along the shores of what's now known as Stone Lagoon. Over time the highway was improved and a small inn and restaurant—the Little Red Hen—was established near the lagoon. It continued to house and serve visitors to the area until 1979. Today this building is home to a museum, park office, bookstore, and the Humboldt Lagoons Visitor Center.

This is a very unique and beautiful stretch of coast.

Now the farms and ranches are gone and this area is a protected marshland. The lagoons are habitat for numerous species of marsh plants, birds, and other animals. The Humboldt Lagoons are a great place to go hiking, boating, or fishing, or just to walk on the beach. Picnic areas are located near the visitor center and on the beach at the north end of Stone Lagoon. There's a 3-mile trail to explore as well as prime birding and whale-watching opportunities.

Other Information

Local Surf Shops: Salty's Surf and Tackle, 332 Main St., Trinidad; (707) 677-0300.
Places to Stay: Patrick's Point State Park, 4150 Patrick's Point Dr., Trinidad; (707) 677-3570. Lost Whale Inn, 3452 Patrick's Point Dr., Trinidad; (707) 677-3425. There are also several motels along Patrick's Point Drive.
Places to Eat: Seascape, at the pier off of Main Street in Trinidad; (707) 677-3762. Larrupin' Cafe, 1658 Patrick's Point Dr., Trinidad; (707) 677-0230. Ocean Grove Restaurant, 480 Patrick's Point Dr., Trinidad; (707) 677-0394.

Lucia Griggi

Big Lagoon is a winter spot that can handle huge swell. It's located between the towns of Orick and Trinidad, just north of Patrick's Point, off US 101. Big Lagoon gets its name because it breaks outside a sandy peninsula that contains a large lagoon. It needs a strong northwest or west swell and can hold waves from chest high to triple overhead. Big Lagoon isn't the most consistent spot in the area. If you're looking for monstrous waves, however, and the conditions are favorable, it's definitely worth visiting.

SUPDATE: KLAMATH RIVER TO HUMBOLDT HARBOR

The coastline from Klamath River down to Eureka is also loaded with SUPportunities by land and sea. Trolling for salmon on the Klamath from a SUP could be a good way to go for a Nantucket sleigh ride. Drive into Gold Bluff's park and launch, and you will find miles and miles of empty coast that are accessible only by SUP—just remember this is great-white-shark territory. Go with friends and tell people where you are going. It would be a good day's adventure to standup-paddle across Big Lagoon, hump your board across the sand berm on the other side, and get some waves all to yourself. Trinidad is a cool little Popeye town that would be fun for a cruise, and the lineups at Trinidad and Camel Rock look like great SUP waves: Just behave yourself, please. And from Moonstone on down is 20 miles of empty beach break. All the solitude you can handle. SUP makes this possible. If you are complaining about crowds up here, you do not understand the power of a standup paddleboard.

Agate Beach

This is a right beach break at Patrick's Point State Park.

Best tide: Low
Best swell direction: Northwest
Best wave size: Chest high to double overhead
Bottom: Sand and rock
Type of break: Right beach break
Skill level: Intermediate to advanced
Best board: Shortboard
Best seasons: Fall and winter
Crowds: Not crowded
Water quality: Clean
Hazards: Sharks, dangerous shore break
Fees and permits: According to oregonstateparks.org, there is no fee to enter the state park, or you can park outside the entrance and hike in through the forest.

Locked in and caught inside at Agate Beach.

Finding the Break

From Eureka: Follow US 101 north for about 25 miles. Take the Patrick's Point Drive exit and enter Patrick's Point State Park, roughly 5 miles north of the town of Trinidad. Inside the park, head toward the Agate Campground and take the Agate Beach Trail down to the beach. GPS: N41 08.123 / W124 09.354

Surf Description

Agate Beach is a large, pristine, and very beautiful beach. As with most beach breaks, it can produce a wide range of surfing conditions. Depending on the swell, this spot can range from fun and friendly to a heavy, aggressive beach break. It faces northwest and as a result sees some serious winter swell. The break at Agate Beach is usually a well-shaped and consistent wave that can produce quality barrels. On bigger days you'll definitely want to beware of the heavy shore pound.

Agate Beach is located within Patrick's Point State Park, a 640-acre park 25 miles north of Eureka. This park is home to many types of trees, such as redwood, fir, pine, spruce, hemlock, and red alder. There are also large meadows here filled with wildflowers as well as wildlife including bears, skunks, and raccoons. The shoreline is just as diverse. You can find wide sandy beaches such as Agate Beach, dramatic cliffs, and rocky tide pools all within close proximity. Six miles of hiking trails wind through the park and offer great ocean views. The Rim

Agate Beach is one of the most picturesque beaches around.

Trail is a great hike if you hope to see some harbor seals, sea lions, or gray whales. The Octopus Tree Trail is a loop that will lead you through an old-growth grove of Sitka spruce. There are two steep trails to Lookout Rock and Ceremonial Rock, ancient sea stacks that were once submerged underwater. And there are trails you can take out to Mussel Rocks, Wedding Rock, Patrick's Point, Rocky Point, Abalone Point, and Palmers Point to get away from it all, picnic, or check out the sunset.

You can also visit a reconstructed Yurok village within the park called Sumeg Village. This attraction consists of traditional family houses, changing houses, a sweat house, a dance house, and a redwood canoe. Local Yuroks use the village as a way to educate their children and share their culture with visitors. Right next to the village is a garden filled with plants native to this unique part of the coastal fog belt that several generations of Yuroks used for food, medicine, ceremonies, and basket making. Called the Native American Plant Garden, it was established in 1973 by the Patrick's Point Garden Club.

Other Information

Local Surf Shops: Salty's Surf and Tackle, 233 Main St., Trinidad; (707) 677-0300.
Places to Stay: Patrick's Point State Park, 4150 Patrick's Point Dr., Trinidad; (707) 677-3570. Lost Whale Inn, 3452 Patrick's Point Dr., Trinidad; (707) 677-3425. There are also several motels along Patrick's Point Drive.
Places to Eat: Seascape, at the pier off of Main Street in Trinidad; (707) 677-3762. Larrupin' Cafe, 1658 Patrick's Point Dr., Trinidad; (707) 677-0230. Ocean Grove Restaurant, 480 Patrick's Point Dr., Trinidad; (707) 677-0394.

Patrick's Point

This is a consistent outside left at Patrick's Point State Park.

Best tide: High
Best swell direction: West
Best wave size: Chest high to triple overhead
Bottom: Rock
Type of break: Outside left
Skill level: Intermediate to advanced
Best boards: Funshape, gun
Best seasons: Fall and winter
Crowds: Not crowded
Water quality: Clean
Hazards: Sharks, submerged rocks, dangerous entry and exit
Fees and permits: There's a small fee to enter the state park, or you can park outside the entrance and hike in through the forest.

California doesn't have a whole lot of left point breaks so Patrick's Point is a bit of an anomaly. Chris Burkard

Finding the Break

From Eureka: Follow US 101 north for about 25 miles. Take the Patrick's Point Drive exit and enter Patrick's Point State Park, roughly 5 miles north of the town of Trinidad. Inside the park take the Mussel Rock Trail down to the beach. GPS: N41 07.761 / W124 09.781

Surf Description

This state park, one of the most beautiful parks in all of California, is about 300 miles north of San Francisco. It took its name from Patrick Beegan, who settled here in 1851. The break at Patrick's Point is a thick, outside, rocky left. This spot can handle waves up to 25 feet, making it a stellar winter break. However, the beach break here closes out when it gets big, so getting out and getting back in can be hazardous. And the submerged rocks in this area limit surfing to higher tide windows. Overall, the wave at Patrick's Point is not for the inexperienced. This spot should be taken seriously and requires that you plan your session ahead of time.

Geologists have taken a keen interest in Patrick's Point State Park over the years. There are 245-million-year-old rocks and million-year-old sedimentary deposits exposed here. Students from the College of the Redwoods and Humboldt State University come to the park to study both geology and seismic activity. A fault runs through Patrick's Point State Park, and the boundary between the Gorda and North American Plates is located roughly 25 miles west, beneath the ocean. It's believed that the Gorda Plate has been converging with the western portion of the North American Plate for more than 200 million years.

Patrick's Point State Park is a great place to hike, camp, and hang out.

The plates converge during the large earthquakes that occur in this region; some of the rocks you can see at the park have been deformed as a result of this plate movement. Geologists gain information by studying rocks here such as greenstone, conglomerate, graywacke, chert, and metamorphic rock. They can learn about glacially controlled sea-level fluctuations by examining the sediment. The earth in Patrick's Point State Park is also of interest to them as they seek understanding of progressive uplift and tilting of terraces.

On November 11, 1980, a large earthquake of magnitude 7.1 occurred about 30 miles west of the park. The quake is thought to have originated roughly 12 miles beneath the earth's surface within the Gorda Plate. It seems to have been caused by a lateral slip along a 60-mile-long vertical fault. The force of the earthquake collapsed a freeway overpass just south of Eureka and resulted in nearly $2 million worth of damage in the region.

Left, College Bowl is a beach break located around 1.5 miles north of Trinidad. It works best with a waist- to chest-high swell from the south or west at a medium tide. Due to shifting sandbars, College Bowl can produce peaks in various areas on the beach, which also makes wave shape somewhat unpredictable. Nonetheless, if you're looking for a fun, small-wave beach break, College Bowl is worth visiting.

Below, Trinidad State Park is a rock reef break that's roughly due west of the town of Trinidad. The state park actually borders the town of Trinidad and is very easy to find. From Main Street, head north on Stagecoach Road, then take a left to the Trinidad State Park parking lot. Once you drop off your vehicle, look for signs and the dirt trail that heads down to the beach. Because of submerged rocks, you'll want to surf this break at higher tides. It's not the most consistent break in the area, but it's definitely worth checking out.

Lucia Griggi

Chris Burkard

Other Information

Local Surf Shops: Salty's Surf and Tackle, 233 Main St., Trinidad; (707) 677-0300.
Places to Stay: Patrick's Point State Park, 4150 Patrick's Point Dr., Trinidad; (707) 677-3570. Lost Whale Inn, 3452 Patrick's Point Dr., Trinidad; (707) 677-3425. There are also several motels along Patrick's Point Drive.
Places to Eat: Seascape, at the pier off of Main Street in Trinidad; (707) 677-3762. Larrupin' Cafe, 1658 Patrick's Point Dr., Trinidad; (707) 677-0230. Ocean Grove Restaurant, 480 Patrick's Point Dr., Trinidad; (707) 677-0394.

Camel Rock

This is a fun and protected beach break just south of Trinidad.

Best tides: Low to medium
Best swell direction: Northwest
Best wave size: Chest high to just overhead
Bottom: Sand and rock
Type of break: Beach break
Skill level: Novice to intermediate
Best boards: Funshape, longboard
Best seasons: Fall and spring
Crowds: Can get crowded when it's good
Water quality: Clean
Hazards: Sharks
Fees and permits: None

Finding the Break

From Arcata: Head north on US 101 toward the town of Trinidad. Take the Westhaven Drive exit just south of Trinidad and drive south along Scenic Drive until you see the sign for Camel Rock. The break is guarded by a large rock that looks like the back of a camel with two humps. There's parking on Scenic Drive and easy access down to the beach. GPS: N41 03.289 / W124 07.918

Surf Description

Camel Rock is a beach break that faces southwest. As a result, it's protected from the northerly winds that are often felt in this region. Camel Rock can be an especially good spot to scope out during a bigger swell when the winds are blowing from the north. This is a very picturesque stretch of coast just south of Trinidad. Large rocks dot the shore, and from the bluff overlooking this break, you can clearly see how this spot got its name.

The town of Trinidad has an interesting history that can be traced back several hundred years. The Tsurai Indians are thought to have discovered and become the first inhabitants of this area. Their descendants still live here and continue some of their ancestors' traditions, such as carving seaworthy canoes out of redwood logs.

Trinidad is a small fishing area that attracts a fair number of tourists. The surrounding area has some nice hiking trails with great vistas, rocky coves, headlands, and forests to explore.

Over the last few hundred years, Trinidad has been visited by explorers, gold miners, whalers, fur traders, fishermen, crabbers, and lumberjacks. In 1595 a sea captain from Portugal, Sebastian Rodriguez Cermeno, was the first European to lay eyes on what's now known as Trinidad Bay. In 1775 two captains from Spain, Juan Francisco la Bodega y Quadra and Bruno Hezeta, anchored here and named the port La Santisima Trinidad. Eighteen years later, in 1793, Captain George Vancouver also landed in this bay. And numerous fur traders from places such as Russia are known to have anchored in Trinidad Bay in the early 1800s. In 1849 Josiah Gregg discovered Trinidad in his search for gold, and before long the gold rush was in full swing. Trinidad became a supply port for gold miners from all over the world as they sought riches in the nearby Salmon, Klamath, and Trinity Rivers. Trinidad has also been a hub of activity for the timber industry. During the gold rush, ships from San Francisco would bring the miners and supplies to Trinidad and carry lumber back to use in building the rapidly growing city.

Today Trinidad is a quaint seaside town about 25 miles north of Eureka. There are several beautiful beaches surrounding the town and numerous shops and restaurants for tourists to enjoy. You can walk the Trinidad Head Trail and visit the historic lighthouse located on the end of the bluff. There's also great hiking in Trinidad State Park and nearby Patrick's Point State Park, a few minutes to the north. Overall, Trinidad is a great place to relax, get away from it all, and hopefully score some quality surf.

Other Information

Local Surf Shops: Salty's Surf and Tackle, 233 Main St., Trinidad; (707) 677-0300.
Places to Stay: Ocean Grove Lodge, 480 Patrick's Point Dr., Trinidad; (707) 677-3543.

Camel Rock on a nice spring day, with no northwest winds—yet—and a couple of humps coming around the corner to a waiting crowd.   Elizabeth Pepin Silva

Trinidad Inn, 1170 Patrick's Point Dr., Trinidad; (707) 677-3349.
Places to Eat: Larrupin' Cafe, 1658 Patrick's Point Dr., Trinidad; (707) 677-0230. Ocean Grove Restaurant, 480 Patrick's Point Dr., Trinidad; (707) 677-0394.

Moonstone Beach

This is a large beach just south of Trinidad with numerous right and left peaks.

Best tides: Low to medium
Best swell direction: West
Best wave size: Chest high to head high
Bottom: Sand
Type of break: Outside rights and lefts

Skill level: Novice to intermediate
Best boards: Funshape, longboard
Best seasons: Fall and spring
Crowds: Can get crowded when it's good
Water quality: Clean
Hazards: Sharks
Fees and permits: None

Finding the Break

From Arcata: Head north on US 101 toward the town of Trinidad. Take the Westhaven Drive exit just south of Trinidad and drive south along Scenic Drive. Head west on Moonstone Beach Drive and park by the beach. There's plenty of parking in the Moonstone Beach parking lot, and it's an easy walk to the beach. GPS: N41 01.751 / W124 06.667

Surf Description

Moonstone Beach is just south of Trinidad, a small fishing town that attracts a fair number of tourists. The surrounding area is very beautiful and has some nice hiking trails with great vistas, rocky coves, headlands, and forests to explore. This beach used to be called Merriman's, after a restaurant of the same name that overlooked the beach. The restaurant is now called Moonstone, and as a result, the name of the beach was changed.

Moonstone is a large beach with plenty of peaks to enjoy—there should be no reason to surf in a crowd here. If you walk up or down the beach a little, you're bound to find a relatively empty spot. Several outer sandbars along this beach create long, peeling lines. Most of the waves at Moonstone Beach are rights, but you can find the occasional left. Overall, the waves here are well suited to novice and intermediate surfers. Waves tend to be forgiving and not as hollow as many sand-bottomed breaks. The winter surf can be big and fun, though spring and fall months tend to bring waves with less size but better shape.

For a taste of Trinidad's nightlife, visit Ocean Grove Lounge, 480 Patrick's Point Dr., Trinidad; (707) 677-3238.

This area has also generated a few shark stories over the years. On October 18, 1976, a surfer was attacked at Moonstone Beach. Luckily, no major injuries were inflicted. Then, almost exactly four years later, on October 17, 1980, another surfer

An empty pocket at Moonstone Beach.   Chris Burkard

was attacked here and was also very lucky to escape with no major injuries. However, years later a third surfer wasn't quite as lucky. On August 24, 1997, a surfer reportedly sustained major injuries after being attacked at Moonstone Beach. In 1990 there were also two attacks, about a week apart, near the town of Trinidad. The first came on August 28, 1990, on a 22-year-old surfer at Trinidad Head. This incident involved a great white shark that was estimated to be more than 18 feet long. Not only was the shark scarily long, it was also very large in girth. The attack occurred about 30 yards from shore and left a deep laceration in the victim's leg. And on September 5, 1990, a kayaker was attacked by a shark at Trinidad State Beach. Fortunately, this victim got away with no major injuries.

As we've mentioned earlier, your odds of being attacked by a shark while surfing are very low. Still, it's advisable to surf with a buddy for a variety of reasons. And it makes even more sense if you're surfing a break that could be occasionally patrolled by sharks.

Elizabeth Pepin Silva

Nikki Brooks

Above, Clam Beach is a beach break just north of the town of Arcata. To reach it, follow the signs for Clam Beach off US 101. It's an exposed break that's best during a south swell in summer. Winter surf can be good, but getting out can be difficult.

Left, Samoa Beach is a beach break just outside Arcata Bay. From Arcata, follow Samoa Boulevard and look for the signs for Samoa Beach. Like Clam Beach, Samoa is best during a summer south swell. The winter peaks here can be well shaped with the right conditions.

Other Information

Local Surf Shops: Salty's Surf and Tackle, 233 Main St., Trinidad; (707) 677-0300.
Places to Stay: Ocean Grove Lodge, 480 Patrick's Point Dr., Trinidad; (707) 677-3543.
Trinidad Inn, 1170 Patrick's Point Dr., Trinidad; (707) 677-3349.
Places to Eat: Larrupin' Cafe, 1658 Patrick's Point Dr., Trinidad; (707) 677-0230. Ocean
Grove Restaurant, 480 Patrick's Point Dr., Trinidad; (707) 677-0394.

North Jetty

This is a very consistent, high-quality beach break on the north side of the entrance
to Humboldt Bay.

Best tides: Low to medium
Best swell direction: Northwest
Best wave size: Chest high to triple overhead
Bottom: Sand
Type of break: Left and right outside
Skill level: Intermediate to advanced
Best boards: Shortboard, gun
Best seasons: Fall and winter
Crowds: Crowded
Water quality: Average to clean
Hazards: Sharks, localism
Fees and permits: None

Finding the Break

From Eureka or Arcata: Take Samoa Boulevard (Route 255) until you reach the ocean
at Samoa. There are places to park along Jetty Road, and it's a short walk to the beach.
GPS: N40 45.216 / W124 13.959

Surf Description

North Jetty is the best wave in the Humboldt area. There's a semipermanent sandbar
here that's been carved out by the current and creates a great wave. The best waves
break 200 to 300 feet from shore and go farther out as the swell size increases. There
are two main waves at North Jetty—a short hollow right and a longer bowling left.
Have fun, but surf with a buddy because in October 1993 a shark attack on a surfer at
North Jetty resulted in major injuries.

The beach breaks on both sides of Humboldt Harbor have heaps of power. This peak is breaking off the north side, as two paddlers watch from out of position.

In 1991 the Surfrider Foundation brought a $5.8 million lawsuit against two pulp mills in Humboldt County. The case is referred to as "the North Jetty lawsuit" and was won in 1992. The pulp mills were charged with more than 40,000 violations of the federal Clean Water Act—the second biggest Clean Water Act suit in US history. It was a major victory for the environment and for the sport of surfing, and pulp mills have since been forced to change their practices.

The Surfrider Foundation is an environmental organization that was founded in 1985. Glen Hening, a history teacher from Ventura, and cofounder Tom Pratte wanted "to make a statement about the extraordinary character of riding waves." They had a vision of providing "a way for wave riders everywhere to take an active role in shaping the future of something we love with a passion." The Surfrider Foundation currently has chapters all over the world and is "committed to conservation, research, and education."

This break can be world-class with the right swell.

The North Jetty is the north side of the entrance to Humboldt Bay. This area was once a seasonal food-gathering site for the Wiyot Indians. In the 1850s the US government built a lighthouse in the center of what is now a recreation area. However, the beacon was too low to be seen from the ocean, and the lighthouse was abandoned in 1867. During World War II the Coast Guard constructed ammunition bunkers in this area as part of its surveillance of the Pacific coastline. Today the beach on this side of the harbor entrance is part of the Samoa Dunes Recreation Area and is managed by the Bureau of Land Management as a multiple-use recreation site. This 300 acre park offers a wide variety of activities but is most popular with all-terrain vehicle users. Riders have access to more than 200 acres of "open" terrain, including trails, as well as the beach.

Other Information

Local Surf Shops: Humboldt Surf Company, 817 H St., on the Arcata Plaza, Arcata; (707) 822-2680. The Shop, 939 Eighth St., Arcata; (707) 498-3637.

Places to Stay: Samoa Boat Ramp County Park, 5 miles south of Samoa Bridge near Navy Base Road, call for directions; (707) 445-7651. There are many major hotel chains in Eureka and Arcata.

Places to Eat: Crosswinds Restaurant, 860 10th St., Arcata; (707) 826-2133. Hey Juan's, 1642 G St., Arcata; (707) 822-8433. Weatherby's, 1906 Fourth St., Eureka; (707) 442-0683.

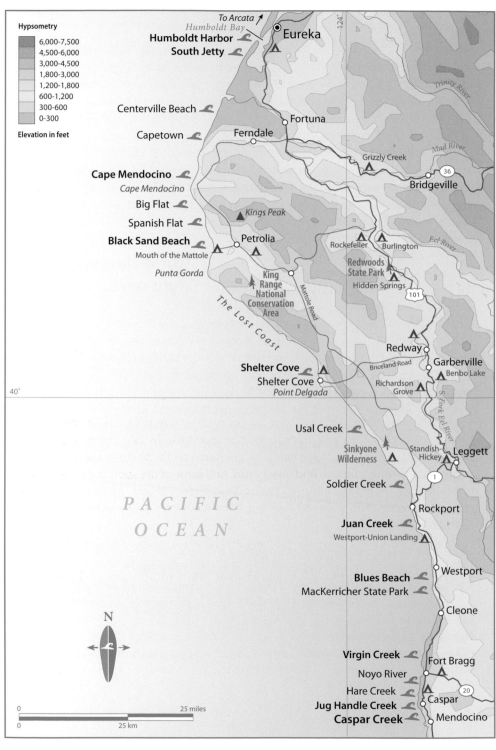

Hypsometry

6,000-7,500
4,500-6,000
3,000-4,500
1,800-3,000
1,200-1,800
600-1,200
300-600
0-300

Elevation in feet

To Arcata ↗
Humboldt Bay
Eureka
124°

Humboldt Harbor
South Jetty

Trinity River

Centerville Beach

Fortuna

Capetown
Ferndale

Grizzly Creek
Mad River

Cape Mendocino
Cape Mendocino

36

Bridgeville

Big Flat
Kings Peak

Spanish Flat
Rockefeller
Burlington
Eel River

Black Sand Beach
Petrolia

Redwoods
State Park

Mouth of the Mattole

Hidden Springs

Punta Gorda
King
Range
National
Conservation
Area

Mattole Road

101

The Lost Coast

Redway

Shelter Cove
Briceland Road
Garberville

Shelter Cove
Benbo Lake

Point Delgada
Richardson
Grove

40°

S. Fork Eel River

Usal Creek

Sinkyone
Wilderness
Standish-
Hickey
Leggett

PACIFIC

1

OCEAN

Soldier Creek

Rockport

Juan Creek
Westport-Union Landing

Blues Beach
Westport

MacKerricher State Park

N

Cleone

Virgin Creek
Fort Bragg

Noyo River
20

Hare Creek
Caspar

Jug Handle Creek

Caspar Creek
Mendocino

0   25 miles

0   25 km

Region 2 (Eureka to Mendocino)

REGION 2: EUREKA TO MENDOCINO

This part of California's coast Is as beautiful as it gets. It's a little more populated than the region north of here but still mellow and relatively undeveloped. The scenery and feel of this region vary considerably. There are coastal ridges filled with Douglas fir, sand dunes, beach grass, lush rain forests, rolling green hills, and flatland marshes. The middle of this region, called the Lost Coast, is a long stretch of dramatic sheer cliffs and rock. There are parts of this stretch that feel extremely remote, with no homes, towns, or cars anywhere in sight. Yet other sections have a much more touristed feel to them. No matter where you go in this region, though, you're bound to find a beautiful spot to camp, hang out, or hike and a friendly place to eat.

Humboldt Bay, near Eureka, is California's largest port north of San Francisco. Humboldt State University in Arcata draws many surfers to this region. However, you probably won't encounter crowds unless It's a weekend or a stellar sunny day. If you steer clear of the popular spots, you can surf by yourself any day of the week.

Overall Surf Description

As with the area north of here, a lot of the spots in this region can be hit or miss. This part of California gets a lot of north and northwest winds. As a result, a lot of the better breaks can get blown out quickly. Depending on the weather conditions, you might need to drive a little to find quality surf. And some of the spots are several miles from the main highways. If you're not in a hurry, however, you can definitely score some sweet waves here nearly year-round. Bring two or three different boards so you can adapt to the conditions. If you truly want to get to know the surf here, or just want to relax and escape it all, give yourself ample time to experience this region. You just might find yourself making an annual surf trip here for years to come.

Every surf spot along this section of coast has seen its share of sharks. River mouths are sharks' favorite places, but the creatures can also hang out at reefs and point breaks. It's a good idea to surf with a buddy whenever possible.

Fall Surf

Fall is usually the best season for both swell and weather. The water tends to be a little warmer, the winds weaker. The autumn months are your best chance to surf ideal waves with no one else in sight.

Rugged coastline, rugged surf, and rugged conditions. A Mendo-scenic slice of surfing life at the mouth of Big River, as the local surfers experience it. The surf isn't always perfect, but the land is always beautiful.   Chris Burkard

Winter Surf
The winter season can mean big surf at some spots. However, you definitely need to know where to surf, depending on the swell size and direction. Wind and tides can also play a big role in the conditions at many of the spots in this region.

Spring Surf
Spring tends to be windy but also sunny. The surf can get big but usually isn't as consistent. As with the region north of here, the south-facing spots are best this time of year.

Summer Surf
Summer's usually not the best season in this area; the surf tends to be small and mushy as onshore winds prevail.

Average Temperatures for Region (Eureka to Mendocino)		
	Air (Mendocino)	Water (Mendocino)
Jan	55	52
Feb	57	52
Mar	58	50
Apr	59	50
May	62	50
June	64	51
July	65	51
Aug	65	52
Sept	66	53
Oct	64	54
Nov	60	53
Dec	56	53

Humboldt Harbor

This is a big wave that breaks inside the entrance to Humboldt Harbor.

Best tide: Low
Best swell direction: Northwest
Best wave size: Head high to quadruple overhead
Bottom: Sand
Type of break: Left and right
Skill level: Advanced
Best board: Gun
Best seasons: Fall and winter
Crowds: Can get crowded when it's good
Water quality: Average to clean
Hazards: Sharks, getting caught in the impact zone
Fees and permits: None

Finding the Break

From Eureka or Arcata: Take Samoa Boulevard (Route 255) and drive until you see the ocean at the harbor entrance. There's parking near the jetty. You have to jump off the jetty and climb back on afterward. GPS: N40 45.935 / W124 13.891

Surf Description

Humboldt Harbor can be one of the heaviest waves in the area. Some liken the left to Pipeline, and the right is steep and dredging. This wave only breaks with a big swell and gets better as the swell size increases. Surfing here on an incoming tide can be hazardous—you can get pulled toward the bay and into the impact zone. In general, Humboldt Harbor requires experience and demands respect.

Humboldt Bay is the only deepwater port between San Francisco and Coos Bay, Oregon. No other coastline in the continental United States goes so far without a deepwater harbor. For hundreds if not thousands of years, several Indian tribes such as the Yuroks and Hupas lived along Humboldt Bay and the nearby rivers. This area went undiscovered by outsiders for many years because the coastline is rugged and the bay isn't easily seen from the ocean, making it a difficult place to approach by ship. Humboldt Bay is also protected by 150 miles of coastal mountains, which means it's an equally daunting spot to reach by land.

Arcata is a fun little town that's been called "the Santa Cruz of Northern California."

The first non-Indians whom Native inhabitants encountered were probably Japanese and Chinese. Their primitive boats were more than likely caught in the eastern flow of the Japanese Current and deposited upon the rocky shoreline near here. Indian legends describe "yellow-skinned men" cast ashore and adopted by tribes hundreds of years before the first white men's ships came here. According to historians, the first European to discover California was Juan Rodriguez Cabrillo, a Portuguese explorer, in 1542. The Cabrillo expedition is believed to have also been the first European venture into Northern California.

From 1565 to 1815 the Spanish made frequent voyages to trade with the Philippines. Ships would sail from Mexico to the Philippines and return along the coast of California. During this time the Spanish were looking for harbors in order to repair their ships, replenish their supplies, and seek protection from pirates. However, records of these explorers include no mention of Humboldt Bay. It's possible that the treacherous coastline, fog, wind, and storms kept their ships far from shore and prevented them from exploring this area.

When Elizabeth I became queen of England in 1558, she sent Sir Francis Drake to raid Spain's Pacific ports and to explore the northeast region of the Pacific Ocean. It's believed that Drake did visit the Humboldt coastline—but he, too, seems never to have found Humboldt Bay. For several decades other Spanish explorers continued to look for a safe place to harbor in this area, and in the 1700s Russian fur traders established outposts along the Pacific Coast, but neither ever noticed Humboldt Bay. It wasn't until 1806 that one Jonathan Winship, who worked for the Russian-American Fur Company, stumbled upon the bay while searching for sea otters.

Harbor Entrance is an unusual wave that breaks on a sandbar inside the entrance to Humboldt Harbor. There are very dangerous currents when it's big, as all that raw power is constricted into a man-made channel that is about 2,000 feet wide and 3,000 feet long. Chris Burkard

Other Information

Local Surf Shops: Humboldt Surf Company, 817 H St., on the Arcata Plaza, Arcata; (707) 822-2680. The Shop, 939 Eighth St., Arcata; (707) 498-3637.

Places to Stay: Samoa Boat Ramp County Park, 5 miles south of Samoa Bridge near Navy Base Road, call for directions; (707) 445-7651. There are several major hotels in Eureka and Arcata.

Places to Eat: Crosswinds Restaurant, 860 10th St., Arcata; (707) 826-2133. Hey Juan's, 1642 G St., Arcata; (707) 822-8433. Weatherby's, 1906 Fourth St., Eureka; (707) 442-0683.

South Jetty

This is a fun and consistent beach break just south of the entrance to Humboldt Bay.

Best tide: Medium
Best swell direction: South
Best wave size: Waist to head high
Bottom: Sand
Type of break: Left and right beach break
Skill level: Intermediate to advanced
Best board: Short
Best season: Summer
Crowds: Can get crowded when it's good
Water quality: Average to clean
Hazards: Sharks
Fees and permits: None

Finding the Break

From Eureka: Follow US 101 south. Head west on Hookton Road until it turns into Table Bluff Road, then follow the signs to the South Jetty. You can park along the road and walk to where the break looks best. GPS: N40 41.840 / W124 16.512

Surf Description

South Jetty is a long beach with numerous well-shaped peaks. It works best with a strong south swell, making it a favored summer spot. Winter surf can be big but not as organized or predictable. Medium-size waves at South Jetty are generally fast and clean, making them the most fun.

The quest for gold and fur resulted in the development of several Northern California settlements in the 1800s, many located on the eastern side of the coastal mountains protecting Humboldt Bay. Miners and trappers needed a way to get supplies from ships as well as ship gold and fur out. This prompted Josiah Gregg to lead an expedition seeking a route through the mountains to the Pacific Ocean. The group started from the gold camp in Weaverville, a distance of roughly 150 miles from the coast. They brought a two-month supply of food and, due to the dense forests, were able to travel an average of only 2 miles per day.

The members of the Gregg expedition nearly starved but managed to eventually reach the Pacific. A short time later they found Humboldt Bay and walked back to San Francisco in order to report on what they had discovered. Josiah Gregg can be

All the conditions come together for this barrel at South Jetty, Humboldt.

credited with overcoming the Humboldt region's isolation. Armed with the knowledge that a northern port existed, two ships from San Francisco headed north to find Humboldt Bay in 1850. The sailors from one of the ships, the *Laura Virginia,* bestowed the name Humboldt Bay after a famous naturalist named Baron Von Humboldt. They can also be credited with founding Humboldt City.

Humboldt County grew tremendously from 1860 to 1900 thanks to the timber and fishing industries. Giant redwoods were cut down at a frenzied pace with no concern for reforestation, and the lumber was soon sent all over the world. Records show that more than 1,000 ships entered Humboldt Bay in 1876—at the time, they provided the only transportation to and from the growing cities in the area. In 1914 a railroad was constructed between Eureka and San Francisco. Although some sections were unpaved until 1925, US 101 was completed in 1920. And in 1942 the US Navy built an airport in McKinleyville.

Chris Burkard

Centerville Beach is located south of Eureka and west of the town of Ferndale. This is a very remote area of the California coast and a few miles from US 101. There are outside peaks with long lines and a powerful beach break that works best from waist to chest high.

Nikki Brooks

The Capetown area is an isolated and undeveloped stretch of coast south of Eureka. There are a series of rock reefs with numerous quality breaks that can work with virtually any size swell from any direction. As the swell size increases, the peaks move farther out. However, Capetown's versatility also makes it susceptible to becoming easily blown out by northwest winds. The currents and cleanup sets in this area can be strong and hazardous.

Despite the advances in transportation made in the last several decades, Humboldt County has managed to remain somewhat isolated. In 1991 the city of Eureka and Humboldt County published a development plan for the region. The report suggested ways to use the bay to off-load Japanese containers in order to create more jobs and reduce the local economy's dependence on the timber industry. However, because it takes so long to get products from this area to more populated parts of the country, it's unlikely that such ideas will be successful anytime in the near future. Humboldt County could very well stay relatively small and underdeveloped for years to come.

Other Information

Local Surf Shops: Humboldt Surf Company, 817 H St., on the Arcata Plaza, Arcata; (707) 822-2680. The Shop, 939 Eighth St., Arcata; (707) 498-3637.

Places to Stay: Samoa Boat Ramp County Park, 5 miles south of Samoa Bridge near Navy Base Road, call for directions; (707) 445-7651. There are several major hotels in Eureka and Arcata.

Places to Eat: Crosswinds Restaurant, 860 10th St., Arcata; (707) 826-2133. Hey Juan's, 1642 G St., Arcata; (707) 822-8433. Weatherby's, 1906 Fourth St., Eureka; (707) 442-0683.

SUP DATE: HUMBOLDT HARBOR TO CAPE MENDOCINO

In a lot of ways, SUPs were made for coastlines like this. Most of this coastline is either off-limits or hard to get to for most surfers—the highway doesn't come close, there is private farm land as a barrier, and there is no place to park. So standup paddlers with the skill, right equipment and experience, and caution can have a blast along here.

For example. Launch in Humboldt Harbor, then paddle out of the entrance, turn left, and paddle along the beach breaks at South Jetty for 8 or so miles. Check out the sandbars at the mouth of the Eel River, ride waves to *The Theme from Jaws,* and then paddle through the sandbar and into the Eel River estuary and go upriver as far as you want.

That's a big adventure right there, and there are many others. Farther south, the Mattole is a beautiful, isolated river that empties into the ocean south of Cape Mendocino. It would be fun to launch from Petrolia on the Mattole, paddle 6 beautiful miles downriver to the mouth of the Mattole, and see what's breaking along the sandbar there. Then paddle along the coast as far as the conditions—and your nerve—allow.

Cape Mendocino

Miles of quality reef and point breaks on an undeveloped and isolated stretch of coast.

Best tide: Any
Best swell direction: Any
Best wave size: Any
Bottom: Sand and rock
Type of break: Beach, outside, reefs, points, lefts and rights
Skill level: Novice to advanced
Best boards: Longboard, shortboard, funshape
Best seasons: Spring and winter
Crowds: Not crowded
Water quality: Clean
Hazards: None
Fees and permits: None

The westmost point in California, Cape Mendocino is hammered by a lot of swell and a lot of wind, and sometimes the two come together into cold, lonely, quality surf.

Finding the Break

From Eureka: Head south on CA 101. Follow CA 211 west until the road runs parallel to the ocean. CA 211 is a long and winding road that runs from CA 101 to Petrolia. From Petrolia it continues southeast back to CA 101, but it's a very slow drive on a narrow and twisting road. You can park along the road and walk to the breaks. GPS: N40 26.408 / W124 24.570

Surf Description

Cape Mendocino has miles of reef and beach breaks to surf. This is a very beautiful, undeveloped, and isolated stretch of coast; it's home to numerous bays and points that can serve up excellent waves. Cape Mendocino can capture swell year-round but is especially good in spring and winter. If you're looking to surf well-shaped, quality waves all by yourself, this is the place to visit. There are no nearby services, however, so make sure you have plenty of gas, food, and water before you venture out here.

In an average year the coastal areas of Humboldt and Del Norte Counties experience an average of one hundred earthquakes of a magnitude 3.0 or higher and roughly twenty with a minimum magnitude of 4.0. The Cape Mendocino region in particular is known as one of the most seismically active areas of the United States. The Mendocino Fault—the boundary between the Pacific Plate to the south and the Gorda Plate to the north—is very active and is responsible for about 30 percent of the seismic energy released in the North Coast area each year.

There have been several large earthquakes in this region in recent years. In September 1991 an earthquake estimated at 6.2 on the Richter scale occurred roughly 13 miles southeast of Cape Mendocino. More than 60 percent of the homes in the nearby town of Honeydew

> **Cape Mendocino is a very beautiful and incredibly isolated stretch of coast.**

sustained structural damage. In April 1992 a 7.1-magnitude quake was centered near Petrolia, the closest town to Cape Mendocino. This quake was a result of the North American Plate being thrust over the Gorda Plate and caused coastal uplift of up to 5 feet in the vicinity of Cape Mendocino. The movement of the 1992 quake triggered a small tsunami that was recorded at tide gauges from Port Orford, Oregon, to San Luis Obispo, California. This earthquake and the large aftershocks caused more than $60 million in damage and resulted in a federal disaster declaration. In September 1994 a 7.2-magnitude quake occurred roughly 90 miles west of Cape Mendocino. Felt from south of San Francisco to Roseburg, Oregon, this earthquake also triggered a small tsunami. However, because the quake was located so far offshore, there were no reports of damage. In February 1995 a 6.6-magnitude temblor was recorded 80 miles west of Cape Mendocino. This quake was very similar to the one experienced in 1994 and fortunately resulted in no major damage.

Nikki Brooks

Left, Big Flat is the next spot worth surfing south of Cape Mendocino. It's located on a southwest-facing stretch of completely isolated and undeveloped shoreline dubbed the Lost Coast. This section of beach is part of the King Range National Conservation Area and as a result is difficult to access.

Below, Spanish Flat is the next area to check out south of Big Flat. It's a little more south-facing than Big Flat but just as isolated and undeveloped. Spanish Flat is also part of the Lost Coast and the King Range National Conservation Area, and it is just as difficult to access. You can find quality outer-reef breaks as well as inside beach breaks here. Again, winter surf can be big and unpredictable, but summer surf is well shaped and consistent.

Nikki Brooks

Other Information

Local Surf Shops: Humboldt Surf Company, 817 H St., on the Arcata Plaza, Arcata; (707) 822-2680. The Shop, 939 Eighth St., Arcata; (707) 498-3637.
Places to Stay: Samoa Boat Ramp County Park, 5 miles south of Samoa Bridge near Navy Base Road, call for directions; (707) 445-7651. There are several major hotels in Eureka and Arcata.
Places to Eat: Crosswinds Restaurant, 860 10th St., Arcata; (707) 826-2133. Hey Juan's, 1642 G St., Arcata; (707) 822-8433. Weatherby's, 1906 Fourth St., Eureka; (707) 442-0683.

Black Sand Beach

This is a large, mostly west-facing, black-sand beach with offshore reefs just north of the town of Shelter Cove.

Best tides: Incoming to high
Best swell direction: West
Best wave size: Waist high to double overhead
Bottom: Rock and sand
Type of break: Outside
Skill level: Novice in summer, intermediate to advanced in winter
Best boards: Shortboard, longboard
Best season: Any
Crowds: Not crowded
Water quality: Clean
Hazards: Sharks
Fees and permits: None

Finding the Break

From Eureka: Head south on US 101 to the Redway–Shelter Cove exit near Garberville. Drive through Redway onto Briceland Road. Follow Briceland Road for about 23 miles and look for the signs to Black Sand Beach. The road from Redway through Briceland to Black Sand Beach is long and winding. There's plenty of space in the Black Sand Beach parking area, and it's an easy stroll down to the beach. GPS: N40 02.730 / W124 04.650

Surf Description

Black Sand Beach is a picturesque and relaxing beach. The black sand that covers the beach and has given the spot its name is very unusual. There are offshore reefs in this area that can create peeling lines of consistent and well-shaped surf. The winter months can bring big swell from the west and northwest. In general, the winter season requires skill and experience and isn't the best time of year for novice surfers to visit. The summer months can mean smaller surf with fun south swells that are much less intimidating. Regardless of the season, this is definitely a beach worth checking out even when there's not a visiting swell.

Black Sand Beach is near the south end of the King Range National Conservation Area—a stretch of California coast that's still relatively undeveloped, with few towns and roads. The terrain here is steep and rocky with several large elevation gains. The highest peak, called Kings Peak, is more than 4,000 feet high. This part of the coast is so rugged that it forced the combined US 1/101 about 30 miles inland.

The conservation area is a great place to check out if you have time. It consists of roughly 52,000 acres of public land managed by the Bureau of Land Management; an additional 8,000 acres are privately owned. There's a lot of wildlife here including

On the way from Shelter Cove to Big Flat: temptation along Black Sands Beach.

harbor seals, sea lions, black bears, black-tailed deer, Roosevelt elk, pelicans, bald eagles, spotted owls, woodpeckers, gulls, and roughly 300 other species of native and migratory birds. You can also see California gray whales migrating very close to this beach, especially in January and February.

The King Range receives some of the most rainfall of any spot on the Pacific Ocean. If you're visiting from October to April, you can expect rain as a result of the moist ocean air and storms that frequently hit this coastal mountain range. There's a 24-mile section of the Lost Coast Trail that leads north from Black

Stop by the Shelter Cove information bureau (707-986-7069) for other things to do in the area.

Sand Beach to the Mattole River. This hike can be challenging and even strenuous at times, but it's known as one of the best ways to experience the King Range National Conservation Area.

Other Information

Local Surf Shops: Tsunami Surf and Sport, 818 Redwood Dr., Garberville; (707) 923-1965 (they also have a small shop by the air strip in Shelter Cove).
Places to Stay: Beachcomber Inn, 412 Machi Rd., Shelter Cove; (800) 718-4789. Ocean Front Inn, 26 Seal Ct., Shelter Cove; (707) 986-7002. Inn of the Lost Coast, 205 Wave Dr., Shelter Cove; (888) 570-9676.
Places to Eat: The Cove Restaurant, 10 Seal Ct., Shelter Cove; (707) 986-1197.

Shelter Cove
This is an area of coast with several rock reefs far removed from any major town.

Best tides: Incoming to high
Best swell direction: West, northwest
Best wave size: Waist high to double overhead
Bottom: Rock
Type of break: Left and right
Skill level: Novice in summer; intermediate to advanced in winter
Best boards: Shortboard, longboard
Best season: Fall
Crowds: Not crowded
Water quality: Clean
Hazards: Sharks, submerged rocks
Fees and permits: None

Finding the Break

From Eureka: Head south on US 101 to the Redway–Shelter Cove exit near Garberville. Drive through Redway onto Briceland Road. Follow Briceland Road for about 23 miles and look for the signs to Shelter Cove. The road from Redway through Briceland to Shelter Cove is long and winding. There are plenty of places to park in the town of Shelter Cove, and it's an easy walk to the beach to check out the breaks. GPS: N40 02.079 / W124 04.706

Surf Description

Shelter Cove is a unique and quiet coastal town surrounded by several quality reefs. There are inside and outside point breaks and reef breaks all within close proximity. The best break to surf for the conditions will become obvious when you check them out from the bluff above. The breaks on the north end of Shelter Cove can handle bigger swell but are also more exposed to north and northwest winds. The breaks on the south end of the cove are best from waist to head high and are much more protected.

There's evidence that Shelter Cove may have been inhabited by Sinkyone Indians as early as the thirteenth century. It's believed that they came to the coast every spring to escape the summer heat of the inland valleys; they were probably attracted by the abundance of food in the area as well. Some believe that these Indians may have even stayed here during the winter months. However, the winters on this stretch of coast can be cold and rainy.

> **Shelter Cove is a mellow town on the "Lost Coast."**

Spanish trade ships and Russian seal traders are also known to have stopped in this cove over the years. Eventually, non-Indians began to settle here, and sheep and cattle ranching became popular in this region. Later on, the tanbark industry thrived here, and a wharf was built in order to ship the bark. When the fishing and tourist industries became popular in Shelter Cove, this wharf saw a lot of traffic from fishing boats and passenger ships from places like San Francisco.

When CA 1 was constructed in the early years of the twentieth century, the decision was made to keep the road inland in this area due to the coastal mountains. And as the tanbark industry declined, people started to abandon Shelter Cove. Shortly thereafter, this portion of the California shoreline became known as the Lost Coast. However, the Machi brothers are credited with the revival of the town. These three young men had worked summer jobs in Shelter Cove in the 1930s and returned to the area to start the community you'll find today. They made a living by renting out rooms and boats to tourists and fishermen. In time Shelter Cove became a land speculation and development project that resulted in a great deal of infrastructure. It continues to grow, and the tourism and fishing industries here are still strong.

Looking south from Shelter Cove along the Sinkyone Wilderness on a perfect fall day.

Other Information

Local Surf Shops: Tsunami Surf and Sport, 818 Redwood Dr., Garberville; (707) 923-1965 (they also have a small shop by the air strip in Shelter Cove).

Places to Stay: Beachcomber Inn, 42 Machi Rd., Shelter Cove; (800) 718-4789. Ocean Front Inn, 26 Seal Court, Shelter Cove; (707) 986-7002. Inn of the Lost Coast, 205 Wave Dr., Shelter Cove; (888) 570-9676.

Places to Eat: The Cove Restaurant, 10 Seal Court, Shelter Cove; (707) 986-1197.

Bryce Johnson

Usal Creek is a remote, mostly west-facing creek break between Shelter Cove and Rockport. The best way to access this break is to head northwest from CA 1 just north of Rockport. Usal Creek has the ability to catch swell any time of year and is best from waist to head high at a medium tide. Peaks can be well-shaped with the right conditions but are dependent on the consistency of the sandbar.

Bryce Johnson

Soldier Creek is a beautiful and protected outer sandbar break. It's located north of Juan Creek on CA 1. If you're driving southwest on CA 1 from the town of Leggett, Soldier Creek is the first break you'll see once you reach the ocean. Swell lines roll into this creek break and produce fast, well-shaped peaks. As with many creek breaks, Soldier Creek is best after heavy rains have deposited fresh sand into the channel.

SUPDATE: THE LOST COAST

You don't want to walk all the way to Big Flat? Then go by SUP! Pack surf gear, camping equipment, and food, keep an eye on the wind, and stroke from Shelter Cove up to Big Flat—to find out if the legend is true. If there are already surfers there, give them a wide berth. Outsiders are often told to get lost along the Lost Coast and SUPs are even less welcome. If it's too windy to head north, then go south from Shelter Cove along the Sinkyone Wilderness. This stretch of coast isn't even accessible by foot, and the adventurous SUPista will find waves and wonders along here.

Juan Creek

This west-facing beach—where Juan Creek empties into the ocean—is located about 22 miles north of Fort Bragg.

Best tide: Medium
Best swell direction: Any
Best wave size: Any
Bottom: Rock
Type of break: Outside
Skill level: Intermediate to advanced
Best boards: Shortboard, funshape
Best seasons: Fall and winter
Crowds: Not crowded
Water quality: Clean
Hazards: Rocks along shoreline
Fees and permits: None

Finding the Break

From Eureka: Follow US 101 south to Leggett. In Leggett follow CA 1 southwest toward Westport. Juan Creek is between Rockport and Westport off CA 1; look for the sign posted on the bridge. You can park along CA 1 and walk down to the beach. GPS: N39 42.176 / W123 48.218

Juan Creek as seen from the unblinking helicopter of Kenneth Adelman, the man behind **californiacoastline.org.** californiacoastline.org

Surf Description

Juan Creek is a west-facing beach that catches swell coming from any direction. This break can create thick walls that peak on a reef about 100 yards out. The big rocks along the shoreline can make entry and exit hazardous at higher tides. And wave shape here is best at a medium tide. Overall, Juan Creek is a consistent spot not to be taken lightly.

We all know that the state of California was originally inhabited by a people we refer to as the American Indians. The state is said to have been discovered by Europeans in 1542 by J. R. Cabrillo, a Portuguese navigator who was sailing for Spain. In 1578 Sir Francis Drake landed at what's now known as Drake's Bay. He is believed to have communicated with the natives who lived here at the time, and when he took possession of the region in the name of England, he named it New Albion. Several years later, in 1602, a Spaniard by the name of Sebastián Vizcaíno explored the region extensively. However, it wasn't until 1769—when Franciscan fathers built a mission in San Diego—that the state was colonized. In the next few decades, more than twenty missions were established in the state, and the lives of more than 20,000 American Indians around those missions changed drastically. California eventually became part of the United States, and the gold rush of 1848 proved devastating for the natives who weren't affected by the Spanish. The huge influx of immigrants that poured into this part of the country in the 1800s resulted in systematic displacement and extermination of the American Indians in the state of California. Today the ancestors of the Native peoples of the state live on reservations that were set aside for their tribes or are scattered throughout the country living as squatters or on land that they've managed to purchase.

> **Westport, a town of fewer than 300 people, is the only beach town between Cleone and Shelter Cove.**

The Indian tribe that lived in the Juan Creek area is part of the Yukian tribes; they referred to themselves as Ukohtontilka, or "ocean tribe." They were the early inhabitants of the stretch of California coast between Cleone and a point halfway between Rockport and Usal. The tribe was known to have hunted and fished in this region, but the majority of their diet came from vegetation near the coast. Following the gold rush, this coastal tribe of Yuki Indians came in contact with whites on several occasions. Each conflict resulted in significant casualties for these natives. In 1864 the Round Valley Reservation was established for this tribe as well as a few others. By 1902 there were fewer than twenty tribe members living on the reservation.

Other Information

Local Surf Shops: None.

Places to Stay: Howard Creek Ranch Inn, 40501 N. CA 1, Westport; (707) 964-6725. The Westport Inn, 37040 N. CA 1, Westport; (707) 964-5135. Westport-Union Landing State Beach, 18200 N. CA 1, Westport; (707) 937-5804.

Places to Eat: Westport Inn and Deli, 37040 N. CA 1, Westport; (707) 964-5135. Westport Community Store, 37001 N. CA 1, Westport; (707) 964-2872.

Blues Beach

This can be a superb right outside reef break and is located roughly 15 miles north of Fort Bragg.

Best tide: Medium
Best swell direction: West
Best wave size: Chest high to head high
Bottom: Sand and rock
Type of breaks: Right outside reef
Skill level: Intermediate
Best boards: Shortboard, funshape, longboard
Best seasons: Fall and summer
Crowds: Not crowded
Water quality: Clean
Hazards: Sharks
Fees and permits: None

Finding the Break

From Eureka: Follow US 101 south to CA 1 at Leggett. Follow CA 1 southwest toward Westport. Blues Beach is near milepost 75.4. Look for a short dirt road that leads to the beach from CA 1. Blues Beach is roughly 1.6 miles south of Westport. There's parking at the end of the dirt road, and it's a short walk to the beach. GPS: N39 36.828 / W123 46.913

Surf Description

Blues Beach is a beautiful sandy beach protected by a few very large rocks. There's some decent beach break here, but the best surf is a right outside reef break. With an organized west swell at medium tide, Blues Beach can be graced by peaky, fast tubes—but the surf here can also get mushy at higher tides. If you have the time, and the weather cooperates, Blues Beach is one of those places worth hanging out at for a few hours.

The closest town to Blues Beach is a small, quaint village called Westport. Today the population of Westport is less than 300. In the late 1800s and early 1900s, however, 3,000 people lived here, making it the largest coastal town in California north of San Francisco at the time. In those days Westport served as an important shipping port and was home to the longest logging chutes in the state. A 1,000-acre sheep and cattle ranch and a lumber company were also located near Westport back then.

Lonely surf check at Blues Beach.   Chris Burkard

Eventually, the rancher moved south and the lumber company closed down. The village of Westport was destroyed by a fire in 1920, and the town church has fallen off the cliff into the ocean twice. A lot of people have since left this once bustling community to find work elsewhere; it's now just another quiet little California coastal burg.

Although there has never been an attack reported at Blues Beach, sharks are known to patrol these waters. There were two attacks north of here in Shelter Cove, one in 1991 and the other in 1995. And three free divers sustained major injuries after being attacked near

Blues Beach and the surrounding coast is truly awe-inspiring.

here. One attack occurred at Usal Creek in 1975; another was at a place called Bear Harbor to the north of Westport in 1982; the third was in Westport in 1993. A more recent attack happened at a place called Kibesillah Rock near Westport on August 15, 2004. The victim was a 50-year-old man who was diving for abalone. His friend

Lucia Griggi

MacKerricher State Park is located off CA 1 near the town of Cleone. The park has a sandy 6-mile stretch of beach and dunes with decent beach-break surf. A northwest swell at medium tide can produce waves with steep drops and tubes. However, the best break in MacKerricher is in a small cove that can experience clean rights peeling into a channel. There's also a left that can be good, but the right is usually better. The bottom here is a combination of sand and rock, which makes the peak fairly consistent. Watch for submerged rocks if you surf at lower tides.

apparently saw a large fish shortly before the man disappeared; the diver's headless body was found the next day. According to the Department of Fish and Game, there have been 106 shark attacks on the West Coast since the 1950s. Ten resulted in fatalities. The last fatal attack before this one occurred in August 2003 when an 18-foot-long great white killed a swimmer at Avila Beach.

Other Information

Local Surf Shops: None.
Places to Stay: Howard Creek Ranch Inn, 40501 N. CA 1, Westport; (707) 964-6725. The Westport Inn, 37040 N. CA 1, Westport; (707) 964-5135. Westport-Union Landing State Beach, 18220 N. CA 1, Westport; (707) 937-5804.
Places to Eat: Westport Inn and Deli, 37040 N. CA 1, Westport; (707) 964-5135. Westport Community Store, 37001 N. CA 1, Westport; (707) 964-2872.

Virgin Creek
This is a small beach where Virgin Creek meets the ocean just north of Fort Bragg.

Best tide: Medium
Best swell direction: West, northwest
Best wave size: Waist high to head high
Bottom: Sand and rock
Type of breaks: Left and right, outside, and beach break
Skill level: Intermediate to advanced
Best boards: Shortboard, funshape, longboard
Best season: Any
Crowds: Can get crowded on weekends when it's good
Water quality: Clean
Hazards: None
Fees and permits: None

Finding the Break

From Fort Bragg: Head north 5.6 miles on CA 1. Look for a dirt lot on the east side of the highway about 0.3 mile north of Airport Road. You can park here and follow the path down to the beach. GPS: N39 27.904 / W123 48.357

Surf Description

The beach at Virgin Creek is a few-minutes' walk from where you can park on CA 1. If it's on, you'll probably see at least one car with surf racks parked in the lot where the path begins. Once you get to the bluff overlooking the break, you'll be able to see where the creek comes in and where the waves are breaking best. This beach is mostly west facing, so it works best with energy from the west and northwest. With an organized swell, the peaks at Virgin Creek can be nicely shaped and the waves fast.

Virgin Creek is just north of Fort Bragg and just south of MacKerricher State Park. The 9-mile stretch of beach in this state park is beautiful and pristine, with rocky head-lands, sand dunes, coves, and sandy beaches. The Northern Pomo and Coast Yuki Indians are believed to have inhabited this part of the California coast for thousands of years. The natural resources here are plentiful; these tribes lived off fish, seaweed, shellfish, and a variety of coastal vegetation.

In 1865 a Canadian by the name of Duncan MacKerricher moved to this area and within a few years was able to purchase a 1,000-acre ranch. He called it Rancho de la Laguna and raised cattle, horses, and hogs. A wharf was later built on Laguna Point, just north of Virgin Creek, and MacKerricher allowed a local lumber-mill owner to construct a gravity-fed railway from Cleone to Laguna Point. MacKerricher's heirs ended up selling the land to the state in 1949.

MacKerricher State Park is filled with wildlife. From December to April Laguna Point is a popular whale-watching spot. Gray whales can be seen during this time as they migrate between Baja California and the Bering Sea. There's also a seal-watching station on Laguna Point where visitors can check out harbor seals that enjoy basking in the sun on the rocks near here. Black-tailed deer, raccoons, foxes, rabbits, squirrels, and more than ninety species of birds live in the park as well.

There's a beach in Fort Bragg aptly named Glass Beach—a former bottling company used it as a dump. The Skunk Train in Fort Bragg is a great way to learn a little about Mendocino Coast history; call (707) 964-6371.

The town of Fort Bragg, just south of Virgin Creek, was originally established as a military post. Today it has a cool small-town feel with numerous shops, restaurants, and lodging options. The Skunk Train is popular among tourists, taking you on a tour from downtown Fort Bragg through some of the area's redwood forests.

The go-to spot for surfers in the Fort Bragg area, Virgin Creek has as many moods as the Pacific Ocean—from flat and gloomy in summer to raging Victory at Sea in winter. Best to get it somewhere in between.   californiacoastline.org

Other Information

Local Surf Shops: Lost Surf Shack, 319 N. Franklin St., Fort Bragg; (707) 961-0889. North Pacific Productions, 22991 CA 1, Fort Bragg; (707) 961-0314.

Places to Stay: There are several motels and hotels in Fort Bragg to fit any budget. Surf and Sand Lodge, 1131 N. Main St., Fort Bragg; (800) 964-0184. MacKerricher State Park campgrounds, 24100 MacKerricher Rd., Fort Bragg; (707) 937-5804.

Places to Eat: North Coast Brewing Company, 444 Main St., Fort Bragg; (707) 964-3400. Egghead's, 326 N. Main St., Fort Bragg; (707) 964-5005. Home Style Cafe, 790 S. Main St., Fort Bragg; (707) 964-6106.

Chris Burkard

Noyo River is a left that breaks off the Noyo Harbor seawall in Fort Bragg. It's not very consistent and works best during a large winter swell. The Noyo River break is a slow wave and needs a lower tide to be worth surfing.

Chris Sardelis

Hare Creek is a creek break just south of Fort Bragg. The waves are best here when they're small and peeling. Wave shape comes closest to ideal when the creek is flowing strongly. Hare Creek works best with waist-high waves at a medium tide.

Jug Handle Creek

This is an outer sandbar break that can create well-shaped peaks in a small cove.

Best tide: Medium
Best swell direction: West
Best wave size: Waist high to chest high
Bottom: Sand
Type of break: Outside sandbar
Skill level: Intermediate
Best boards: Shortboard, funshape, longboard
Best season: Winter
Crowds: Can get crowded on weekends when it's good
Water quality: Clean
Hazards: Sharks
Fees and permits: None

Finding the Break

From Fort Bragg: Head south on CA 1. Turn right into Jug Handle State Park just before the small town of Caspar. You can leave your vehicle in the parking lot and walk down to the beach on a small dirt trail. GPS: N39 22.608 / W123 49.037

Surf Description

Jug Handle Creek is an outer sandbar break within a protected cove. The cove faces west, making it a good winter spot. West and northwest swell can enter the cove, but wave shape is enhanced as a result of being protected from northwest wind. Jug Handle Creek is best after a rain when the creek deposits fresh sand and builds the outer sandbar.

Jug Handle Creek is within the Jug Handle State Reserve, a 769-acre park on the Mendocino coast. There's a 2.5-mile nature trail here called the Ecological Staircase that allows you to walk along five different terraces. Each wave-cut terrace represents a stage of ecological succession and landscape evolution formed by the same glacial, sea, and tectonic activity that created the Coastal Range. Every terrace was uplifted above sea level 100,000 years before the one below it. The plants you can see on each terrace are more advanced than the ones below and represent what the next level will look like in 100,000 years.

These terraces at Jug Handle State Reserve are a result of the movement of the earth's crust as well as the fluctuation of the sea level over time. Scientists believe that in the last few million years, the continent of North America has moved northwest,

Keren Katz slides a rare sunny, glassy day at Jug Handle Creek.   Elizabeth Pepin Silva

while the Mendocino coast has risen in relation to the sea-level fluctuation caused by the melting of glaciers. There's evidence that during the Pleistocene period, glaciers were moving northward and the sea level was rising faster than the land was. Wave action then resulted in the creation of these once-underwater terraces. Eventually, the glaciers re-formed, the sea level dropped—and now we can walk on this Ecological Staircase.

There are some good hiking trails at Jug Handle State Reserve.

As the sea level and the waves decreased, sand and other materials were spread along the top, emerging terrace. The uplifting of the earth's crust and the rise of the coastline continued to elevate the first terrace, and new terraces were created where the first one had been originally shaped. The highest and oldest terrace—terrace number five—was once at the elevation of number four, and so on down the line. This sequence of events is believed to have occurred over the course of about 100,000 years, resulting in roughly 100 feet of uplift to form each terrace.

Other Information

Local Surf Shops: Lost Surf Shack, 319 N. Franklin St., Fort Bragg; (707) 961-0889. North Pacific Productions, 22991 CA 1, Fort Bragg; (707) 961-0314.

Places to Stay: Caspar Beach RV Park and Campground, 14441 Point Cabrillo Dr., Caspar; (707) 964-3306. Caspar Inn, 14957 Caspar Rd., Caspar; (707) 964-5565.

Places to Eat: North Coast Brewing Company, 444 Main St., Fort Bragg; (707) 964-3400. Egghead's, 326 N. Main St., Fort Bragg; (707) 964-5005. Home Style Cafe, 790 S. Main St., Fort Bragg; (707) 964-6106.

Caspar Creek

This outer sandbar break produces small, peeling waves inside a well-protected cove.

Best tide: Medium

Best swell direction: West

Best wave size: Waist high

Bottom: Sand

Type of break: Outside sandbar

Skill level: Novice to intermediate

Best boards: Longboard, funshape

Best season: Winter

Crowds: Can get crowded on weekends when it's good

Water quality: Clean

Hazards: Sharks

Fees and permits: None

Finding the Break

From Fort Bragg: Head south 5.7 miles on CA 1. Turn right onto Point Cabrillo Drive, south of the town of Caspar, and drive down to the beach. There's an area to park by the beach, and it's a very short walk from there to the break. GPS: N39 21.580 / W123 48.960

Surf Description

The break at Caspar Creek is located within a large, picturesque cove. The bluffs on either side of this cove protect its beach and waves from northwesterly wind. However, being sheltered also means that the break at Caspar Creek doesn't get a

Dave Silva slides left inside the protection of Caspar Creek.   Elizabeth Pepin Silva

lot of swell energy. As a result, the waves are slow and peeling, making it a very safe learning spot. Unless there's a strong west swell visiting, you'll want a longboard to surf here. Like most creek breaks, Caspar Creek is best after a rain when the creek deposits fresh sand.

The village of Caspar is located about 160 miles north of San Francisco, roughly halfway between Fort Bragg and Mendocino. The town got its name from Siegfried Caspar, who once lived in a little shack down by the beach. In the late 1800s and early 1900s, the Mendocino coast was a bustling logging area due to the demand for lumber in the development of the San Francisco Bay Area as well as the rebuilding effort following the 1906 quake. In those days Caspar was a thriving mill town with a population several times larger than you'll find today.

Numerous ships were transporting goods to and from the area during those years. As they plied the coast, the need for a lighthouse became evident. In 1906 construction of the Point Cabrillo Light Station began; it was completed in 1909. This lighthouse is unusual in that it uses a third-order Fresnel lens that was built in Britain and has a range of nearly 15 miles. The Point Cabrillo Light Station was originally powered by a kerosene oil lamp and is one of only three British-built lenses in operation in the United States today.

While it has shrunk considerably since its logging heyday, Caspar has managed to survive with a little help from the timber, fishing, and tourism industries. The community here has been active in the protection of local wildlife, opposition to off-shore oil drilling, and prevention of the aerial herbicide broadcasting by tree farmers. Many "Casparados"—as the locals are called—are also very concerned with the management of their water supply and are opposed to the efforts of multinational corporations to buy and ship water from here elsewhere.

Visit the Caspar Inn in the evening to hear some live music.

Other Information

Local Surf Shops: Lost Surf Shack, 319 N. Franklin St., Fort Bragg; (707) 961-0889. North Pacific Productions, 22991 CA 1, Fort Bragg; (707) 961-0314.

Places to Stay: Caspar Beach RV Park and Campground, 14441 Point Cabrillo Dr., Caspar; (707) 964-3306.

Places to Eat: North Coast Brewing Company, 444 Main St., Fort Bragg; (707) 964-3400. Egghead's, 326 N. Main St., Fort Bragg; (707) 964-5005. Home Style Cafe, 790 S. Main St., Fort Bragg; (707) 964-6106.

SUPDATE: LOST COAST TO FORT BRAGG TO MENDOCINO

As the pelican flies, it's about 45 miles from Shelter Cove to Mendocino, but if you paddled this coast on a SUP, the mileage would be much greater. And what would you find if you paddled that distance? In the first 20 miles, you'd find nothing but nature and maybe some epic surf from Shelter Cove along the Sinkyone Wilderness, past Usal Creek to Rockport—where CA 1 once again meets the ocean. The next 15 miles is rough, rocky coastline that is accessible only by boat or SUP, all the way down to Ten Mile Beach and MacKerricher State Park. A diver was killed by a great white shark here, so keep your eyes peeled. There are small creeks for exploring all along here but no major rivers until you get to Fort Bragg. If you're tired of stressing about sharks, wind, and currents, paddle up Noyo Bay into the Noyo River—say hello to the fishermen in their boats and maybe to some salmon and steelhead heading upriver to spawn. And the same for Mendocino: Launch on the north side, paddle around the town, see if there is any surf at Big River, and then keep going up the river as far as you want. It's warm, protected, and quiet up there, and it winds inland for miles.

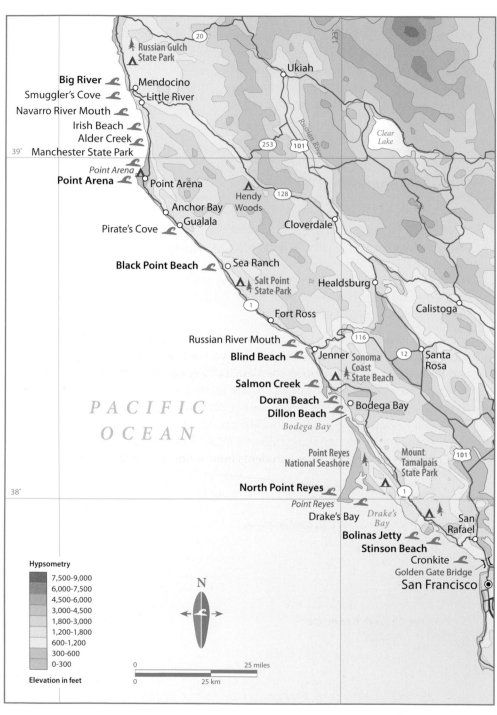

Region 3 (Mendocino to San Francisco)

REGION 3: MENDOCINO TO SAN FRANCISCO

This region is popular with Bay Area vacationers who have second homes in the quaint, isolated coastal towns. They visit the coast to beat the heat and escape their busy urban lives. You won't find monstrous homes and strip malls here, just a lot of rolling green hills filled with cattle, sheep, and horses.

The tiny towns on the Mendocino coast are all unique and popular with tourists in summer. They come to relax, eat great food, stroll along the coast, hang out at the beach, visit art galleries, listen to good music, and taste fine wine. In winter, however, these towns are quiet and left to the locals.

The Sonoma coast is mostly rural and is home to some of the most renowned wine country in the world. The towns are few and far between, and there are many inaccessible beaches with waves that cannot be surfed.

Overall Surf Description

The surf spots are spread out in this region, and you should be prepared to encounter some heavy tourist traffic on weekends. This part of California isn't overly populated and there's a lot of undeveloped coastline, but the key spots do become crowded when the waves are good. The really good breaks are few and far between, so surfers tend to congregate when the conditions are just right.

For the visitor, only a few spots will be obvious, and finding the rest will require some effort; the forests and steep cliffs along CA 1 keep a lot of spots hidden. Lower NorCal surfers range from college students from Sonoma State University to yuppies from Marin to Mendocino construction workers. Localism is prevalent at many spots, so be respectful. The Red Triangle (home to numerous great white sharks) stretches from Ano Nuevo Island to the Farallon Islands to Point Reyes. It's not advisable to surf by yourself or at a beach loaded with seals.

Fall Surf

Fall is the best season for clean surf and sunny days, although the season can also see some heavy, winter-like storms, with 20-foot waves and heavy rainfall. The winds are usually the lightest this time of year, so if you're going to visit this region, come in September through November.

Winter Surf

Winter usually brings harsh weather and big waves. Waves can reach upward of 25 feet, with 50-knot winds and stinging rain. If you want to witness some burly conditions, visit this area in winter. If you're looking to score good waves though, wait for summer or fall.

Spring Surf

Spring here tends to bring stiff, cold wind, cold water, and big, junky surf. You might get lucky and experience a quality session, but—like winter—it's not the best time of year to visit this region.

Summer Surf

Summer is often foggy, the waves are small, and tourism is at its heaviest. The water's also colder due to the upwelling that follows the springtime winds. In general, the more-exposed beach breaks see the best surf from June through August.

Ocean Beach (and everything north, for that matter) has many moods. But this is the flavor locals love best: clear, sunny skies, offshore winds, and a clean swell a-framing from Playland to Fleishacker's Pool.   Lucia Griggi

Average Temperatures for Region (Mendocino to San Francisco)		
	Air (Bodega Bay)	Water (Bodega Bay)
Jan	57	52
Feb	59	52
Mar	59	52
Apr	61	51
May	63	50
June	66	51
July	66	52
Aug	67	53
Sept	68	54
Oct	66	55
Nov	62	54
Dec	58	53

Big River

This is an easy point and beach break in Mendocino Bay.

Best tides: Low to medium
Best swell direction: West, southwest
Best wave size: Waist high to chest high
Bottom: Sand
Type of break: Point and beach break, lefts and rights
Skill level: Novice to intermediate
Best boards: Funshape, longboard
Best season: Summer
Crowds: Can get crowded on weekends when it's good
Water quality: Clean
Hazards: None
Fees and permits: None

Finding the Break

From Mendocino: Find Main Street in downtown Mendocino. There's also a Main Street exit off CA 1. Between CA 1 and downtown on Main Street, you'll see a small church next to a Chevron gas station. There's a dirt lot behind the church that you can park in for free. The trail that heads toward the Big River Bridge will lead you to the beach. GPS: N39 18.317 / W123 47.837

Surf Description

Big River is the break in front of the Big River Bridge in Mendocino Bay. The outer sandbars are shaped in part by the Big River, which empties onto this beach. As a result, it's best with a south swell in summer, when the bottom is the most consistent. The beach at Big River is well protected from northwest winds and is a great place to hang out on a sunny day.

Geologists believe that 10,000 years ago, the sea level here was roughly 300 feet lower than it is today. There was no Mendocino headland, and Big River would have been about 3.5 miles longer. Because the sea level was lower, Asians are thought to have crossed over to North America via the Bering Strait (then a land bridge), eventually moving south to settle in California. The earliest inhabitants of Mendocino are known as the Pomos and may have begun living here on a coast that is now submerged.

Mendocino is a cool little town with a great feel.

The beginning of what is now known as the town of Mendocino can be traced back to the 1850s. During the California gold rush, thousands of people came to California in search of wealth. In San Francisco an enterprising black teenager named Nathaniel Smith started a ferry service between Sausalito and the bustling city. He is believed to have become very wealthy, charging $16 per person. Lured by stories of plentiful game and fish, Nathaniel sold his ferry and moved up the coast. In 1852 he moved to a cabin on the Mendocino headlands said to have been built by a German sailor who was shipwrecked here. Soon thereafter Nat sold the cabin and moved to the south shore of the mouth of the Big River. He is believed to be the first non-Pomo to live in this area, and he watched the first bridge over Big River being built in 1860. Loggers soon arrived to cut down the giant redwoods above Big River, which they floated down to a sawmill once located on Big River Beach. Nathaniel Smith raised his family here and made a living by providing game for the loggers.

The timber and fishing industries have kept Mendocino alive ever since. In the 1950s the town became a popular destination for artists, and it has maintained its reputation as a thriving arts community. Today it's filled with tourists who enjoy the numerous shops, inns, restaurants, and festivals.

Going big at Big River. Elizabeth Pepin Silva

Other Information

Local Surf Shops: Mendocino Board Sports, 45090 Main St., Mendocino; (707) 937-2197.

Places to Stay: Van Damme State Park, just south of Mendocino off of CA 1, call for directions; (707) 937-5804. Stanford Inn, 44850 Comptche-Ukiah Rd., Mendocino; (707) 937-5615.

Places to Eat: Bay View Cafe, 45040 Main St., Mendocino; (707) 937-4197. Raven's Vegetarian Restaurant at the Stanford Inn, 44850 Comptche-Ukiah Rd., Mendocino; (707) 937-5615.

Chris Burkard

Smuggler's Cove is a small and protected cove on the south end of Mendocino Bay. From Mendocino, head south on CA 1 and park at the first vista-point turnout. A steep trail will take you down to the break. The waves break at Smuggler's Cove on an outside rock reef, allowing it to hold large swell. It's a thick and often mushy peak with flat shoulders. It works best at low tide, with a strong west swell in winter.

Chris Burkard

The Navarro River Mouth is an outer sandbar break south of Mendocino where the Navarro River meets the ocean. This can be a powerful wave with a well-shaped peak. The Navarro River Mouth is best with a waist-high to head-high winter swell at medium tide. The shape of the waves is dependent upon how much sand flows out from the river. Remember that sharks like to feed at the mouths of rivers such as this; avoid surfing here alone.

Chris Burkard

Irish Beach is a small, mostly west-facing beach between Mendocino and Point Arena. There are signs for the beach off CA 1, making it easy to find. Because of the way it's positioned, Irish Beach can work with swell from any direction. The left peak in the middle of the beach is the most consistent. And wave shape is best with a waist- to chest-high swell at a medium tide.

Alder Creek is a northwest-facing creek break between Irish Beach and Manchester State Park. There's a small road that leads to the beach from CA 1 where the creek passes under the highway. Alder Creek has outer sandbar peaks on either side of the creek mouth. Winter surf is best here with a waist- to head-high swell at a medium to low tide. Summer surf can also be fun, but it's much smaller and slower.

Elizabeth Pepin Silva

Manchester State Park is a beach break north of Point Arena. There are signs for the park on CA 1. Winter surf here can be big, steep, heavy, and powerful. Manchester State Park is best from waist to chest high at a medium tide. Summer swells can produce well-shaped and much-less-intimidating surf.

Point Arena

This is a world-class surf spot south of Mendocino.

Best tide: Medium
Best swell direction: West
Best wave size: Head high to double overhead
Bottom: Rock
Type of break: Right and left point breaks
Skill level: Advanced
Best boards: Shortboard, gun
Best season: Fall
Crowds: Can get crowded on weekends when it's good
Water quality: Clean
Hazards: Sharks, localism
Fees and permits: None

Finding the Break

From Mendocino: Head south on CA 1 to the town of Point Arena. Go right on Iverson Avenue toward the wharf. It's about 1 mile from CA 1 to the pier. There's plenty of parking near the pier, and you can paddle out from there. GPS: N38 54.860 / W123 42.587

Surf Description

Point Arena is home to two excellent breaks: a classic outside right on the north side of the pier and a quality left point break just south of it. The right is thick and fast with a steep takeoff and can hold up to 20 feet. The left is more of a peeling wave and can hold a 10-foot swell. The right is more protected and can produce a longer ride than the more exposed left. The safest and easiest way to access either break is to paddle out through the channel by the pier.

Point Arena is a small town about 130 miles north of San Francisco. In 1906 the earthquake that leveled San Francisco was even more violent in Point Arena. The town was virtually destroyed, and the original Point Arena lighthouse, which began operation in 1870, sustained so much damage that it had to be torn down. Shortly thereafter, the US government hired a company that specialized in the construction of factory smokestacks to build an earthquake-proof lighthouse. In 1908 the first steel-reinforced, concrete lighthouse in the United States was put into service.

The Pomo Indians, a tribe of coastal hunter-gatherers, are believed to have been the first inhabitants of this area. Unfortunately, they suffered greatly over the years. In the

ere invaded by Russian fur traders, who would attack a village and kidnap the women and children, requiring the Pomo men to bring them meat and fish.

The US government eventually forced the Pomos onto federal reservations or rancherias. One such reservation was the Manchester/Point Arena Pomo rancheria. There were also numerous Pomo rancherias around Clear Lake, the largest freshwater lake in California. In 1850 a little-known US Army massacre occurred on an island on the north side of the lake, now called Bloody Island by the Pomos—the first army massacre of a village filled with peaceful inhabitants. Most of the newspapers of the time covered the story with a very pro-army slant. However, one paper, the *Northern Californian*, described the event as an "indiscriminate massacre of innocent Indians" and reported that "women and children" had been "butchered." The editor, Bret Harte, had to leave town to escape a lynch mob that smashed his printing press.

In the twentieth century the United States was still a very hostile place for American

Point Arena offers world-class surf with no crowds.

The rumors are true. Point Arena is now a federally mandated, "Kneeboarders Only" preserve. This means both the right reef and the left on the other side are off-limits to all standup surfers, shortboarders, longboarders, and SUPpers. Violators will be used as crab bait. (Psyche!)   Chris Burkard

Indians. The Pomos were one of the first tribes to take legal action in an effort to gain rights and maintain their land. In 1907 Ethan Anderson, an Eastern Pomo, won a court case giving non-reservation Indians the right to vote in California. This was quite an accomplishment considering that natives in some states weren't given that right until the 1960s.

Other Information

Local Surf Shops: Cove Coffee and Tackle, 790 Port Rd., Point Arena; (707) 882-2665. Family Surf N Skate, 195 Main St., Point Arena; (707) 882-1981.
Places to Stay: Seashell Inn, 135 Main St., Point Arena; (707) 882-2000. Rollerville Junction Campground, Lighthouse Road and CA 1, Point Arena; (707) 882-2440
Places to Eat: Point Arena Cafe, 206 Main St., Point Arena; (707) 882-2110. Rollerville Cafe, 22900 Shoreline Hwy., Point Arena; (707) 882-2077.

Elizabeth Pepin Silva

Pirate's Cove is a sheltered cove just north of Gualala Point. It's protected from northwest winds, which can result in glassy conditions. The break at Pirates Cove is consistent and well shaped with the right conditions. It works best with a waist- to chest-high winter swell at a medium to low tide.

Black Point Beach

This is a mostly west-facing beach break between Point Arena and Bodega Bay.

Best tide: Medium
Best swell direction: Southwest, west, northwest
Best wave size: Waist high to slightly overhead
Bottom: Sand
Type of break: Beach break
Skill level: Intermediate
Best boards: Shortboard, funshape
Best seasons: Fall, winter, summer
Crowds: Not crowded
Water quality: Clean
Hazards: Sharks
Fees and permits: According to redwoodcoastchamber.com, there is a nominal fee for parking at Black Point Beach parking lot.

Finding the Break

From Santa Rosa: Head west on CA 12 to CA 1. Go north on CA 1 to the town of Sea Ranch. Black Point Beach is located at mile marker 50.85. Leave your vehicle in the beach parking lot (for a nominal parking fee) and walk 0.25 mile to the beach. GPS: N38 41.1078 / W123 25.951

Surf Description

Black Point Beach is a consistent beach break that can hold some decent-size swell. Paddling out can become a challenge on bigger days, but if you do venture out, you're bound to have a good time. Wave shape can be decent, and the waves here get hollow under certain conditions. Black Point Beach is positioned to catch a lot of swell but seems to work best with a southwest. Unfortunately, this beach is also exposed to northwest winds and can get blown out easily. Overall, if you're in the area, Black Point Beach is worth a quick look.

The Pomo Indians are believed to have made seasonal trips to this part of the coast hundreds of years ago. They came to this region to gather kelp and shellfish but apparently never chose to actually live here. In fact, settlement of this area of California isn't believed to have occurred until 1846. That year a naturalized Mexican citizen named Ernest Rufus received one of the last Mexican land grants before California broke away from Mexico. The property spanned from the Gualala River to

Black Point Beach on a blue-sky day.

Ocean Grove and was mainly used for ranching from 1855 to 1937. In 1941 the Ohlson family bought the land for $125,000. In 1963 a company called Oceanic California Inc. bought the 10-mile stretch of land, including the 5,200-acre Del Mar Ranch, for $2.3 million. The Del

If you feel like playing golf, check out the Sea Ranch Golf Links; (707) 785-2468.

Mar Ranch became the site for a coastal development, with its name translated from Del Mar into "The Sea" Ranch. Building began in the 1960s with an effort to design houses that blended in with their environment. Construction has involved using natural wood sidings and sod roofs in an attempt to camouflage the homes. Black Point Beach is located within this development.

The Sea Ranch is now loaded with nice homes, miles of hiking trails, restaurants, vacation houses, and shops. There's also a lodge and a premier golf course said to be on the same level as the distinguished courses near Carmel. Gray whales can be seen migrating in fall and spring, and bird watching is especially good here.

Besides surfing, this stretch of coast is also home to some good scuba diving. Abalone diving is the most popular, and there are several local dive shops. On October 2, 1971, a scuba diver was attacked by a shark here—reportedly at a depth of 15 feet—and suffered major injuries.

Other Information

Local Surf Shops: None.
Places to Stay: Gualala Point Regional Park, 42401 CA 1, between Gualala and Sea Ranch; (707) 785-2377. Sea Ranch Lodge, 60 Sea Walk Dr., Sea Ranch; (707) 785-2371.
Places to Eat: Sea Ranch Lodge, 60 Sea Walk Dr., Sea Ranch; (707) 785-2371. There's food at the general store, just south of Sea Ranch in Stewarts Point.

Chris Burkard

The Russian River Mouth is a right beach break. It's located north of Bodega Bay near the town of Jenner where the Russian River meets the ocean. With the right conditions, this beach break can produce a fast right barrel. The Russian River Mouth works best with a southwest swell in summer and fall months. There's a shark danger here due to a large group of harbor seals that call this place home.

Blind Beach

This is a thick and burly beach break just south of the town of Jenner.

Best tides: Medium to high
Best swell direction: Any
Best wave size: Waist high to double overhead
Bottom: Sand
Type of break: Right and left, outside and beach break
Skill level: Intermediate to advanced
Best boards: Shortboard, funshape
Best season: Any
Crowds: Not crowded
Water quality: Clean
Hazards: Sharks, strong currents
Fees and permits: None

Finding the Break

From Santa Rosa: Head west on CA 12 to CA 1. Go north on CA 1 north of Bodega Bay toward the town of Jenner. Just south of Jenner, between mile markers 19 and 20, look for a sign that says SONOMA COAST STATE BEACH/GOAT ROCK. Turn left here and park in the lot for Blind Beach. A steep trail leads from the parking lot to the beach. GPS: N38 26.162 / W123 07.317

Surf Description

Blind Beach is a somewhat protected beach break guarded by large rock outcroppings. This beach can capture large swell from virtually any direction. Blind Beach can hold overhead swell and produce a heavy wave with fast barrels. As a result, this isn't a very good break for novice surfers. The peak here is fairly consistent, and the left and right are equally good. When it's on, Blind Beach is one of those beach breaks that you'll wish you lived near.

The closest town to Blind Beach is a small village called Jenner by the Sea. This area, where the Russian River meets the Pacific Ocean, was once part of a large Spanish land grant that was subdivided into several ranches. The town got its name from an author named Charles Jenner who came to this area in 1868 looking for a quiet place to write. Ranch owner

There are some wineries in the area if you'd like to do some tasting.

The parking lot at the north end of Blind Beach. Goat Rock offers some protection on windy, stormy days, and there's a half mile of beach breaks going south when conditions are good.   californiacoastline.org

John Rule gave Jenner permission to build a small house in a canyon above what's now the Jenner Inn. The canyon became known as Jenner Gulch and was something of a landmark along this stretch of coast. As more people moved in, the town needed a name. Jenner by the Sea was chosen, and it stuck.

In 1904 A. B. Davis built a lumber mill in Jenner. The mill flourished after the huge earthquake of 1906 as it worked to supply lumber to rebuild San Francisco and Santa Rosa. And until Davis died and the mill closed in 1914, Jenner grew considerably. Several more homes, a schoolhouse, and a hotel/post office were built to meet the needs of the developing town.

This part of the California coast is known to be inhabited by sharks; the nearby mouth of the Russian River is a favored shark feeding spot. (A large group of harbor seals resides here.) There have been three reported attacks in the area since 1982. In that year a scuba diver suffered major injuries after being attacked by a shark 15 miles north of here in Stillwater Cove. In September 1990 a free diver also sustained major injuries when attacked just north of Jenner. And in October 1993 a kayaker was attacked at neighboring Goat Rock Beach but was lucky enough to escape without injury. Although none of these attacks involved surfers, it would be a good idea to employ the buddy system when surfing at Blind Beach.

Other Information

Local Surf Shops: Northern Light Surf Shop, 17190 Bodega Hwy., Bodega; (707) 876-3032. Surf Plus/Bodega Bay Surf Shack, 1400 CA 1, Bodega Bay; (707) 875-3944.
Places to Stay: Bodega Dunes Campground, 3095 CA 1, Bodega Bay; (707) 875-3483.
Places to Eat: Gramatzki's River's End Restaurant, 11051 CA 1, Jenner; (707) 865-2484.

Salmon Creek

This is a powerful beach break north of Bodega Bay.

Best tides: Medium to high
Best swell direction: Any
Best wave size: Waist high to double overhead
Bottom: Sand
Type of break: Beach break
Skill level: Intermediate to advanced
Best boards: Shortboard, funshape, gun
Best season: Any
Crowds: Can get crowded on weekends when it's really good
Water quality: Clean
Hazards: Sharks, rip currents
Fees and permits: None

Finding the Break

From Santa Rosa: Head west on CA 12 to CA 1. Go north on CA 1. One mile north of Bodega Bay, you'll find the north Salmon Creek Beach parking lot. Leave your vehicle here and walk down to the beach. GPS: N38 21.168 / W123 03.763

Surf Description

Salmon Creek is a consistent beach break that can hold 10- to 12-foot swells. It can be a big and heavy wave, requiring experience, wave knowledge, and skill. The beach here is wide and sandy, and several peaks offer well-shaped lefts and rights. Sand deposited by the creek plays a large role in how far out waves will begin to break. Even when the waves are good, Salmon Creek Beach usually doesn't seem to get crowded. There's plenty of room to spread out here, and you're bound to find an area all to yourself if you don't mind walking down the beach a few hundred yards in either direction from the main parking area.

This beach is also definitely patrolled by sharks, which like to feed at creek mouths. On August 20, 1961, a swimmer paddling at the surface was attacked and sustained major injuries. After that, nearly thirty-five years went by without a documented attack—although it's likely that some shark encounters occurred but were simply never reported. Then on October 3, 1996, a great white shark struck the board of a 31-year-old surfer. The attack occurred a few hundred feet offshore, and the shark was reportedly around 15 feet long. Luckily, the surfer was uninjured. Less than two months later, on November 29, 1996, another surfer was attacked by a shark at Salmon Creek Beach, escaping with minor injuries. However, on November 28, 2002, another surfer wasn't as fortunate, as this attack resulted in major injuries. The most recent shark attack in this area was reported on May 31, 2004, and involved a surfer and a 14- to 18-foot-long great white shark. Several witnesses were convinced this would be a deadly attack: The surfer was supposedly bumped and tossed around as the shark circled around him for about 30 seconds. Immediately following the confrontation, though, the surfer paddled to the beach with no major injuries.

> **Bodega Head is a great place to hike, with fine views of the coast.**

The attacks listed above aren't frequent or serious enough to keep most surfers out of the water when the waves are good. Still, it's advisable that you surf this break with at least one other surfer.

Other Information

Local Surf Shops: Northern Light Surf Shop, 17190 Bodega Hwy., Bodega; (707) 876-3032. Surf Plus/Bodega Bay Surf Shack, 1400 CA 1, Bodega Bay; (707) 875-3944.
Places to Stay: Bodega Dunes Campground, 3095 CA 1, 1 mile north of Bodega Bay; (707) 875-3483. Bodega Harbor Inn, 1345 Bodega Ave., Bodega Bay; (707) 875-3594.
Places to Eat: Sandpiper Dockside Cafe, 1400 Bay Flat Rd., Bodega Bay; (707) 875-2278. The Tides Wharf, 835 CA 1, Bodega Bay; (707) 875-3652.

A windy barrel winds left over a Salmon Creek sandbar as a tow team, or, perhaps, lifeguards (or maybe the shark patrol) hover inside and wait to make their move.

Doran Beach

This is a sheltered and powerful beach break south of Bodega Bay.

Best tides: Medium to high
Best swell direction: South
Best wave size: Waist high to head high
Bottom: Sand
Type of break: Beach break
Skill level: Novice to intermediate
Best board: Shortboard
Best season: Spring
Crowds: Not crowded
Water quality: Clean
Hazards: Shallow
Fees and permits: According to sonoma-county.org, there is a nominal parking fee charged at Doran Beach.

Finding the Break

From Santa Rosa: Head west on CA 12 to CA 1 and Bodega Bay. Doran Beach is 1 mile south of downtown Bodega Bay off Doran Beach Road. Parking at Doran Beach allows you very easy access to the break. GPS: N38 18.812 / W123 02.383

Surf Description

Doran Beach is located within a sheltered cove just south of Bodega Bay. The beach here is clean, large, and beautiful. And if the weather's nice, the weekend can attract a lot of people. Luckily, very few of them come here to surf. You'll find that the majority of visitors are here to beat the inland heat and picnic, build sand castles, or simply lie around and watch the ocean.

This spot is well protected from northwest wind, which can result in picture-perfect glassy surf. However, it's also unable to capture large northwest swell, which makes it more of a spring and summer spot. The wave shape here can be stellar with the right conditions, and the waves can be fast and tubing; it's a good spot to surf when the waves are closing out everywhere else in the area. Because of the relatively small waves that break here, Doran Beach is well suited for novice and intermediate surfers. Still, it's a shallow beach break and requires a bit of respect from surfers of all abilities. You can get injured on a small day at a shallow beach break such as this if the waves are powerful enough and you put yourself in a position to get slammed into the bottom.

We don't intend to scare anyone, but there have been several shark encounters in this area. The first reported shark attack around here occurred on October 4, 1959, at nearby Bodega Rock. The victim was free-diving and was uninjured. At the same place in 1968, however, another free diver was attacked and sustained major injuries. There have been eight shark attacks reported close to Doran Beach at Tomales Point over the years, in 1960, 1961, 1969, 1972, 1974, 1977, 1984, and 1996.

The Bodega Bay area is home to numerous stretches of beautiful beach.

God's-eye view of Doran Beach, which explains why it likes a south swell and why northwest winds blow offshore here. californiacoastline.org

The good news is that none of the victims were surfers. The bad news is that six of these eight attacks resulted in major injuries. On September 28, 1985, a free diver was attacked at Elephant Rock and escaped without injury. However, on October 5, 1996, a surfer suffered major injuries after a shark attack not too far south of here at Dillon Beach. None of the twelve attacks listed above occurred at Doran Beach, and perhaps this sheltered cove doesn't attract many sharks. Therefore, we haven't listed sharks as a hazard at this break. Nonetheless, you might want to surf with a buddy just in case.

Other Information

Local Surf Shops: Northern Light Surf Shop, 17190 Bodega Hwy., Bodega; (707) 876-3032. Surf Plus/Bodega Bay Surf Shack, 1400 CA 1, Bodega Bay; (707) 875-3944.
Places to Stay: Bodega Dunes Campground, 3095 CA 1, 1 mile north of Bodega Bay; (707) 875-3483. Bodega Harbor Inn, 1345 Bodega Ave., Bodega Bay; (707) 875-3594.
Places to Eat: Sandpiper Dockside Cafe, 1400 Bay Flat Rd., Bodega Bay; (707) 875-2278. The Tides Wharf, 835 CA 1, Bodega Bay; (707) 875-3652.

Dillon Beach

This is a fun beach break near Tomales Bay.

Best tides: Medium to high
Best swell direction: West
Best wave size: Waist high to slightly overhead
Bottom: Sand
Type of break: Beach break
Skill level: Novice to intermediate
Best boards: Shortboard, funshape
Best seasons: Summer and fall
Crowds: Not crowded
Water quality: Average
Hazards: Sharks
Fees and permits: According to yelp.com, a nominal fee is charged at Dillon Beach parking lot.

Finding the Break

From Santa Rosa: Head west on CA 12 to CA 1. Go south on CA 1 toward the town of Tomales until you see the sign for Dillon Beach. Turn right onto Valley Ford Franklin School Road and then right again onto Dillon Beach Road. Park in the Dillon Beach parking lot; from there you're only a few steps to the beach. GPS: N38 14.985 / W122 58.019

Surf Description

Dillon Beach can produce some well-shaped and consistent beach breaks. The beach is wide open, and there are numerous peaks that break outside with a bigger swell. Dillon Beach can also experience strange currents as a result of being so close to Tomales Bay.

Dillon Beach is a small town within Bodega Bay. According to geologists, this area used to be underwater—and if you look around, you'll see large, rounded rock formations with names like Elephant Rock serving as evidence. Later on, what is now known as Dillon Beach was inhabited by a coastal tribe of American Indians known as the Miwoks. Numerous archaeological sites contain evidence that the Miwoks used nearby sand dunes to dry shellfish, which they used when trading with other tribes.

Russian sea otter trappers settled in Dillon Beach after the Miwoks. By the mid-1800s, however, there were no more otters to hunt and the Russians left.

In 1859 Irish immigrant George Dillon came to this area and built a small hotel. The business was successful, and he soon bought more land in the area. In 1903 Dillon

> **This is a very relaxing, picturesque, and mellow area—a great place to get away from it all.**

sold a portion of oceanfront property to John Keegan, who divided it into small lots with narrow streets much like the New England fishing villages of the time. San Franciscans who wanted to visit this stretch of coast could take a train to the nearby town of Tomales, then travel the 4 miles to Dillon Beach via stagecoach. Once there, they could stay either in the hotel or in rental cottages by the beach.

Shortly thereafter, in 1911, Keagan sold his property to a San Francisco firm called the California Eucalyptus Plantation Company. And in 1923 a gentleman from Sacramento, Sylvester Lawson, leased the area around Dillon Beach from this company. Three years later, in 1926, Lawson and his sons were able to purchase the resort town. In 1933 the Lawsons loaned a building to the University of California and the University of the Pacific to be used for marine research. The University of California later moved its facility to Bodega Bay, and in 1948 the University of the Pacific

The mouth of Tomales Bay is also known as Shark Pit because Tomales Bay is a breeding ground for white sharks—and we all know how hungry an animal can get after sex. This lineup shows how good it can get out there, but you have to ask yourself a question: "How much fun do you really want to have?" Well do ya, punk?   Chris Burkard

dedicated its operation as a marine biological station. Until the lab was closed in the late 1970s, Dillon Beach was visited by numerous scientists and students who wanted to study marine life.

During World War II the military limited access to Dillon Beach when—a few days after the Pearl Harbor attack—a Japanese submarine was spotted near the entrance to Tomales Bay. The military concluded that the large beach here would be an appealing invasion point for enemy troops. After the war the military paved the roads around Dillon Beach in an effort to repair the damage caused by heavy vehicles.

In the 1960s developers established subdivisions in the area. Such expansion was soon limited, however, when the land surrounding the small town was rezoned for agricultural use only. As a result, Dillon Beach hasn't changed much in the last fifty years or so. As you drive in from Tomales, you'll find acres of pristine grazing land all the way to the ocean.

Other Information

Local Surf Shops: Dillon Beach Resort, 1 Beach Ave., Dillon Beach; (707) 878 2696. Point Reyes Surf Shop, 11101 CA 1, Point Reyes Station; (415) 663-1072. Brotherhood Board Shop, 1240 Mendocino Ave., Santa Rosa; (707) 546-0660. Cali Jones World Wide Surf Co., 1180 Holm Rd., Petaluma; (707) 762-2477. Sonoma Coast Surf Shop, 9 Fourth St., Petaluma; (707) 763-3860.

Places to Stay: Lawson's Landing Campground, 137 Marine View Dr., Dillon Beach, southwest of town; (707) 878-2443.

Places to Eat: William Tell House Restaurant and Bar, 26955 CA 1, Tomales; (707) 878-2403. There's also a bakery, general store, and cafe in the town of Tomales.

North Point Reyes

This is a 10-mile stretch of mostly west-facing beach with numerous peaks on the northwest side of Point Reyes.

Best tide: Medium

Best swell direction: West, northwest

Best wave size: Waist high to chest high

Bottom: Sand

Type of break: Beach break

Skill level: Intermediate to advanced

Best boards: Shortboard, funshape

Best seasons: Summer and fall

Crowds: Not crowded

Water quality: Clean

Hazards: Sharks, rip currents, pounding surf

Fees and permits: None

Finding the Break

From Petaluma: Head southwest to CA 1 and Point Reyes Station. Turn right onto Sir Francis Drake Boulevard just south of Point Reyes Station. Follow the boulevard west until you see a sign for Point Reyes Beach North. Turn right and park in the large lot by the beach. Look for a peak where the waves appear the cleanest. GPS: N37 59.704 / W122 58.779

Surf Description

North Point Reyes is a 10-mile section of exposed beach break also known as "the Great Beach." It faces west-northwest, making it very vulnerable to northwest wind. However, it can also catch a lot of swell and produce quality waves under the right conditions. The main beaches along the west side of Point Reyes are, from north to south: McClures Beach, Kehoe Beach, Point Reyes Beach North, and Point Reyes Beach South. The exposure is similar at all of the beaches, although outer sandbars can produce better surf at one spot or the other depending on the size and direction of the swell. The cold water, big surf, and unpredictable conditions make this beach break an intermediate to advanced surfing spot. This is definitely one of those places that novice surfers should steer clear of until they've gained enough wave knowledge and

Pastoral view of the Great Beach at North Point Reyes.

experience to stay safe under any circumstances. Even advanced surfers should take note of how abruptly the sand drops off along this long stretch of beach and be prepared to encounter strong rip currents and the occasional shore pounding.

Even if the waves are blown out at this beach when you arrive, the Point Reyes National Seashore is a national park well worth the visit. Numerous quality hiking trails of differing lengths and difficulty are found within the park. The Point Reyes Headlands is a great place to cruise around and explore. The Point Reyes Lighthouse is located on the southern tip of the Great Beach and offers spectacular views. This point overlooks rocky shelves and outer rocks filled with sea lions. If you

> **The Point Reyes area is a very pristine and beautiful stretch of coast with much to explore.**

visit between January and April, the observation platform on the lighthouse is supposedly the best spot to view migrating gray whales.

The Point Reyes Peninsula has been of great interest to geologists over the years. The rocks on this stretch of coast match those found in the Tehachapi Mountains more than 300 miles south of here. This is a result of plate tectonics and the continual motion of the earth's crust. The Point Reyes Peninsula is on the eastern edge of the Pacific Plate, which moves northwestward around 2 inches each year. During the San Francisco earthquake of 1906, the peninsula traveled northwest an amazing 20 feet.

The Miwok Indians used to inhabit this area and lived off acorns, berries, salmon, shellfish, deer, and elk. In 1579 Sir Francis Drake, an English explorer for Queen Elizabeth, spent five weeks on the south end of Point Reyes in what's now called Drakes Estero. The Miwoks are said to have helped feed the crew during their stay. Drake named this area Nova Albion, or New England, and then continued his around-the-world journey by sailing west across the Pacific.

Other Information

Local Surf Shops: Point Reyes Surf Shop, 11101 CA 1, Point Reyes Station; (415) 663-1072. Brotherhood Board Shop, 1240 Mendocino Ave., Santa Rosa; (707) 546-0660. Cali Jones World Wide Surf Co., 1180 Holm Rd., Petaluma; (707) 762-2477. Sonoma Coast Surf Shop, 9 Fourth St., Petaluma; (707) 763-3860.

Places to Stay: Point Reyes Hostel, 1390 Limantour Spit Road; 7 miles from Bear Valley Road, 2 miles from end of Limantour Road, call for directions; (415) 663-8811. Point Reyes Station Inn, 11591 CA 1, Point Reyes Station; (415) 663-9372. Point Reyes Hike-In Campgrounds, call for directions; (415) 663-8054.

Places to Eat: Station House Cafe, 11180 CA 1, Point Reyes Station; (415) 663-1515. The Pine Cone Diner, corner of Fourth and B Streets, Point Reyes Station; (415) 663-1536.

Chris Burkard

Drake's Bay is a long stretch of beach on the south side of Point Reyes. To get there, follow the directions to North Point Reyes, but instead of turning right off Sir Francis Drake Boulevard, go a little farther and turn left toward the Kenneth C. Patrick Visitor Center. Since it faces south, Drake's Bay works best with a strong south swell.

Bolinas Jetty

This is a beach break near the mouth of Bolinas Lagoon.

Best tide: Low
Best swell direction: South
Best wave size: Waist high to chest high
Bottom: Sand
Type of break: Beach break, left and right
Skill level: Novice to intermediate
Best boards: Funshape, longboard
Best seasons: Summer and spring
Crowds: Can get crowded on weekends

Water quality: Average

Hazards: Sharks, localism

Fees and permits: None

Finding the Break

From Petaluma: Head southwest to CA 1 and Point Reyes Station. Go south on CA 1 toward the town of Bolinas. Around mile marker 17 turn right onto Olema-Bolinas Road; the locals make sure there's no road sign. However, if you find Bolinas Lagoon on your right, you've just passed the turnoff. At the small town of Bolinas, head toward the beach. There's very limited parking, and the roads are narrow. Once you find a place to park, walk to the beach and you'll see the break. GPS: N37 54.289 / W122 41.158

Too-high tides, not much swell, a little crowded, and god knows how many white sharks prowling close by. This is not an A+ angle on the surf at Bolinas, but regardless of what the surf conditions are like, the place is just knockout gorgeous.   Elizabeth Pepin Silva

Surf Description

The break near the mouth of Bolinas Lagoon is south facing and very protected from the wind. The surf is best when the waves are small, making it a good spring and summer spot. The east side of the lagoon mouth has good rights; the west side has some good lefts. Wave shape is best when the tide is relatively low.

Bolinas is a unique town with a peculiar vibe. Some of the locals make an effort to remove any road signs directing you to their town. In their effort to keep people away, however, they've managed to attract a great deal of attention. As a result, there are undoubtedly more curious visitors to Bolinas than there would be if the signs were left alone. The town is an interesting mix of million-dollar homes, sleeping bags on the beach, San Francisco yuppies, and isolation-loving locals. Lieutenant Dennis McQueeny of the Major Crimes Task Force, Marin County Sheriff's Department, has described Bolinas as a town "where drugs are interwoven into the culture."

Bolinas is one of the funkiest towns on the California coast.

When you first enter town, one of the first businesses you'll notice is Smiley's Schooner Saloon—one of the only bars in the state to be in continuous existence for more than one hundred years. The building is thought to have been erected during the California gold rush by Captain Isaac Morgan in 1851. In the 1870s Morgan went back east to find a wife, and Niles Ogden ran the bar for a few decades. In the 1920s, when Prohibition forced most US drinking establishments to close, this saloon managed to stay open. The front of the building was made to look like a barbershop, while the bar was located behind a second door in the back. Since then the saloon has changed ownership several times and is now a happening place with live music on Friday and Saturday nights.

The Bolinas Lagoon is apparently in danger of shrinking as channels get smaller, which could result in the lagoon being closed off. It's home to a large population of harbor seals, whose numbers continue to grow each year and have become a source of controversy for some of the locals. Many folks favor letting the population keep on expanding by protecting the seals and preventing them from being disturbed. There are other residents, however, who are working to repopulate the streams that feed the lagoon with steelhead and salmon. They argue that the seal colony has become overpopulated, disrupting the ecosystem's natural balance. In either case, it seems that unless something is done to protect the lagoon itself, both the fish and seals will suffer.

Other Information

Local Surf Shops: Bolinas Surf Shop, 52 Wharf Rd., Bolinas; (415) 868-1935. 2 Mile Surf Shop, 22 Brighton Ave., Bolinas; (415) 868-0333. Live Water Surf Shop, 3448 Shoreline Hwy., Stinson Beach; (415) 868-0333.

Places to Stay: Grand Hotel, 15 Brighton Ave., Bolinas; (415) 868-1757. Blue Heron Inn, 11 Wharf Rd., Bolinas; (415) 868-1102.

Places to Eat: Bolinas Bay Bakery and Cafe, 20 Wharf Rd., Bolinas; (415) 868-0211.

Stinson Beach

This is a friendly beach break north of San Francisco.

Best tide: Any

Best swell direction: Southwest

Best wave size: Waist high to head high

Bottom: Sand

Type of break: Beach break, left and right

Skill level: Novice to intermediate

Best boards: Shortboard, funshape, longboard

Best seasons: Spring and fall

Crowds: Can get crowded on weekends

Water quality: Clean

Hazards: Sharks

Fees and permits: None

Finding the Break

From San Francisco: Head north on CA 1 and follow the signs to Stinson Beach. The road twists and turns as it follows the foothills along the coast. The drive is slow but the views are incredible. Once you get to Stinson Beach, there's a large parking lot. Drop off your vehicle, walk to the beach, and look for a peak. GPS: N37 54.029 / W122 38.666

Surf Description

Stinson Beach is a large, crescent-shaped white-sand beach. It faces southwest and usually has its best surf in spring and fall. The beach break here is forgiving and consistent, with some fun peaks. Wave shape can vary depending on the size of the swell,

An empty curl beckons somewhere along Stinson Beach. Elizabeth Pepin Silva

direction of the swell, and tide height. You might want to bring two or three different boards.

Stinson Beach has had numerous shark sightings over the years, but there have been only two reported attacks, one in August 1998 and the other in May 2002. Unfortunately, both victims were surfers, and each attack resulted in major injuries.

There's a nude beach between Muir Beach and Stinson Beach called Red Rock. There's also a Shakespeare festival in Stinson Beach every summer and fall.

The 2002 attack occurred about 50 yards from shore; other surfers watched as the victim punched a "very, very big shark" in an attempt to fight it off.

Captain Alfred Derby Easkoot is recognized as the founder of Stinson Beach. He was born in Massachusetts in 1820 and began going to sea when he was young. In 1851 he came to San Francisco to captain a ship, but he was unable to take charge when he fell ill with Panama fever. During his recuperation he met Captain Isaac Morgan, who was living in Bolinas, and went to work on Morgan's ranch. In 1871 he came to Stinson Beach, then known as Willow Camp, to retire. He had managed to buy a portion of the beach with some money he had saved over the years. Captain Easkoot's friends started traveling by horse and buggy to visit him over a road that had been built in 1870 from Sausalito. Shortly thereafter, "Easkoot's Beach" became a popular place to camp in summer. In 1880 Nathan Stinson started a beach resort here that competed with Captain Easkoot's camp; later on, the town became known as Stinson Beach.

UPDATE: MENDOCINO TO CRONKITE BEACH

According to Google Earth, it's about 150 miles from Mendocino to Cronkite Beach. But that's if you go by US 101, and if you do that, you'll be missing out on a world of SUPportunities by land and sea. Most of the coastline from Big River in Mendocino down to the entrance to the Golden Gate Bridge is rough and open and hard to access. For those who like to dive or explore, the possibilities are endless—but keep an eye on the weather because help can be far away. For slightly safer adventures, Little River, Albion Cove, the Navarro River, Alder Creek, the Gualala River, and the mighty Russian River are all just awaitin' to be explored—either launch from somewhere inland and stroke to the ocean, or vice versa. There are also great SUP and dive opportunities at protected coves like Stump Beach, Gerstle Cove, Ocean Cove, Stillwater Cove, Fort Ross Cove, and a dozen more—take a look on Google Earth and then go explore. Many of the surf spots along the Sonoma Coast are hard to get to, and a SUP is the way to adventure and lonely waves. Bodega Harbor would be fun to explore on a SUP and you can go outside as far as you dare. But maybe the biggest adventures for a SUP along this coast are in southern Sonoma. Tomales Bay would take a couple of days to see from one end to the other; Bolinas Lagoon at high tide is about as scenic as Nor-Cal gets; or you can launch at Drakes Bay Oyster Company and paddle down Drake's Estero to surf the sandbars at the ocean. Being on a SUP might make you feel a little safer in these sharky waters because you can at least see what's coming. And hopefully your SUP is bigger than the shark—because they're pretty dumb.

Cronkite is an inconsistent beach break just north of the entrance to San Francisco Bay. It can capture virtually any swell and breaks year-round. However, it works best in summer with a south swell and can be a lot of fun when the breaks around it are flat. In fall and winter Cronkite can produce well-shaped and tubing waves but maxes out at around head high.   Elizabeth Pepin Silva

Captain Easkoot built a large, two-story house for his wife in 1883, which still stands. Life was quite good for the couple until Mrs. Easkoot died of a ruptured heart in 1886. The captain subsequently withdrew from his friends and was said to have become a "brooding old man," known to threaten children with a shotgun. Captain Easkoot died in 1905 and was buried in Bolinas.

Other Information

Local Surf Shops: Live Water Surf Shop, 3450 Shoreline Hwy., Stinson Beach; (415) 868-0333. Stinson Beach Surf & Kayak, 3605 CA 1, Stinson Beach; (415) 868-2739. Proof Lab, 254 Shoreline Hwy., Mill Valley; (415) 380-8900.
Places to Stay: Steep Ravine Cabins and Environmental Campground, 11 miles north of US 101 on CA 1 and 1 mile south of Stinson Beach, call for directions; (415) 388-2070. The Sandpiper, 1 Marine Way, Stinson Beach; (415) 868-1632. Marin Headlands Hostel, 941 Fort Barry, Sausalito; (415) 331-2777.
Places to Eat: Guaymas, 5 Main St., Tiburon; (415) 435-6300. Parkside Cafe, 43 Arenal Ave., Stinson Beach; (415) 868-1272.

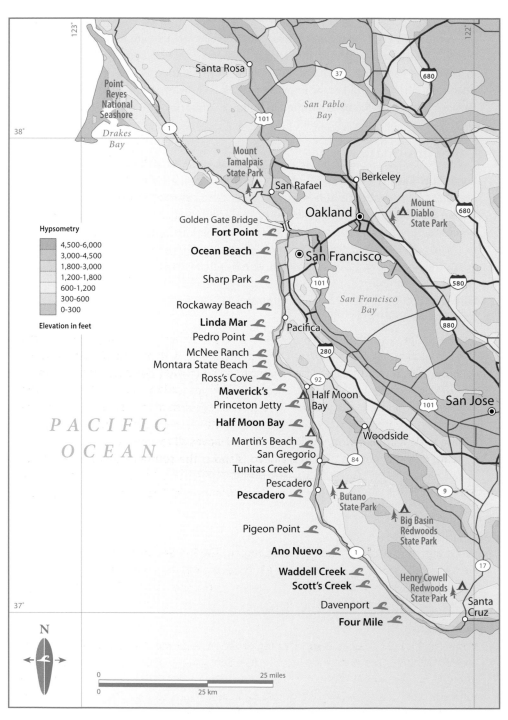

Region 4 (San Francisco to Santa Cruz)

Hypsometry

4,500-6,000
3,000-4,500
1,800-3,000
1,200-1,800
600-1,200
300-600
0-300

Elevation in feet

PACIFIC
OCEAN

Point Reyes National Seashore
Drakes Bay
Santa Rosa
San Pablo Bay
Mount Tamalpais State Park
San Rafael
Berkeley
Golden Gate Bridge
Fort Point
Oakland
Mount Diablo State Park
Ocean Beach
San Francisco
Sharp Park
Rockaway Beach
San Francisco Bay
Linda Mar
Pedro Point
Pacifica
McNee Ranch
Montara State Beach
Ross's Cove
Maverick's
Half Moon Bay
Princeton Jetty
San Jose
Half Moon Bay
Woodside
Martin's Beach
San Gregorio
Tunitas Creek
Pescadero
Pescadero
Butano State Park
Big Basin Redwoods State Park
Pigeon Point
Ano Nuevo
Waddell Creek
Scott's Creek
Henry Cowell Redwoods State Park
Davenport
Santa Cruz
Four Mile

N

0   25 miles
0   25 km

REGION 4: SAN FRANCISCO TO SANTA CRUZ

This region begins in San Francisco, then heads along Ocean Beach and on down the coast through Pacifica and Pedro Point to Maverick's in Half Moon Bay. From Half Moon Bay to the end of this region, just north of Santa Cruz, you'll find 50 miles of open, relatively undeveloped coastline.

This stretch ranges from the big-city experience of San Francisco to the tranquillity of the San Mateo coast. The money and talent flowing into San Francisco have made it a very happening place to be, and the ocean is never more than a few minutes away from any point in the city. The Half Moon Bay area has become a popular town among surfers, and Maverick's has earned respect as a quality big-wave spot. The vibe from Half Moon Bay to Santa Cruz is very mellow. This area is very sparsely populated, beautiful, and can offer quality waves.

Overall Surf Description

There are spots within this region that are very crowded and competitive. Yet the same stretch of coast also offers lonely, isolated breaks with miles and miles of beach and reef with no one around. If you want to avoid crowds, the best time to come is midwinter, midweek, midday. Cold water, big waves, school, and work all limit the crowds. Year-round, if you go north of Santa Cruz or south of San Francisco during the week, you will rarely see more than a handful of other surfers out. If you're flexible and willing to do a little driving, you'll get plenty of waves all to yourself.

One thing to note is that Ano Nuevo Island is the southern tip of what's been called the Red Triangle. Since the early 1990s, shark attacks on surfers, swimmers, and divers in this area have become a yearly occurrence. Avoid surfing alone or near beaches populated by seals.

Fall Surf

Fall is a great season for surfing in this region. The fog and onshore winds leave, to be replaced by blue skies and offshore breezes. September and October tend to see early northern Pacific swells and late southern hemisphere swells. The result is a high likelihood of good surf and conditions.

Winter Surf

Winter is the best season to surf this region. The winter months deliver a lot of consistent, quality swell from local storms, Aleutian storms, and low-pressure systems. The tides are extreme in winter with very low lows and very high highs—you have to time your sessions accordingly. The water and air can get pretty cold, but if you bring a good wet suit and some big boards, you'll have a blast.

Spring Surf

Spring in this region is a combination of winter and summer conditions. The beginning of spring is usually accompanied by northwest winds; the season ends when the summer fog starts rolling in. There can be good surf in spring if you know where to look. The area just north of Santa Cruz can see big and consistent south swells with no wind and plenty of sun all season long. And the occasional northwest swell can roll in as late as June. Maverick's has even been known to go off into May and June some years.

Summer Surf

Summer usually brings fog, flat spells, and onshore winds to this region. For the most part, it's a season to be endured and not the best time to score waves here.

There are a lot of famous and infamous surf spots between Fort Point at the northern frontier of San Francisco, and Pleasure Point at the eastern frontier of Santa Cruz. But somewhere in the middle, Maverick's has come to define both fame and infamy for Northern California surfing. Nikki Brooks

Average Temperatures for Region (San Francisco to Santa Cruz)		
	Air (Fort Point)	**Water (Fort Point)**
Jan	57	53
Feb	60	53
Mar	60	54
Apr	61	54
May	61	55
June	63	57
July	63	58
Aug	64	53
Sept	66	59
Oct	66	60
Nov	62	59
Dec	58	55

Fort Point

This is a left point break on the southeast side of the Golden Gate Bridge.

Best tides: Low and incoming

Best swell direction: West, northwest

Best wave size: Waist high to slightly overhead

Bottom: Rock

Type of break: Left point

Skill level: Intermediate to advanced

Best board: Shortboard

Best season: Winter

Crowds: Can get crowded when it's good

Water quality: Average

Hazards: Locals, boulders, currents, dangerous entry and exit

Fees and permits: None

Finding the Break

From San Francisco: Head north toward the Golden Gate Bridge; Fort Point is near the southeast end. It's located within the Golden Gate Recreation Area between the bridge and the Marina district. From the Marina district, take Lincoln Boulevard toward the bridge. You'll see a sign for Fort Point as you turn right onto Long Avenue. There's parking at the end of the road and directly in front of the break. Look for a safe place to walk down the rocks and paddle out around the break. GPS: N37 48.632 / W122 28.624

Surf Description

Fort Point is a left point break that can be a good wave with the right conditions. Swell comes in toward San Francisco Bay and wraps around the point, finally breaking on the southeast end of the Golden Gate Bridge. It's heavily affected by changes in wind and tide. However, the inside section of this point can be protected from the wind even when there are whitecaps on the west side of the bridge. The currents here can be strong, and on bigger swells entry and exit from the rocks can be a little sketchy.

Hard to argue that Fort Point isn't the most unusual surf spot in California. Fort Point breaks under the Golden Gate Bridge, 3 miles inside the entrance to San Francisco Bay. A spectacular view, no matter which way you look. And Fort Point can be a barreling left when the swell and winds come together. Chris Burkard

Fort Point has an interesting history that dates back to the 1800s. In 1847 the US government acquired all of the land formerly claimed by Mexico as well as Angel and Alcatraz Islands and the area now known as the Presidio. A year later, in 1848, the gold rush began, and increased trade motivated the military to construct coastal defenses for San Francisco Bay. The plan was to mount cannons on the north and south shores of the Golden Gate in order to prevent enemy ships from entering the bay.

In 1853 building started on Fort Point at the south shore of the Golden Gate. The brick-and-mortar design consisted of four tiers with room to accommodate 126 very large cannons. Construction was completed in 1861, and fifty-five cannons were mounted. During the Civil War the military budget for San Francisco Bay was increased and much more artillery was added at Fort Point. This was in response to the reinforcement of Vancouver Island by the British. The fear was that British forces might attempt to seize California while the United States was fighting a Civil War on the East Coast.

In 1886 troops were withdrawn from Fort Point; the advent of more powerful rifled cannons had made brick-and-mortar forts obsolete. The last cannon was removed in 1900, but Fort Point was used as a storage and training facility by the military for several more years. From 1933 to 1937 the fort was used as a base of operations for the construction of the Golden Gate Bridge. And during World War II several soldiers were stationed at Fort Point to protect a submarine net strung across the entrance to San Francisco Bay.

Fort Point is the only brick fort of its kind on the US West Coast and became a National Historic Site on October 16, 1970.

> **Even people who don't like cities like San Francisco. There are countless tourist attractions. If you want to play golf, call the Presidio Golf Course at (415) 561-GOLF.**

Other Information

Local Surf Shops: Wise Surfboards, 800 Great Highway 1, before Golden Gate Park, San Francisco; (415) 750-9473. SF Surf Shop, 3809 Noriega St., San Francisco; (415) 661-7873. Mollusk Surf Shop, 4500 Irving St., San Francisco; (415) 564-6300. Aqua Surf Shop, 2830 Sloat Blvd., San Francisco; (415) 242-9283. Sunset Shapers, 3896 Noriega St., San Francisco; (415) 665-7873.

Places to Stay: There are numerous hotels all over San Francisco. For budget accommodations, go to norcalhostels.org.

Places to Eat: Mas Sake (sushi), 2030 Lombard St., San Francisco; (415) 440-1505. Guaymas (Mexican), 5 Main St., Tiburon; (415) 435-6300.

Ocean Beach

This is a 3-mile stretch of exposed beach break in San Francisco.

Best tide: Medium
Best swell direction: Anything but south
Best wave size: Waist high to triple overhead
Bottom: Sand
Type of break: Outside and beach break, lefts and rights
Skill level: Intermediate to advanced
Best boards: Shortboard, funshape, gun
Best seasons: Fall and winter
Crowds: Can get crowded on weekends
Water quality: Average
Hazards: Strong currents, getting out on a big day
Fees and permits: None

Finding the Break

From San Francisco: Head west on Geary Boulevard to Great Highway. Turn left onto Great Highway; Ocean Beach is the large stretch of beach on your right. There are numerous large parking lots on the west side of the road. Park anywhere you see well-shaped peaks. GPS: N37 45.138 / W122 30.526

Surf Description

Ocean Beach is home to 3 miles of beach break that can be excellent on a good day. However, this beach is also exposed to northwest wind, which can significantly affect the wave shape. Even though Ocean Beach is located on the outskirts of a major city, it rarely gets crowded. A lot of people visit on the weekend when the weather's nice, but very few of them surf. If the waves aren't too intimidating, wave shape is good, and it happens to be a sunny, windless, weekend day, you'll find a fair number of surfers in the water. Luckily, it's a large beach with numerous peaks, so it's easy for people to spread out. Ocean Beach isn't a very good break for novice surfers. It's a powerful beach break, and the outer sandbars can hold large waves in winter. Be prepared for shifting peaks, strong currents, and conditions that change significantly from hour to hour.

For nightlife information, visit sfclubs.com.

On the wild west end of a great city, from Kelly's Cove to Sloat Boulevard, Ocean Beach is 3 miles of wind, swell, tide, sandbars, currents, and raw energy. The surf at Ocean Beach is a complex equation that doesn't always add up. But when it all comes together, the result is glorious.   Chris Burkard

If you have the time and the chance to cruise around San Francisco, you'll experience one of the most diverse cities on the planet. There are countless tourist areas to check out: Fisherman's Wharf, the Golden Gate Bridge, Alcatraz, Lombard Street, Ghirardelli Square, the Legion of Honor, the Palace of Fine Arts, Golden Gate Park, the Marina district, the Presidio, Pacific Heights, and Chinatown. You'll also discover numerous cool little areas and hundreds of restaurants off the beaten path that don't feel nearly as touristy.

Very few people know that respected big-wave surfer Laird Hamilton was born in San Francisco. He bounced back and forth between California and the Hawaiian Islands for several years; by the late 1980s he'd become known as an aggressive and powerful surfer at Backdoor and Pipeline on the North Shore of Oahu. Although talented, Laird wasn't interested in taking the traditional competitive surfing route and

CLIFF AND SURF AREA
EXTREMELY DANGEROUS
People have been swept
from the rocks and drowned

Elizabeth Pepin Silva

Sharp Park is a large sandy beach between San Francisco and Pacifica. There are signs for it off CA 1. It works best with a west or northwest swell in fall or spring. The break at Sharp Park can hold large overhead waves and requires some skill and experience during big swells.

Elizabeth Pepin Silva

Rockaway Beach is a consistent outside break that can catch swell from virtually any direction. It's located just north of Pacifica at Rockaway Avenue off CA 1. Rockaway is worth checking out year-round. Wave shape can be excellent with the right conditions. The waves can be big and fast and the currents strong.

instead focused his attention on conquering big surf. When waves on the outer reefs of the North Shore were too big to paddle into, he began using a Jet Ski to tow into them. Eventually, Hamilton started towing into a reef break called Peahi—now known as Jaws—on the island of Maui. Jaws holds monstrous surf but at the time had not yet been ridden when it got big. Over the years Laird has been pushing the envelope of big-wave surfing, at Jaws and other big-wave spots, and has been designing and experimenting with a variety of equipment innovations.

Other Information

Local Surf Shops: Wise Surfboards, 800 Great Highway 1, before Golden Gate Park, San Francisco; (415) 750-9473. SF Surf Shop, 3809 Noriega St., San Francisco; (415) 661-7873. Mollusk Surf Shop, 4500 Irving St., San Francisco; (415) 564-6300. Aqua Surf Shop, 2830 Sloat Blvd., San Francisco; (415) 242-9283. Sunset Shapers, 3896 Noriega St., San Francisco; (415) 665-7873.

Places to Stay: Ocean View Motel, 4340 Judah St., San Francisco; (415) 661-2300. Ocean Park Motel, 2690 46th Ave., San Francisco; (415) 566-7020.

Places to Eat: The Beach Chalet, 1000 Great Highway 1, San Francisco; (415) 386-8439. The Sea Biscuit, 3185 Noriega St., San Francisco; (415) 661-3784. Java Beach, 2650 Sloat Blvd., San Francisco; (415) 731-2965.

Linda Mar

This is a mostly west-facing beach in Pacifica.

Best tides: Low and incoming

Best swell direction: West, north, northwest

Best wave size: Waist high to slightly overhead

Bottom: Sand and rock

Type of break: Beach break and outside lefts and rights

Skill level: Novice to intermediate under head high; advanced when it's head high and over

Best boards: Longboard, funshape

Best seasons: Fall, winter, spring

Crowds: Crowded

Water quality: Average

Hazards: Shore pound on a big day

Fees and permits: None

Finding the Break

From San Francisco: Head south on CA 1 to Pacifica. The parking lot for Linda Mar is off CA 1 behind the oceanfront Taco Bell. Drop off your vehicle and walk a few steps to the beach. GPS: N37 35.825 / W122 30.215

Surf Description

Linda Mar is a mile-long stretch of beach just north of Pedro Point. It's a very picturesque area and somewhat protected from the wind. The break here is usually fairly forgiving, and on a nice weekend it can attract a fair number of novice surfers. However, Linda Mar can also produce a fun and challenging wave with a bigger swell. The outer peaks tend to be the best shaped and often produce the longest rides.

Decent little lefts peel past the Boat House on a sunny, windless day at Linda Mar.
Elizabeth Pepin Silva

No shark attacks have been reported at Linda Mar, but there have been numerous sightings over the years. Great white sharks are known to patrol the waters near this beach, and it's common to see seals cruising around the lineup. The most recent reported shark sighting was in July 2004 when several surfers said they saw a shark twisting in the water as if feeding. In 1990 a surfer was attacked at nearby Montara, and in 1993 a diver was attacked at Pedro Point. Luckily, neither attack resulted in major injuries.

Linda Mar Beach is located in the town of Pacifica. Pacifica means "peace" in Spanish and was adopted during a contest in 1957 to find a name for the town. Ohlone Indians were the first known settlers of this area, but their village was wiped out by disease in 1791. In 1834 Mexico seized this land; in 1839 a large area of this coast, known as Rancho San Pedro, was granted to Francisco Sanchez. In 1842 Sanchez was appointed mayor of San Francisco and in 1846 he built a country home on his land, which is now known as Pacifica. Sanchez died in 1862; the adobe changed ownership several times until 1947, when it was sold to San Mateo County. The Sanchez adobe became a historic landmark in 1953.

Linda Mar is a very popular beach and can get crowded on weekends.

There have been three well-known shipping accidents in this area over the years. In 1851 the paddle steamer *Republic* struck Pedro Point. In 1900 the schooner *Bonita* was sunk by a whale off the coast here. And in 1910 a schooner named *James Rolph* was wrecked on Pedro Point.

In 1985 the first Pacifica Fog Fest was held. The festival is held every September to celebrate the foggy weather in this area. However, September is usually one of the sunnier months of the year, so if you come to this festival, prepare to experience some beautiful days.

Other Information

Local Surf Shops: Norcal Surf Shop, 5460 Cabrillo Hwy., Pacifica; (650) 738-9283. Sonlight Surf Shop, 575 Crespi Dr., Pacifica; (650) 359-0353.
Places to Stay: Howard Johnson, 2160 Francisco Blvd., Pacifica; (650) 359-9494.
Places to Eat: La Playa Mexican Food, in Pedro Point Shopping Center, off CA 1, Pacifica; (650) 738-2247. Gorilla Barbeque, 2145 Coast Hwy., Pacifica; (650) 359-7427.

Pedro Point is another year-round spot that can catch a lot of swell. It's located just south of Linda Mar. There's a small, inside break with a sand bottom and a larger, outside reef break. The outside break at Pedro Point can hold swell well overhead and is not to be taken lightly on a big day. There's limited parking here and this place can get crowded on weekends, especially when the weather's nice and the waves are good.

McNee Ranch is a sandy, protected cove between Pedro Point and Montara State Beach. Swell wraps around a point on the north end of the cove and produces a two-way peak on the inside. CA 1 is well above the beach at this point in the coast. However, there's a parking lot on the east side of CA 1 with a sign that says McNee Ranch. You can leave your vehicle there and walk down to the beach.

Chris Burkard

Montara State Beach is a beach break between Pacifica and Half Moon Bay. It's positioned to catch swell from any direction and can produce surf of varying size and quality year-round. You can park in the Chart House restaurant parking lot on the north side of the beach off CA 1 and walk down.

Lucia Griggi

Ross's Cove is a left that breaks into a small cove on the north side of Pillar Point. You can access this cove by parking near Moss Beach, just north of Half Moon Bay, and walking south along the beach. Ross's Cove needs a swell from the west, northwest, or north, which makes it best in fall, winter, and spring.

Maverick's

This is a world-renowned big-wave break in Half Moon Bay.

Best tide: Varies

Best swell direction: Varies

Best wave size: Overhead to many times overhead

Bottom: Rock

Type of break: Outside left and right

Skill level: Advanced

Best board: Gun

Best season: Winter

Crowds: Not crowded

Water quality: Clean

Hazards: Sharks, hold-downs, ending up on the rocks

Fees and permits: None

Brock Little is one of the best surfers in the world, but he has been saying for a long time that Shane Dorian is the best big-wave surfer in the world. This is Dorian boldly going where few men have the skills or the courage—pulling into the barrel at Maverick's on February 13, 2010.   Nikki Brooks

Finding the Break

From San Francisco: Head south on CA 1 toward Half Moon Bay. The breaks at Maverick's are outside Pillar Point in Half Moon Bay. There's an Air Force base overlooking the break. The best way to access the break is to park by Pillar Point Harbor break wall and paddle out through the lagoon. GPS: N37 30.199 / W122 28.991

Surf Description

Maverick's is located just north of Half Moon Bay and is about 0.25 mile from Pillar Point Harbor. It has earned a reputation as one of the best big-wave spots in the world. Big-wave surfers from Southern California, Hawaii, and Australia travel to this break when there's a massive swell visiting. There are two main peaks at Maverick's. The peak on the north end of the break is ridden the most. The other break, known as the outer bowl, can be a monstrous, nearly perfect two-way peak. Hold-downs can be particularly frightening here on a big day due to the cold water and large submerged boulders. And many a big-wave gun has ended up on the Pillar Point rocks. With a small swell, Maverick's will appear virtually flat and serene. Given a large winter swell, however, this deepwater break can hold waves that are several times overhead. When it's on, Maverick's is definitely not a break for the timid or inexperienced surfer.

It's believed that this break wasn't ridden until the 1970s and was known by only a few locals until 1990. In the early 1990s the word got out, and surfers from Santa Cruz to San Francisco began coming here to score some heavy, cold-water waves. In 1994 Maverick's started to experience a great deal of press. *Surfing* and *Surfer* magazines both featured cover shots of the wave that year. And in December 1994 several well known big-wave surfers came to California from Hawaii to surf Maverick's during a large winter swell. One of those surfers, Mark Foo, caught an edge on an 18- to 20-foot wave, resulting in what observers described as a standard wipeout. Unfortunately, Foo was found dead as a result of the wipeout, and Maverick's was suddenly thrust into the international spotlight.

> **Half Moon Bay is a very busy town on weekends.**

The winter of 1997–1998 was an El Niño season and an especially good year for surf on the West Coast. That same year a clothing company offered a $50,000 prize for paddling into the largest wave of the winter. Surfers began taking huge risks at Maverick's in an attempt to win the money. The next year tow-in surfing began to take hold at this break, and Quiksilver held its first Maverick's Big Wave Invitational with a $15,000 purse. In the winter of 1999–2000, the prize money was doubled, rewarding the winner with a $30,000 check.

Other Information

Local Surf Shops: Cowboy Surf Shop, 2830 Cabrillo Hwy., Half Moon Bay; (650) 726-6968. Half Moon Bay Board Shop, 3032 Cabrillo Hwy., Half Moon Bay; (650) 726-1476. Mavericks Surf Shop, 25 Johnson Pier, Pillar Point Harbor, Half Moon Bay; (650) 560-8088.

Places to Stay: There are numerous places to stay in Half Moon Bay, including a youth hostel on the north side of town: Point Montara Lighthouse Hostel, 16th Street CA 1, Montara; (650) 728-7177. Or you can camp at Half Moon Bay State Park, a state campground on the south side of town; (650) 726-8819.

Places to Eat: Moss Beach Distillery, 140 Beach Way, Moss Beach; (650) 728-5595. Half Moon Bay Brewing Company, 390 Capistrano Ave., Princeton-by-the-Sea (Pillar Point Harbor); (650) 728-2739. Creekside Smokehouse, 280 Avenue Alhambra, Half Moon Bay; (650) 712-8862; creeksidesmokehouse.com.

Chris Burkard

Princeton Jetty is a right that breaks on the south side of the jetty in Half Moon Bay. It's located just steps from CA 1; there are numerous places to park. The break at Princeton Jetty works best with a medium-size swell from the south or west. It can be a well-shaped wedge and a fun wave with the right conditions.

Half Moon Bay Beaches

This is a 4-mile stretch of beach with numerous breaks in Half Moon Bay.

Best tide: Varies

Best swell direction: Anything but southwest

Best wave size: Waist high to overhead

Bottom: Sand and rock

Type of break: Beach break, outside, lefts and rights

Skill level: Novice to advanced

Best boards: Shortboard, funshape, longboard

Best season: Any

Crowds: Some breaks can get crowded on weekends

Water quality: Average

Hazards: Rip currents, shore-break poundings

Fees and permits: None

Finding the Break

From San Francisco: Head south on CA 1 to Half Moon Bay. Once you're in Half Moon Bay, almost any road that goes west from CA 1 will take you to the beach. There are large signs along CA 1 telling you what beach is at the end of each road. Some of the roads end in state parks, others in parking lots. Leave your vehicle on the bluff overlooking the beach and walk down the stairs. GPS: N37 27.020 / W122 25.795

Surf Description

Half Moon Bay is a 4-mile crescent of beach with several breaks. Some are exposed to northwest wind, but they can all be great with the right conditions. The best spots are (from north to south): El Granada Beach, Vallejo Beach, Miramar Beach, Naples Beach, Dunes Beach, Venice Beach, Elmar Beach, and Francis Beach. The three main parking and access points are at Francis Beach, Venice Beach, and Dunes Beach. Francis Beach is located at the end of Kelly Avenue in the heart of the town of Half Moon Bay. Venice Beach is at the end of Venice Boulevard off CA 1. And Dunes Beach is at the end of Young Avenue off CA 1.

The Half Moon Bay area was originally inhabited by the Costanoan Indians. Later the Spanish came and divided the land into cattle and horse ranches called ranchos. Eventually, the land became part of the United States; after the gold rush the first Americans began to settle here. Half Moon Bay became known as Spanish Town due to the large number of Spanish-speaking people who lived in this area in those days.

An aerial view of about a mile of the beach breaks of Half Moon Bay from Pilarcitos Avenue in the south to Young Ave in the north. californiacoastline.org

Back then this part of the coast was very isolated by coastal mountains. Before the turn of the twentieth century, only two narrow and winding roads led to Half Moon Bay. Despite the difficult access, loggers, whalers, and farmers gradually started to call this place home.

In the late 1800s the Ocean Shore Railroad planned to lay tracks linking San Francisco and Santa Cruz. The goal was to develop and bring tourists to this beautiful section of shoreline. Many Half Moon Bay locals at the time resisted this development plan and were disturbed by the thought of a West Coast Coney Island with numerous hotels and resorts. The railroad started the project in San Francisco and encountered numerous geographic obstacles that proved to be very expensive. The 1906 earthquake cost the railroad a great deal

There's an air show in Half Moon Bay each spring. The Half Moon Bay golf course is also nice.

of money when thousands of dollars in equipment fell into the ocean in the Devils Slide area. The railroad plans spurred the development of beach towns between San Francisco and Half Moon Bay. However, the tracks never made it beyond Tunitas Creek, a few miles south of Half Moon Bay, and the project was eventually abandoned in the early 1920s.

Other Information

Local Surf Shops: Cowboy Surf Shop, 2830 Cabrillo Hwy., Half Moon Bay; (650) 726-6968. Half Moon Bay Board Shop, 3032 Cabrillo Hwy., Half Moon Bay; (650) 726-1476. Mavericks Surf Shop, 25 Johnson Pier, Pillar Point Harbor, Half Moon Bay; (650) 560-8088.

Places to Stay: There are numerous places to stay in Half Moon Bay, including a youth hostel on the north side of town, Point Montara Lighthouse Hostel 16th Street CA 1, Montara; (650) 728-7177. Or you can camp at Half Moon Bay State Park, a state campground on the south side of town; (650) 726-8819.

Places to Eat: Moss Beach Distillery, 140 Beach Way, Moss Beach; (650) 728-5595. Half Moon Bay Brewing Company, 390 Capistrano Ave., Princeton-by-the-Sea (Pillar Point Harbor); (650) 728-2739. Creekside Smokehouse, 280 Avenue Alhambra, Half Moon Bay; (650) 712-8862; creeksidesmokehouse.com.

Elizabeth Pepin Silva

Martin's Beach is a two-way reef break south of Half Moon Bay. There are signs for this beach off CA 1. It works best with a waist- to head-high swell from the southwest at a medium tide. The surf at Martin's Beach has the best shape in fall, spring, and summer.

Chris Burkard

Tunitas Creek is a beach break just south of Martin's Beach. It's one of those breaks that looks better from afar than it is in actuality. Tunitas Creek can break with swell from virtually any direction and is best from waist to head high. Due to various shark sightings and stories, this creek break has earned the nickname "Don't Eat Us Creek" from some of the locals.

Pescadero

This is an area of beach breaks and rocky reefs 14 miles south of Half Moon Bay.

Best tides: Incoming to high
Best swell direction: South, west, northwest
Best wave size: Waist high to overhead
Bottom: Sand and rock
Type of break: Beach break, outside, lefts and rights
Skill level: Intermediate to advanced
Best board: Shortboard
Best season: Any
Crowds: Not crowded
Water quality: Clean
Hazards: Sharks
Fees and permits: None

Finding the Break

From San Francisco: Head south on CA 1. Pescadero is 14 miles south of Half Moon Bay. There are signs directing you to Pescadero State Beach. There's a parking lot at the beach and it's an easy stroll down to the break. GPS: N37 15.925 / W122 24.728

Surf Description

Pescadero is a very remote-feeling area of the California coast even though it's really not that far from San Francisco or Santa Cruz. There are both beach breaks and reef breaks that you can surf all by yourself. The beach breaks are on the north end of Pescadero State Beach, and there are rocky reefs all along Pescadero Point. If there's a swell and the wind is favorable, the surf is bound to be good somewhere in this area.

The Pescadero area has developed a reputation over the years for being inhabited by sharks. There have been four reported attacks and numerous shark sightings around here in the last few decades. In 1969 a diver was attacked at Pigeon Point, just south of here. A surfer was attacked at nearby San Gregorio State Beach in 1974. And in 1987 another surfer was attacked at Tunitas Creek just north of Pescadero. Luckily, all three of these shark attacks resulted in minor

Butano State Park has miles of good hiking trails. There's a lighthouse at Pigeon Point, a few miles south of Pescadero, that's worth a visit.

A windy peak along the beach at Pescadero. This is what it looks like, most of the time: A lot of wind, a lot of swell, few takers.

injuries. However, a diver in 1984 wasn't nearly as lucky: That shark attack at Pigeon Point proved to be fatal.

Nearby Pigeon Point was originally named *Punta de las Balenas* or "whale point," in recognition of the groups of gray whales that pass by here during their migration periods. In 1853, however, a ship called *Carrier Pigeon* was destroyed on the rocks here, and the land was renamed Pigeon Point in memory of the accident. Soon after that the Coast Guard recommended that a lighthouse be built on this point. Unfortunately, three more ships and forty-nine more lives were lost on Pigeon Point due to dense fog and heavy seas before any construction began.

In 1870 the government purchased the land at Pigeon Point; the lighthouse was completed in 1872. Still, three ships were wrecked on this point between 1896 and 1913. In the Prohibition years this stretch of California coast became a favored spot for bootleggers due to its isolation and proximity to San Francisco. Rumrunners used the derrick at the Pigeon Point Lighthouse to hoist their crates up from their boats at night. The 1989 Loma Prieta earthquake caused only minimal damage to the Pigeon Point Lighthouse, and in 1992 it benefited from a major restoration project. Today the lighthouse is leased to American Youth Hostels Incorporated; tours of the station are available.

Other Information

Local Surf Shops: None.
Places to Stay: Butano State Park on San Mateo Coast of CA 1, 4.5 miles southeast of Pescadero; for directions call (650) 879-2040. There are also some places to stay in the town of Pescadero. Pigeon Point Lighthouse Hostel, 210 Pigeon Point Rd., Pescadero; (650) 879-0633. Costanoa Lodge, 2001 Rossi Rd., Pescadero; (650) 879-1100.
Places to Eat: Duarte's, 202 Stage Rd., Pescadero; (650) 879-0464.

Pigeon Point is a right point break located between Pescadero and Ano Nuevo. This isn't a very consistent break, but when it's on you'll see lines just south of the Pigeon Point Lighthouse. The right at Pigeon Point works best during a strong winter swell at a medium tide. This area is known for being populated by sharks.

SUPDATE: SAN FRANCISCO TO SANTA CRUZ

Pigeon Point is a perfect example of a surf spot that was mostly over-looked by surfers and has been adopted by standup paddleboarders. Pigeon Point shifts around, there are a lot of rocks, and it's really not that great of a wave for conventional surfers. But SUPs can make mountains from molehills, and Pigeon Point is a spot that more and more standup paddlers are flocking to—because it's a decent wave, and there aren't many surfers there. But there are lots and lots of possibilities between San Francisco and Santa Cruz for standup paddlers wanting to seek the perfect wave on the perfect day and be alone with the surf and their thoughts.

Riding a SUP at Ocean Beach can be a huge advantage because a standup paddler has 30+ seconds of early warning and can get in position twice as fast—and Ocean Beach is a place where an advantage is needed. Fort Point would be fun on a SUP but might cause unrest, and if you want to just go for a leisurely cruise, the Tiburon coast is one possibility in the vastness of San Francisco Bay. If you're a baseball fan, check out McCovey Cove near ATT Park when the world champion San Francisco Giants are opening a can of whupass on whoever is in town. Back along the coast there are a few adventurous standup paddlers challenging Maverick's on the big days and again, being able to see what's coming and getting there twice as fast is a big advantage in big surf. But if you don't want to have that much fun, take a paddle around Pillar Point Harbor, and don't be spooked when a big skate or a leopard shark swims around in front of you. There is a decent secret spot inside of Maverick's that is popular with SUPs, but that's all that will be said about that. The truth is, there are many, many miles of empty surf between Half Moon Bay and Santa Cruz that are wide-open to a SUP surfer wanting to put in the effort.

Ano Nuevo

This protected beach about 19 miles north of Santa Cruz can produce incredible surf.

Best tides: Incoming to high

Best swell direction: South, north, northwest

Best wave size: Waist high to slightly overhead

Bottom: Sand and rock

Type of break: Beach break, outside, left and right

Skill level: Intermediate to advanced

Best boards: Shortboard, funshape

Best season: Any

Crowds: Can get crowded on weekends

Water quality: Clean

Hazards: Sharks

Fees and permits: According to parks.ca.gov, a nominal parking fee is charged for passenger vehicles.

Dead center in the middle of the Red Triangle, Ano Nuevo is a good place to hide out from the northwest winds and tuck into a barrel wedging off the rocks. It's also a good place to have a close encounter with **Mr. White.**   Chris Burkard

Finding the Break

From Santa Cruz: Head north on CA 1 for 19 miles. Ano Nuevo State Park is clearly marked and is right off CA 1. Enter the state park, pay the nominal fee, and walk down the trail to the beach. The walk down takes 5 or 10 minutes. GPS: N37 09.984 / W122 21.712

Surf Description

The two main breaks at Ano Nuevo can be world-class with the right conditions. You'll find the most people surfing the protected right breaking on the south side of Ano Nuevo Point. This break can get very hollow and fast, with excellent shape.

There's also a big left on the north side of Ano Nuevo Point. However, that break is notorious for being patrolled by large sharks. The good news is that there has never been a reported attack on a surfer here. The bad news is there have been three shark attacks on scuba divers and one on a kayaker within the Ano Nuevo State Reserve. Because Ano Nuevo is the southernmost point of what is referred to as the Red Triangle, most surfers opt for the more sheltered break on the south side of the point.

The Ano Nuevo State Reserve is definitely worth checking out. Just don't try to pet the elephant seals. They move faster than you might suspect.

The Red Triangle is an imaginary zone whose other two points are Tomales Bay to the north and the Farallon Islands to the west. This area is known for being home to a large number of great white sharks, in large part due to the number of seals that live here.

In early January 1603, Spanish explorer Sebastián Vizcaíno sailed by this point. His diarist named it *Punta de Ano Nuevo,* or "New Year's point." It hasn't changed much since then—it's still a beautiful and undeveloped area of coast filled with sea lions and elephant seals.

In the 1800s elephant seals were almost hunted to extinction. In 1892 it was believed that there were fewer than one hundred seals left. Mexico passed a law protecting them in 1922, and the United States soon did the same. The population began to grow, and in the 1950s the first elephant seal pups were born at Ano Nuevo Island. Now there are more than 150,000 elephant seals, and a lot of them make the yearly pilgrimage to Ano Nuevo. This makes the Ano Nuevo State Reserve home to the largest northern elephant seal mainland breeding colony in the world. The males reach sizes of 14 to 16 feet long and can weigh as much as 5,000 pounds. They fight with one another to establish dominance and mating rights. Their breeding season is from December to March; guided walks are available if you want to watch the males battle or see newborn pups waddling around.

Other Information

Local Surf Shops: None between Half Moon Bay and Santa Cruz.
Places to Stay: Davenport Inn Bed and Breakfast, 31 Davenport Ave., Davenport; (831) 425-1818. Pigeon Point Lighthouse Hostel, 210 Pigeon Point Rd., Pescadero; (650) 879-0633. Costanoa Lodge, 2001 Rossi Rd., Pescadero; (650) 879-1100.
Places to Eat: Davenport Bakery Bar and Grill, 490 CA 1, Davenport; (831) 423-9803. Davenport Roadhouse Restaurant and Inn, 1 Davenport Ave.; (831) 426-8801.

Waddell Creek

This is an exposed beach 16 miles north of Santa Cruz.

Best tides: Incoming to high
Best swell direction: Anything but southwest
Best wave size: Waist high to slightly overhead
Bottom: Sand and rock
Type of break: Beach break, outside, lefts and rights
Skill level: Novice to advanced
Best board: Shortboard
Best season: Any
Crowds: Can get crowded on weekends
Water quality: Clean
Hazards: Sharks
Fees and permits: None

Finding the Break

From Santa Cruz: Head north on CA 1 for 16 miles. There's a large sign for Waddell Creek Beach. Park in the lot off CA 1 and walk a few steps to the beach. GPS: N37 05.825 / W122 16.814

Surf Description

Waddell Creek can catch swell from nearly any direction and transform into a quality wave. The area where Waddell Creek flows into the ocean has both outer reefs and beach breaks producing numerous peaks. This beach is very exposed to northwest wind, so it's usually best to surf here in the morning before the wind picks up. This break used to be a popular windsurfing spot, but when the wind is blowing these days, you can expect Waddell Beach to become very crowded with kite surfers. This section of the California coast has generated its share of shark stories. However, Waddell Creek has had only one reported shark attack. It involved a surfer in November 1999.

In the late 1700s this area was referred to as "Canada de la Salud" by campers and hikers who felt that the climate had healthful effects. In the 1860s a man named William Waddell built a lumber mill here, and the beach has retained his name ever since. Waddell Beach is within what is now known as the Big Basin Redwoods State Park. Established in 1902, it's California's oldest state park. Big Basin Redwoods State Park is aptly named as it consists of more than 18,000 acres of old-growth and recovering redwood forest. This is a great park to hike in, with more than 80 miles of trails, waterfalls, and a variety of environments. The trails vary in elevation from sea level to 2,000 feet, and the climate can change drastically from foggy and cool near the beach to warm and sunny on the ridgetops. The park is also known as a good place

Beginning at the San Mateo/Santa Cruz county line, Waddell Creek is 1.5 miles of exposed beach breaks, ending at the Waddell Reefs. This beach gets a lot of wind year-round and is as popular with kite surfers and sailboarders as it is with surfers. Conditions change from season to season, day to day, hour to hour. This is the beach break south of the main parking lot showing some class. Chris Burkard

to do some bird watching and is home to such species as jays, egrets, herons, and woodpeckers. You may also spot numerous other animals, including deer, raccoons, and bobcats.

One section of the state park is known as Rancho Del Oso and contains a nature and history center. This was once a working ranch and home to the Hoover/McLean family. The Rancho Del Oso Nature and History Center is located near Waddell Creek and provides educational and recreational activities that focus on the natural and cultural history of the area. Exhibits and activities concentrate on such subjects as astronomy, Ohlone Indian culture, nocturnal wildlife, and the grizzly bears that once ruled this section of California's coast.

The wind blows steadily here in the afternoon, making it a great place to learn how to kite-surf.

Other Information

Local Surf Shops: None between Half Moon Bay and Santa Cruz.
Places to Stay: Davenport Inn Bed and Breakfast, 31 Davenport Ave., Davenport; (831) 425-1818. Pigeon Point Lighthouse Hostel, 210 Pigeon Point Rd., Pescadero; (650) 879-0633. Costanoa Lodge, 2001 Rossi Rd., Pescadero; (650) 879-1100.
Places to Eat: Whale City Bakery, 490 CA 1, Davenport; (831) 423-9803.

Scott's Creek
This is a right reef break 13 miles north of Santa Cruz.

Best tides: Incoming to high
Best swell direction: Anything but southwest
Best wave size: Waist high to overhead
Bottom: Rock and sand
Type of break: Outside, right
Skill level: Intermediate to advanced
Best board: Shortboard
Best season: Any
Crowds: Can get crowded on weekends
Water quality: Clean
Hazards: Sharks
Fees and permits: None

Finding the Break

From Santa Cruz: Head north on CA 1 for 13 miles. There's a large sign for Scott's Creek Beach. You can park off CA 1 and walk a few steps to the beach. GPS: N37 02.365 / W122 13.668

Savannah Shaughnessy giving it heaps at Scott's Creek—a top turn to set up the inside bowl and then finish off with a big carving cutback to drench that guy on the inside.
Nikki Brooks

Surf Description

Scott's Creek is a right reef break that can be good year-round. The waves here can get big and powerful with well-shaped peaks. The reef on the north end is usually the best. In winter, however, the creek can help create outer sandbars all along the beach, resulting in numerous peaks that can be surfed. Like Waddell Creek Beach north of here, Scott's Creek is also exposed to northwest wind. As a result, the best times to surf here are usually either early or late in the day. The breaks at Scott's Creek are generally better suited for intermediate to advanced surfers. With the right conditions at lower tides, the wave can get fast and hollow—and not too forgiving for novice surfers.

We all know that creek and river mouths are popular places for sharks to feed. And a lot of shark stories have originated in this area. However, there has only been one reported attack at Scott's Creek. It occurred in 1991 and unfortunately resulted in a surfer sustaining major injuries. Nearby Davenport Landing, just south of Scott's Creek, is considered by surfers in the area to be one of the most shark-populated breaks around. In 1991 a surfer suffered major injuries as a result of a shark attack at Davenport. In 1995 a great white shark attacked a windsurfer in the same place, causing minor injuries. Given the history of attacks and reputation for sharks in the area, it would be a good idea to surf Scott's Creek with a buddy.

This section of California's coast is very beautiful and varies a great deal from mile to mile. You'll find green hills, rocky bluffs, sand dunes, and rugged coastal mountains all within a short distance. Scott's Creek Beach is especially picturesque with a wide-open sandy beach and at times a wide creek that runs down from the hills and into the ocean. In spring large pods of whales often travel close to the beach here, making this a good whale-watching spot. It's not surprising that decades ago this part of the coast was popular among whalers. The gray whales were hunted for their meat, bones, and oil. Nowadays whales are protected, and numerous people will stop along the cliffs to catch a glimpse of these huge mammals during their migration.

Other Information

Local Surf Shops: None between Half Moon Bay and Santa Cruz.
Places to Stay: Davenport Inn Bed and Breakfast, 31 Davenport Ave., Davenport; (831) 425-1818. Pigeon Point Lighthouse Hostel, 210 Pigeon Point Rd., Pescadero; (650) 879-0633. Costanoa Lodge, 2001 Rossi Rd., Pescadero; (650) 879-1100.
Places to Eat: Whale City Bakery, 490 CA 1, Davenport; (831) 423-9803.

Chris Burkard

Davenport is an exposed beach a few miles north of Santa Cruz. You'll see a sign for Swanton Road off CA 1 in the town of Davenport. Follow Swanton Road to the beach and walk to the breaks. There's a left on the south end of the beach and a right on the north end. Both breaks can produce some well-shaped waves but are vulnerable to northwest wind. Davenport is not a place you'll want to surf alone due to numerous shark sightings.

Four Mile

This is a right reef and point break 4 miles north of Santa Cruz.

Best tides: Incoming to high
Best swell direction: West, north, northwest
Best wave size: Waist high to overhead
Bottom: Rock
Type of break: Right, reef, point
Skill level: Intermediate to advanced
Best boards: Shortboard, funshape, longboard
Best seasons: Winter, spring, and fall
Crowds: Can get crowded on weekends
Water quality: Clean

Hazards: Locals, parking-lot thieves
Fees and permits: None

Finding the Break

From Santa Cruz: Head north on CA 1 for roughly 4 miles. You can park on CA 1 in one of a couple of large turnouts in that area. Once you've parked, walk down the trail toward the beach. It's about a 5-minute walk to the break. GPS: N36 59.514 / W122 09.976

Surf Description

Four Mile can be a great right reef and point break. It breaks very consistently in winter but can get blown out. The wave shape here can be phenomenal with the right conditions; on a bigger day you can catch waves at the point and ride them almost to the beach.

The nearby town of Davenport was established in the year 1868. In 1851 John Davenport, a sea captain from Rhode Island on his way to San Francisco, supposedly sailed by a pod of whales swimming close to shore here. He is said to have gotten the idea that these whales would be easy to harpoon and their blubber used for oil. In 1852 he got married and moved from Rhode Island to California to start a family and a whaling business. The couple first moved to Monterey, where they lived in the first brick house in California and started the first coastal whaling business. Eventually they decided to move the business closer to San Francisco and moved to Soquel's Landing, the area now known as Capitola.

In 1868 the family moved to this part of the coast and built a wharf where ships could load items to be transported to San Francisco.

Cars have been broken into in the parking area for this beach. Avoid leaving anything of value in your vehicle.

The wharf was known as Davenport's Landing and was one of the best ship landings along the California coast at the time. Shortly thereafter a village grew around the wharf, complete with a general store, hotels, a stable, and a blacksmith shop. The whaling industry was thriving during this time, and whalers would come here for gear and supplies as well as to melt down whale blubber. Captain Davenport and his wife, Ellen, raised ten children in this area and built a house on a high bluff near Agua Puerca Creek cove. In 1880 the wharf at Davenport's Landing was abandoned due to a decline in business and high operational costs. John and Ellen Davenport then moved to Santa Cruz; the captain passed away in 1892.

Kim Mayer hotdogging the inside at Four Mile.   Elizabeth Pepin Silva

In 1906 the Santa Cruz Portland Cement Company was established in this area. The Coast Dairies and Land Company then began developing what is now the town of Davenport to house the cement plant workers. A large fire destroyed nearly everything in 1915, but the town was able to rebuild. In 1998 the Coast Dairies and Land Company's 7,000-acre ranch was purchased for preservation. The town of Davenport is now surrounded by miles of open coastal space.

Other Information

Local Surf Shops: There are numerous surf shops in Santa Cruz including Pearson Arrow Surf and Sport, 2324 Mission St., Santa Cruz; (831) 423-8286.

Places to Stay: There are numerous places to stay in Santa Cruz including Best Western, 500 Ocean Ave., Santa Cruz; (831) 458-9898.

Places to Eat: Zachary's, 819 Pacific Ave., Santa Cruz; (831) 427-0646. Gigi's Bakery and Cafe, 550 River St., Santa Cruz; (831) 425-4800. Pizza My Heart has three locations in Santa Cruz: downtown, Capitola, and 41st Avenue. Paula's Café, 3500 Portola Dr., Santa Cruz; (831) 464-0741.

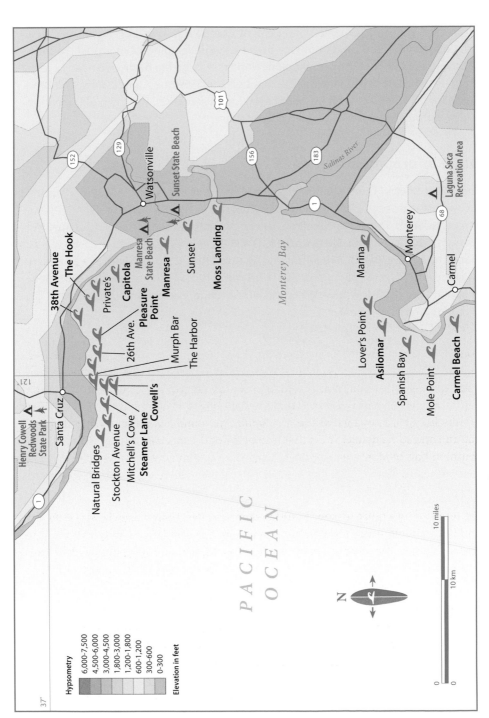

Region 5 (Santa Cruz to Carmel)

Hypsometry

- 6,000–7,500
- 4,500–6,000
- 3,000–4,500
- 1,800–3,000
- 1,200–1,800
- 600–1,200
- 300–600
- 0–300

Elevation in feet

Henry Cowell Redwoods State Park

Santa Cruz

38th Avenue

The Hook

Private's

Capitola

Pleasure Point

26th Ave.

Murph Bar

The Harbor

Cowell's

Steamer Lane

Mitchell's Cove

Stockton Avenue

Natural Bridges

Manresa State Beach

Manresa

Sunset

Moss Landing

Watsonville

Sunset State Beach

Salinas River

Monterey Bay

Lover's Point

Marina

Asilomar

Spanish Bay

Mole Point

Carmel Beach

Monterey

Carmel

Laguna Seca Recreation Area

PACIFIC OCEAN

N

10 miles

10 km

0

37°

121°

152

129

101

156

183

1

1

68

REGION 5: SANTA CRUZ TO CARMEL

This region covers the surf spots within Monterey Bay. At the northern end is Santa Cruz, a town blessed with a lot of good surf, a great vibe, and a fun downtown. As you move south along the cliffs, you travel through the small and touristy coastal village of Capitola on your way to a long stretch of consistent beach breaks. Agricultural land occupies the most inland part of the bay, making it difficult to access the beach for several miles. CA 1 rejoins the coast again at the sand dunes of Moss Landing on the way to Monterey. The coastline becomes rocky and very scenic as you move south through Lover's Point and the famous golf courses along 17 Mile Drive. The southern end of the bay is marked by the quaint, affluent village of Carmel, where you'll find some of the most beautiful sand beaches in California.

Overall Surf Description

You'll find some spots in this region that become very crowded and competitive. Paddle out at Steamer Lane on a head-high sunny weekend day, for example, and you'll get the impression that everyone in Santa Cruz surfs. A lot of good surfers do live in this region, and when the conditions are ripe, surfing heads to the top of the priority list. Still, as you move south of Santa Cruz—and if you know where to go— you can find some quality spots that aren't crowded, especially during the week. The southern half of Monterey Bay doesn't see the same quality or quantity of swell as the northern half, and consequently breaks tend to be less congested and mellower.

Fall Surf

Fall tends to be a great season for surf in Monterey Bay. There's usually very little fog, and both air and water temperatures can reach annual highs in early autumn. The combination of the weather, early northern swells, and late southern swells makes September and October two of the most pleasant months of the year to surf this region.

Winter Surf

Winter is definitely the best season for surf. Conditions are consistently very good and can vary considerably. The water is cold all winter long, but swell size, wave shape, and wind and air temperatures can change several times per week. The quality and quantity of the waves depend on the tides and storms moving through. The key is learning how to predict which spots in Monterey Bay will produce the best surf under certain circumstances.

Spring Surf

Although not as sweet as winter, spring surf can be pretty steady here. There are usually early southern swells and late-winter swells rolling through this time of year to keep things interesting. When the northwest winds blow offshore, wave shape can be exceptionally good.

Summer Surf

As in the region north of here, summer is usually relatively flat. Still, a few times every summer, a big southern hemisphere swell will have enough power to get up to Monterey Bay and produce quality head-high surf. Occasionally the remnants of a smaller south swell will also reach this far north. But the majority of the time, the waves are pretty small; unless you own a 10- or 11-foot longboard, summer surf is rarely very exciting.

Some Santa Cruz surf spots have been famous for decades, some come and go with the seasons and rain. This is the Santa Cruz River mouth in the spring of 2010—right around the time of the Japanese tsunami.   Nikki Brooks

Average Temperatures for Region (Santa Cruz to Carmel)		
	Air (Santa Cruz)	Water (Santa Cruz
Jan	60	53
Feb	62	54
Mar	64	54
Apr	67	54
May	71	55
June	74	57
July	74	59
Aug	75	60
Sept	76	60
Oct	73	59
Nov	66	56
Dec	61	54

Nikki Brooks

Natural Bridges is a right that breaks on a rock shelf. You'll see a sign for it off CA 1 as you head north out of Santa Cruz. It works best during big winter swells at low to medium tides. Natural Bridges can be a world-class break with incredible shape. However, it's also exposed to northwest wind, which can result in it getting blown out. Natural Bridges can hold waves well overhead and can get crowded when the waves are good.

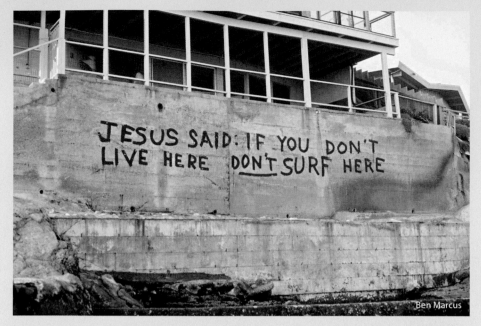

Ben Marcus

Stockton Avenue is a right reef break just east of Natural Bridges. With the right conditions, this break can produce a sweet barrel. Stockton Avenue works best with a small, south swell, although you can find surf here nearly all year long. It closes out when the waves are overhead or larger. This is a very crowded and competitive spot when the waves are optimal.

Nikki Brooks

A right point break between Stockton Avenue and Steamer Lane, Mitchell's Cove works best with a large winter swell at a low to medium tide. It isn't the most consistent spot in the area but can be a great wave with the right conditions. Like the other spots nearby, this break can get crowded when the waves are good. However, since you can find waves here nearly year-round, it's possible to occasionally score this break with only a handful of other surfers.

Steamer Lane

This is a world-class spot located in Santa Cruz.

Best tides: Low to medium
Best swell direction: South, west, northwest
Best wave size: Waist high to double overhead
Bottom: Rock
Type of break: Outside, point, left and right
Skill level: Intermediate to advanced
Best board: Shortboard
Best season: Any
Crowds: Crowded
Water quality: Clean
Hazards: Crowds
Fees and permits: None

Finding the Break

From Santa Cruz: Follow the signs to Ocean Street Beaches from where CA 1 meets CA 17. Go right where the road ends. Follow the coast along the beach and past the boardwalk. Go up the hill to West Cliff Drive and follow it until you see the lighthouse. There are several small, public parking lots along West Cliff Drive. Walk down the stairs near the lighthouse. GPS: N36 57.103 / W122 01.591

Surf Description

There are four main peaks at Steamer Lane. All four can produce well-shaped, consistent, and powerful waves. Indicator is a long, hollow wave inside. Middle Peak breaks a couple of hundred yards out from Lighthouse Point. The Point is the peak at the very tip of Lighthouse Point. And the Slot is the break between the Point and Middle Peak. Although the breaks at Steamer Lane can be incredible, they can also get very crowded and competitive.

Steamer Lane is said to have gotten its name from early surfers back in the 1930s when steamships were prevalent. Ships coming from the north would have to steer clear of the large surf in this area before they turned into Monterey Bay. In the 1950s surfers would travel down from San Francisco to surf Steamer Lane, which began to develop a reputation as a good break to prepare you for the large surf on the North Shore of Oahu. When Jack O'Neill moved his surf shop from San Francisco to Santa Cruz in the late 1950s, Steamer Lane became one of the testing grounds for improving the wet suits he invented.

As surfing became more popular in the 1960s, and wet suits allowed for longer sessions, interest in Steamer Lane also started to grow. In the 1970s and '80s, this break developed numerous quality surfers who could hold their own at the bigger and heavier breaks in Hawaii. Steamer Lane was also the spot that the Association of Surfing Professionals (ASP) O'Neill Coldwater Classic world tour event was held during the 1980s, which served to legitimize this break even further.

A lot of surfing contests take place at Steamer Lane.

Since the 1990s, Steamer Lane has produced countless chargers and has been solidified as one of the world's best breaks. This break gets a lot of media coverage and has earned a reputation for being a hot spot for high-performance, cutting-edge, and big-wave surfing. Unfortunately, all this notoriety has also contributed to the break's crowded and highly competitive vibe. Surfers from throughout California and even around the world come to Santa Cruz to surf Steamer Lane. On smaller days this

SUPs aren't 100 percent welcome in the lineup at Steamer Lane but if SUPpers are polite and make it look good, sometimes the crowd will give them a break.
Colin Brown. Photo courtesy Surftech

break is home to one of the most crowded lineups on the planet as everyone and her brother jockeys for position. Still, when the waves are the heaviest, the cream rises to the top at Steamer Lane and the best local surfers are the only ones you'll see out there.

Other Information

Local Surf Shops: Arrow Surf and Sport, 2324 Mission St., Santa Cruz; (831) 423-8286. Pacific Wave Surf Shop, 1502 Pacific Ave.; (831) 458-9283. Cowell's Beach Surf Shop, 30 Front St., Santa Cruz; (831) 427-2355. O'Neill Surf Shop, 400 Beach St., Santa Cruz; (831) 459-9230. Rip Curl, 1604 Mission St., Santa Cruz; (831) 454-0360. Pearson Arrow Surf Shop, 2324 Mission St., Santa Cruz; (831) 423-8286. O'Neill, 110 Cooper St. 100 D, Santa Cruz; (831) 469-4377. Covewater Paddle Surf, 726 Water St., Santa Cruz; (831) 600-7230. Hotline Wetsuits, 719 Swift St., Santa Cruz; (831) 425-5920. Haut Surf & Sailboards, 345 Swift St., Santa Cruz; (831) 426-7874. Billabong, 4105 Portola Dr., Santa Cruz; (831) 476-7873. Freeline Design Surf Shop, 821 41st Ave., Santa Cruz; (831) 476-2950. O'Neill Surf Shop, 1115 41st Ave., Capitola; (831) 475-4151.

Places to Stay: There are numerous places to stay in Santa Cruz including Best Western, 500 Ocean Ave., Santa Cruz; (831) 458-9898.

Places to Eat: Zachary's, 819 Pacific Ave., Santa Cruz; (831) 427-0646. Gigi's Bakery and Cafe, 550 River St., Santa Cruz; (831) 425-4800. Pizza My Heart has three locations in Santa Cruz: downtown, Capitola, and 41st Avenue. Paula's Café, 3500 Portola Dr., Santa Cruz; (831) 464-0741.

Cowell's

This is a gentle and peeling longboard wave in Santa Cruz.

Best tides: Low to medium
Best swell direction: South, west, northwest
Best wave size: Waist high
Bottom: Sand
Type of break: Outside, right
Skill level: Novice
Best board: Longboard
Best season: Any
Crowds: Crowded
Water quality: Clean
Hazards: Beginners
Fees and permits: None

Finding the Break

From Santa Cruz: Follow the signs to Ocean Street Beaches from where CA 1 meets CA 17. Go right where the road ends. Follow the coast along the beach and past the boardwalk. Go up the hill to West Cliff Drive. Once you pass the Dream Inn, start looking for a place to park in one of the several small, public lots along West Cliff Drive. You'll see the stairs that lead down to Cowell's Beach. GPS: N36 57.458 / W122 01.553

Surf Description

Cowell's is a peeling, gentle wave that breaks for a long time. It's one of the best places you can find to learn how to surf. The wave at Cowell's generally breaks outside and the bottom is sand, making it very safe and inviting for novice surfers. The waves here are slow and small, so bring your longboard. And be prepared to deal with beginners who haven't yet learned how to grab a rail when they fall.

Surfing is an integral part of the culture in Santa Cruz. When the waves are good, it seems like everyone has a board on their roof or in the back of their truck. The first surfers in this area are said to have been young men who moved to the San Francisco Bay Area from Southern California sometime in the early 1930s. They learned how to surf back home and moved north to attend college or find a job, bringing their boards with them. It didn't take long for these transplants to start exploring the coast of Monterey Bay. Cowell's Beach was one of their favorite spots because the conditions at this break are well suited for the heavy and lengthy wooden boards used at the time. Shortly thereafter these young men started introducing the sport to several local teenagers. The visitors gave the local kids some instruction and helped them shape boards of their own.

There's a lot to do in and around Santa Cruz. The Santa Cruz Surf Museum on West Cliff Drive at Steamer Lane is worth visiting, downtown Santa Cruz can be a lot of fun, and the Big Basin Redwoods State Park is beautiful.

In 1936 a Santa Cruz local named David Steward invited these surfers from Southern California to store their boards at his parents' house. Soon the group started forming what was to become the Santa Cruz Surfing Club. The Steward family then moved to a house about 3 blocks from Cowell's Beach that had a barn behind it. Surfers began storing boards and sleeping in the barn; it became a meeting spot for Santa Cruz Surfing Club members. In 1938 a board-storage house was built on Cowell's Beach and a former hamburger stand was rented out to serve as the clubhouse.

One of the best beginner spots in California and the world—Cowell's is part of the Santa Cruz Fun Zone.   Nikki Brooks

Chris Burkard

The Harbor is a break on an outer sandbar near the entrance to the Santa Cruz Harbor. From CA 1, exit Soquel Avenue and head toward the beach. Turn left onto Seventh Avenue and follow it until you see the Harbor. The break here works best with a waist-high to head-high winter swell at a low to medium tide. This wave can produce a powerful barrel with the right conditions.

Nikki Brooks

Murph Bar is a two-way sandbar peak on the east jetty of the Santa Cruz Harbor. From CA 1, exit Soquel Avenue and head toward the beach. Turn left onto Seventh Avenue and follow it until you see the Harbor. This isn't the most consistent spot, but when the conditions are right, you'll find a well-shaped and hollow right and left. Murph Bar works best with a waist- to head-high west, northwest, or south swell. This break can become crowded and competitive but can produce solid waves nearly all year long.

During World War II a lot of the club members served in the military. And when they returned many of them started spending less time with the club and more time focusing on their jobs and starting families. In 1952 the club disbanded and the board house was removed from Cowell's Beach. In 1992 a surfing sculpture was built on West Cliff Drive not far from Cowell's. The monument was inspired by the members of the Santa Cruz Surfing Club and is dedicated to all surfers, past, present, and future.

Other Information

Local Surf Shops: Arrow Surf and Sport, 2322 Mission St., Santa Cruz; (831) 423-8286. Pacific Wave Surf Shop, 1502 Pacific Ave.; (831) 458-9283. Cowell's Beach Surf Shop, 30 Front St., Santa Cruz; (831) 427-2355. O'Neill Surf Shop, 400 Beach St., Santa Cruz; (831) 459-9230. Rip Curl, 1604 Mission St., Santa Cruz; (831) 454-0360. Pearson Arrow Surf Shop, 2324 Mission St., Santa Cruz; (831) 423-8286. O'Neill, 110 Cooper St. 100 D,

Nikki Brooks

26th Avenue is a beach break located at the end of 26th Avenue in Santa Cruz. From CA 1, take the 41st Avenue exit and head toward the beach. Follow 41st Avenue to Portola Road and then turn right. Turn left onto 30th Avenue and right onto East Cliff Drive until you see the beach at 26th. 26th Avenue has a sand-and-rock bottom and can break year-round with varying-size swell. This is a cool little beach but is exposed to northwest wind.

Santa Cruz; (831) 469-4377. Covewater Paddle Surf, 726 Water St., Santa Cruz; (831) 600-7230. Hotline Wetsuits, 719 Swift St., Santa Cruz; (831) 425-5920. Haut Surf & Sailboards, 345 Swift St., Santa Cruz; (831) 426-7874. Billabong, 4105 Portola Dr., Santa Cruz; (831) 476-7873. Freeline Design Surf Shop, 821 41st Ave., Santa Cruz; (831) 476-2950. O'Neill Surf Shop, 1115 41st Ave., Capitola; (831) 475-4151.

Places to Stay: There are numerous places to stay in Santa Cruz including Best Western, 500 Ocean Ave., Santa Cruz; (831) 458-9898.

Places to Eat: Zachary's, 819 Pacific Ave., Santa Cruz; (831) 427-0646. Gigi's Bakery and Cafe, 550 River St., Santa Cruz; (831) 425-4800. Pizza My Heart has three locations in Santa Cruz: downtown, Capitola, and 41st Avenue. Paula's Café, 3500 Portola Dr, Santa Cruz; (831) 464-0741.

Pleasure Point
This is a very consistent spot located in Santa Cruz.

Best tides: Low to medium
Best swell direction: South, west, northwest
Best wave size: Waist high to double overhead
Bottom: Rock
Type of break: Outside, lefts and rights
Skill level: Intermediate to advanced
Best boards: Shortboard, funshape, longboard
Best season: Any
Crowds: Crowded
Water quality: Average
Hazards: Crowds, kelp on the inside at lower tides, dangerous entry and exit at higher tides.
Fees and permits: Parking permits are required on many side streets from late March to early September (weekends and holidays).

Finding the Break

From Santa Cruz: Exit 41st Avenue off CA 1 and head toward the ocean. Turn right onto Portola and then left onto 30th Avenue. Look for parking on any of the side streets off East Cliff Drive. Once you've found a place to park, you can walk down the large steps by the sign that says PLEASURE POINT or down the stairs at 36th Avenue. There's a narrow stretch of beach at lower tides that makes entry and exit easy. At higher tides entry and exit need to be timed between sets—there are a lot of rocks at the base of the stairs. GPS: N36 57.464 / W121 58.131

An aerial view of Pleasure Point from Sewer Peak to 38th Avenue and beyond.   AirPhoto

Surf Description

Aptly named, Pleasure Point is one of the most consistent breaks in California. This part of Monterey Bay is able to capture a lot of swell from many directions and is always worth a look. Wave shape is tide-dependent but generally very good. There are four main peaks at Pleasure Point. Sewer Peak is just right of the point as you're looking out and has a bowling right and a challenging left. Suicides is a small right that breaks a little outside Pleasure Point. First Peak is just to the left of the point as you're looking out and has a long right and short left. Second Peak is just left of First Peak as you're looking out and is a great longboard wave. Sewer Peak and Suicides are the most exposed to northwest wind because they aren't protected by the point, and as a result, they aren't quite as consistent as First and Second Peaks. There's a lot of rock reef at Pleasure Point, and the bigger the swell gets, the farther out waves will break at all four peaks.

Jay Moriarity, a well-known Maverick's surfer, grew up surfing at Pleasure Point. Jay was born in 1978 in Georgia, but his family moved to Santa Cruz when he was young. His dad taught him how to surf at age 11 at Sewer Peak. Moriarity was quickly hooked on the sport and began competing in both shortboard and longboard contests. However, he soon became more interested in surfing big waves than he was in competition. As soon as he found out about Maverick's, the big-wave spot north of Santa Cruz, he began preparing himself physically and mentally for the spot with

Pleasure Point is one of the favorite spots among Santa Cruz locals.

help from a local elder. At the age of 16, Jay Moriarity became known as the most promising big-wave teenager on earth when *Surfer* magazine used a photo of him taking a huge wipeout at Maverick's on the cover. By his early 20s Jay had become one of the most respected regulars in the Maverick's lineup and was sponsored by O'Neill.

Unfortunately, Jay Moriarity drowned a day before his twenty-third birthday while free diving in the Maldives. Moriarity was known as a humble waterman with a great attitude; he is missed by not only his family but also the numerous friends he made in the surfing world in a short period of time.

Other Information

Local Surf Shops: Arrow Surf and Sport, 2322 Mission St., Santa Cruz; (831) 423-8286. Pacific Wave Surf Shop, 1502 Pacific Ave.; (831) 458-9283. Cowell's Beach Surf Shop, 30 Front St., Santa Cruz; (831) 427-2355. O'Neill Surf Shop, 400 Beach St., Santa Cruz; (831) 459-9230. Rip Curl, 1604 Mission St., Santa Cruz; (831) 454-0360. Pearson Arrow Surf Shop, 2324 Mission St., Santa Cruz; (831) 423-8286. O'Neill, 110 Cooper St. 100 D, Santa Cruz; (831) 469-4377. Covewater Paddle Surf, 726 Water St., Santa Cruz; (831) 600-7230. Hotline Wetsuits, 719 Swift St., Santa Cruz; (831) 425-5920. Haut Surf & Sailboards, 345 Swift St., Santa Cruz; (831) 426-7874. Billabong, 4105 Portola Dr., Santa Cruz; (831) 476-7873. Freeline Design Surf Shop, 821 41st Ave., Santa Cruz; (831) 476-2950. O'Neill Surf Shop, 1115 41st Ave., Capitola; (831) 475-4151.

Places to Stay: There are numerous places to stay in Santa Cruz including Best Western, 500 Ocean Ave., Santa Cruz; (831) 458-9898.

Places to Eat: Zachary's, 819 Pacific Ave., Santa Cruz; (831) 427-0646. Gigi's Bakery and Cafe, 550 River St., Santa Cruz; (831) 425-4800. Pizza My Heart has three locations in Santa Cruz: downtown, Capitola, and 41st Avenue. Paula's Café, 3500 Portola Dr., Santa Cruz; (831) 464-0741.

38th Avenue

This is an outside, two-way-peak, longboard break just east of Pleasure Point.

Best tides: Low to medium

Best swell direction: South, west, northwest

Best wave size: Waist high to slightly overhead

Bottom: Sand and rock

Type of break: Outside left and right

Skill level: Intermediate when under chest height; advanced when surf is chest high or larger

Best board: Longboard

Best season: Any

Crowds: Crowded

Water quality: Average

Hazards: Crowds, getting dropped in on by beginners, getting pushed into the rocks inside at higher tides

Fees and permits: None

Finding the Break

From Santa Cruz: Exit 41st Avenue off CA 1 and head toward the ocean. There's a large public parking lot where 41st Avenue ends at East Cliff Drive. Walk to the right from the parking lot, down East Cliff Drive. Then walk down the stairs at 38th Avenue. There's a narrow stretch of beach at lower tides that makes entry and exit easy. At higher tides entry and exit need to be timed between sets—there are a lot of rocks at the base of the stairs. GPS: N36 57.529 / W121 58.036

Surf Description

The break at 38th Avenue is a long, peeling wave that breaks farther outside as the size of the swell increases. The right is generally a longer ride, but the left usually has more juice. This is a great longboard spot. Because Cowell's, the most popular beginner spot in the area, has become so crowded, some novice surfers come here. When the waves are very small and the tide is low, the break at 38th Avenue is fairly forgiving. On bigger days or at higher tides, however, this is definitely not a break for inexperienced surfers.

The green house that overlooks the lineup belongs to Jack O'Neill, the founder of O'Neill Surf Shop and inventor of the modern wet suit. Jack was born in 1923 in Denver, Colorado. His family moved to Portland, Oregon, and eventually ended up in

Some call it Insides. Some call it 38th Avenue. Some call it "that spot in front of the O'Neills' House." Whatever you call it, this spot in front of the O'Neills' house is a popular beginner and longboard spot when it's small. But on a big summer or winter swell, it turns into 38th Avenue—and people get excited. Monica Rose, getting excited at 38th.
Nikki Brooks

Southern California. O'Neill moved to San Francisco in 1949 and worked as a fisherman and a salesman of aluminum, skylights, and fire extinguishers. He used to spend a lot of time at Ocean Beach, which prompted him to begin experimenting with ways to stay a little warmer while he was out in the frigid water there. While on a passenger jet, Jack saw this material called neoprene in the aisle. One thing led to another, and he opened one of California's first surf shops in 1952. The shop was located on the Great Highway in San Francisco, not far from his favorite bodysurfing break.

In 1959 O'Neill moved his shop to Santa Cruz, where the weather and waves were more to his liking. Before long the surfing boom of the 1960s hit, and there were a lot of wet suits being sold. Jack began laminating elastic nylon to the neoprene foam and used a zigzag stitch in his wet suits, which made them more durable as well as easier to get on and off. In the next two decades, O'Neill Surf Shop became an international company selling wet suits and beach sportswear throughout the United States, Australia, Europe, and Japan. Today O'Neill International has licenses and distributors in more than sixty countries.

In 1985 Jack became the chairman of the board of O'Neill Inc.; his son Pat took over as the chief executive officer. He now keeps busy with other projects such as the O'Neill Sea Odyssey program. This venture takes kids out on catamaran cruises in Monterey Bay, teaching them about marine life and the importance of respecting the ocean. Jack O'Neill was inducted into the Huntington Beach Surfing Walk of Fame in 1998 and will be remembered well into the future as one of the most influential innovators in the sport of surfing

Other Information

Local Surf Shops: Arrow Surf and Sport, 2322 Mission St., Santa Cruz; (831) 423-8286. Pacific Wave Surf Shop, 1502 Pacific Ave.; (831) 458-9283. Cowell's Beach Surf Shop, 30 Front St., Santa Cruz; (831) 427-2355. O'Neill Surf Shop, 400 Beach St., Santa Cruz; (831) 459-9230. Rip Curl, 1604 Mission St., Santa Cruz; (831) 454-0360. Pearson Arrow Surf Shop, 2324 Mission St., Santa Cruz; (831) 423-8286. O'Neill, 110 Cooper St. 100 D, Santa Cruz; (831) 469-4377. Covewater Paddle Surf, 726 Water St., Santa Cruz; (831) 600-7230. Hotline Wetsuits, 719 Swift St., Santa Cruz; (831) 425-5920. Haut Surf & Sailboards, 345 Swift St., Santa Cruz; (831) 426-7874. Billabong, 4105 Portola Dr., Santa Cruz; (831) 476-7873. Freeline Design Surf Shop, 821 41st Ave., Santa Cruz; (831) 476-2950. O'Neill Surf Shop, 1115 41st Ave., Capitola; (831) 475-4151.

Places to Stay: There are numerous places to stay in Santa Cruz including Best Western, 500 Ocean Ave., Santa Cruz; (831) 458-9898.

Places to Eat: Zachary's, 819 Pacific Ave., Santa Cruz; (831) 427-0646. Gigi's Bakery and Cafe, 550 River St., Santa Cruz; (831) 425-4800. Pizza My Heart has three locations in Santa Cruz: downtown, Capitola, and 41st Avenue—we suggest you try them all, once a day. Paula's Café, 3500 Portola Dr., Santa Cruz; (831) 464-0741.

The Hook

This is an inside right reef break east of Pleasure Point.

Best tides: Low to medium
Best swell direction: South, west, northwest
Best wave size: Waist high to slightly overhead
Bottom: Rock
Type of break: Inside, right
Skill level: Novice to intermediate
Best boards: Shortboard, funshape, longboard
Best season: Any
Crowds: Crowded
Water quality: Average
Hazards: Crowds, kelp, sharp rocks at lower tides
Fees and permits: None

CJ Nelson sliding a clean, fast little hook at the Wild Hook.   Nikki Brooks

Finding the Break

From Santa Cruz: Exit 41st Avenue off CA 1 and head toward the ocean. There's a large public parking lot where 41st Avenue ends at East Cliff Drive. Directly in front of the parking lot, you'll see the stairs that lead to the Hook. N36 57.611 / W121 57.922

Surf Description

The Hook can be a very consistent right. Wave shape depends a lot on the tide, but it's generally a fast and sometimes hollow break. The waves at the Hook usually break inside and close to the rocks and cliffs, although the peak will move outside as the swell gets bigger. This break can get crowded and competitive when the surf is good, but there are usually enough waves for everyone.

   If you've ever seen a photo of Jack O'Neill, founder of O'Neill Surf Shop, you've noticed that he wears a patch over his left eye. It's a little-known fact that he was surfing at the Hook when he lost that eye. The year was 1971, and O'Neill's son Pat had just invented the surf leash. At the time, the leash consisted of elastic surgical tubing that was fixed to the board with a suction cup and had an attachment for your wrist. Unfortunately, the elastic properties of this early surf leash caused some injuries—boards would come rocketing back toward their riders when the two were separated. Jack was one casualty.

Today leashes are made of non-elastic urethane and Velcro, and most surfers own one. Before 1971, however, if you fell and didn't manage to grab your board, you were more than likely going to do some swimming. And on a big day in places

SUPDATE: SUP'N SANTA CRUZ

Santa Cruz can be heaven or hell for standup paddlers. A lot of surf spots in Santa Cruz are already overcrowded and tense, and paddling into these lineups standing up will get about the same reaction as walking into a passenger jet wearing Muslim robes: Steamer Lane, First Peak and Sewer Peak, the main peak at the Hook, Natural Bridges, the river mouth and harbor when they're breaking—the exception being when the surf is giant, there aren't many surfers in the water and it's human against ocean, not human against human.

Places that are SUPpropriate are the inside of Shark's Cove: This is a weird wave that shifts around and backs off and is perfect for SUP. Most surfers ignore it. Also, Indicator is a spot between Steamer Lane and Cowell's where SUPs seem to have found a home. Indicator is a good place for standup paddlers to pick up energy rolling in from Middle Peak and then re-forming into Cowell's. Because standup paddleboards are mobile, it can be fun to chase down those re-forms and ride as far as you can. If you get one from the statue to the Dream Inn, you're batting a thousand.

North of town there are lots of reef waves that are hard to get to that are open opportunities for standup paddlers, and the same for the beach breaks south of Santa Cruz, from Manresa to Moss Landing and beyond: 90 percent of the waves breaking along there are going unridden, so jump on your SUP, use a good leash, and get some.

If you surf your way all the way down to Moss Landing, you might want to head through the harbor entrance and spend the better part of the day paddling Elkhorn Slough. It's beautiful back there, but watch out for sharks and tides.

like Santa Cruz, where a lot of breaks have rocks lining the shore, a lost board would frequently incur a lot of damage. Despite the widespread use of this innovation today, Pat O'Neill's surf leash wasn't received very well at first and was even referred to as a "kook cord" by many of the top surfers back then.

Shortly thereafter the surf leash caught on. Block Enterprises modified Pat O'Neill's original leash concept using bungee cord instead of surgical tubing, making the attachment at the ankle as opposed to the wrist and fixing the leash through a hole in the fin rather than adhering a suction cup to the board. However, the bungee cord had a tendency to cut off circulation and was found to cut into the fiberglass

Nikki Brooks

Private's is a longboard right reef break between the Hook and Capitola. From CA 1, take the 41st Avenue exit and head toward the beach. Follow 41st Avenue to the end, then turn left onto Opal Cliffs. There's an opening between the oceanfront homes on Opal Cliffs; you'll see a large gate blocking access to the beach. You've now learned why this place is called Private's. The gate is locked, but you can wait around for a local going in or out and charm them, or buy a very expensive key at Freeline Design Surf Shop on 41st Avenue. Private's works best with a large swell from virtually any direction at a medium tide. The waves are usually smaller here than the breaks to the west. Wave shape can be excellent, however, and it's a good place to surf when the other spots are closing out.

of boards. This prompted the use of leather and nylon webbing straps to atta   the bungee to your ankle as well as resin and fiberglass bridges to adhere the other end of the leash to your board. In the late 1970s and early '80s, surf leash manufacturers started replacing the bungee cords with urethane and using Velcro instead of leather and nylon webbing ankle straps. Metal swivels were eventually incorporated in order to improve function.

Whether you're a fan of leashes or not, it's difficult to imagine as many surfers pushing the envelope with the high-risk maneuvers we see today if they lost their board each time they tried something new!

Other Information

Local Surf Shops: Santa Cruz Surf Shop, 753 41st Ave., Capitola; (831) 464-3233. O'Neill Surf Shop, 1115 41st Ave., Capitola; (831) 475-4151.
Places to Stay: Pleasure Point Bed and Breakfast, 23665 E. Cliff Dr., Santa Cruz; (831) 469-6161. Best Western, 1435 41st Ave., Capitola; (831) 477-0607.
Places to Eat: Chill Out Cafe, 860 41st Ave., Santa Cruz; (831) 477-0543. Pink Godzilla Sushi, 830 41st Ave., Capitola; (831) 464-2586. Paula's Café, 3500 Portola Dr., Santa Cruz; (831) 464 0741. Pizza My Heart, 209 Esplanade, Capitola; (831) 475-5714.

Capitola

This is a gentle longboard break south of the pier in Capitola.

Best tides: Low to medium
Best swell direction: South, west, northwest
Best wave size: Waist high to head high
Bottom: Sand and rock
Type of break: Outside, left and right
Skill level: Novice to intermediate under chest height; advanced when the surf is over chest high
Best board: Longboard
Best season: Any
Crowds: Crowded
Water quality: Average
Hazards: Crowds, thick kelp, rocks inside
Fees and permits: Parking may require a fee.

Finding the Break

From Santa Cruz: Head south on CA 1 and take the Bay Avenue/Porter Street exit. Go right onto Bay Avenue and follow it until you see the ocean. There are two large public parking lots in Capitola: a metered lot by the beach and a 12-hour lot a couple of blocks away. Once you park, head toward the beach and walk to the break. GPS: N36 58.313 / W121 57.057

Surf Description

Capitola can produce a very well-shaped, peeling longboard wave. It's protected from the wind but as a result also misses out on a lot of swell. Capitola is a great place to go when the other spots in the area are blown out or are closing out. It works best during a large winter swell, and as the swell gets bigger, the peak moves farther outside. This in turn will make the right a much longer ride than the left. The beach here is filled with medium-size boulders, so entry and exit can be a little tricky at higher tides.

Accomplished Maverick's surfer Peter Mel grew up surfing in Capitola. His family owns Freeline Surf Shop not far from here, and his dad used to shape boards for him. Before Maverick's became popular, Peter was competing as a pro surfer and shaping boards of his own. He would spend winters in Hawaii expanding his comfort zone in large surf and eventually found his niche. Once the word was out about Maverick's, Peter Mel was there. By the late 1990s he had established himself as one of the best big-wave surfers in the world.

Capitola is packed with tourists in the summer.

The El Niño winter of 1997–1998 was Peter's breakthrough year. El Niño is a phenomenon that occurs every three to seven years and can be defined as a disruption of the Pacific Ocean's atmosphere system. It causes significant shifts in the location of high- and low-pressure systems, resulting in what's called a countercurrent. In El Niño years the warm waters and tropical rains of the South Pacific are sent to South America, and the West Coast of the United States experiences huge surf. The most notable winters in which this phenomenon occurred were 1957–1958, 1969–1970, 1982–1983, and 1997–1998. The 1997–1998 winter brought especially big surf to Maverick's, and Peter Mel was one of the surfers who stood out. He was also one of the first surfers to pursue tow-in surfing at Maverick's. In 1999 he towed into one of the largest waves ever ridden at any big-wave spot anywhere.

Downtown Capitola has a lot of cool little shops, restaurants, and nightspots. On summer weekends you'll find a lot of tourists cruising through town and filling the streets. Weekdays mostly belong to the locals, though, and the downtown area takes on a fun and cool vibe. Even when the surf is small, the village of Capitola is worth a visit.

The peak at Capitola on a good day as seen from the cliffs. If Capitola is this good, the rest of Santa Cruz is off its rocker. Boots McGhee

Other Information

Local Surf Shops: Santa Cruz Surf Shop, 753 41st Ave., Capitola; (831) 464-3233. O'Neill Surf Shop, 1115 41st Ave., Capitola; (831) 475-4151.

Places to Stay: Pleasure Point Bed and Breakfast, 23665 E. Cliff Dr., Santa Cruz; (831) 469-6161. Best Western, 1435 41st Ave., Capitola; (831) 477-0607.

Places to Eat: Gayle's Cafe and Bakery, 504 Bay Ave., Capitola; (831) 462-1200. Zeldas, 203 Esplanade, Capitola; (831) 475-4900. Cafe Lido, 110 Monterey Ave., Capitola; (831) 475-6544. Il Pirata, 201 Esplanade, Capitola; (831) 462-1800. Wharf House, 1400 Wharf Rd. (at the end of the pier), Capitola; (831) 476-3534. Pizza My Heart, 209 Esplanade, Capitola; (831) 475-5714. Paula's Café, 3500 Portola Dr, Santa Cruz; (831) 464-0741.

Manresa

This is a classic west-facing beach break south of Aptos.

Best tide: Medium
Best swell direction: South, west, northwest
Best wave size: Waist high to slightly overhead
Bottom: Sand
Type of break: Beach break, lefts and rights
Skill level: Novice to advanced
Best boards: Shortboard, funshape, and longboard
Best season: Any
Crowds: Not crowded
Water quality: Average
Hazards: Shore pound on a big day
Fees and permits: Parking may require a fee.

Finding the Break

From Santa Cruz: Head south on CA 1. Exit at San Andreas/Larkin Valley Road and turn right. Stay on this road until you see the Manresa State Beach parking lot. If they're charging to park in that lot, and you want to save some money, you can go down a couple blocks to Oceanview Road and park for free. Either parking area has stairs that lead down to spacious Manresa Beach. GPS: N36 55.950 / W121 51.711

Surf Description

Manresa is a consistent, mostly west-facing beach that catches a lot of swell year-round. This is a long stretch of beach with numerous well-shaped peaks. Manresa can be a powerful beach break with a big swell. And the wave shape here can be excellent with the right conditions.

Manresa is just south of the mellow community of Aptos. This area was named Awatos or "where the waters meet" by Native Americans who lived in this region for several hundred years. The name refers to two creeks that join here before flowing into Monterey Bay. In 1794 the Spanish built Mission Santa Cruz, and in 1833 the government of Mexico granted a huge parcel of land known as Aptos Rancho to a man named Rafael Castro. Castro used the land for cattle ranching, but once California was declared a US state in 1850, he leased a lot of land to Americans. These Americans built a wharf, lumber mill, and general store in this area. In 1872 a millionaire named Claus Spreckels started to buy land from Castro, building a hotel near the beach,

Dressed in full winter battle gear, a modern man thwaps the lip at Manresa. Matt Doll

a mansion, a ranch, a racetrack for horses, and a deer-hunting park. He was also a major contributor to the Santa Cruz Railroad, which opened in 1876 and caused the town to move to the other side of Aptos Creek. In 1880 the timber industry moved into this part of Santa Cruz County with fervor, and the town of Aptos started to grow. Redwood was harvested heavily from what is now Nisene Marks State Park; the hills surrounding this town were nearly bare by 1920.

Nisene Marks State Park in Aptos has miles of good hiking trails.

Just north of Manresa, in an area of Aptos known as Rio Del Mar, you'll find Seacliff State Beach. This is one of the most beautiful stretches of beach in Santa Cruz County and it connects to Manresa State Beach. At the end of the pier at Seacliff State Beach, you'll find a large cement ship called the *Palo Alto*. In 1918 this ship was built in Oakland to be used as a supply vessel during World War I. The war ended, however, and the ship was used as an oil tanker instead. The Seacliff Amusement Company in Nevada then bought the ship and brought it to this beach in 1929 to be used as a party boat. The ship contained a casino and dance hall with live entertainment. The Great Depression of the 1930s forced the festive *Palo Alto* into retirement; eventually the beach became a state park, which bought the cement ship for $1.

Other Information

Local Surf Shops: La Selva Beach Surf Shop, 308 Playa Blvd., La Selva; (831) 684-0774. **Places to Stay:** Manresa Uplands State Park, 205 Manresa Rd., La Selva Beach; (831) 761-1795. Best Western/Seacliff Inn, 7500 Old Dominion Court, Aptos; (831) 688-7300. **Places to Eat:** Palapas, 21 Seascape Village, Aptos; (831) 662-9000. Pixie Deli, 111 Venetian Rd., Aptos; (831) 688-1115.

Boots McGhee

Sunset State Beach is a mostly west-facing beach between Manresa and Moss Landing, deep in Monterey Bay. There are signs for this beach off CA 1 between Aptos and Watsonville. Sunset is a beach break with numerous well-shaped peaks that works best with a waist-high to head-high west swell at a medium tide. There's rarely anyone here, but this spot can produce quality, well-shaped waves with the right conditions.

Moss Landing

Moss Landing is a consistent beach break south of Watsonville.

Best tide: Any
Best swell direction: West, northwest
Best wave size: Waist high to slightly overhead
Bottom: Sand
Type of break: Beach break, lefts and rights
Skill level: Intermediate to advanced
Best boards: Shortboard, funshape
Best season: Any
Crowds: Can get crowded on weekends
Water quality: Clean
Hazards: Sharks, getting caught inside on a big day
Fees and permits: None

Finding the Break

From Santa Cruz: Head south on CA 1 toward Monterey. Once you pass Watsonville, start looking for a large sign that says MOSS LANDING STATE BEACH. You can park in Moss Landing State Park and walk to the beach. GPS: N36 48.244 / W121 47.208

Surf Description

Moss Landing can be a big and powerful beach break. This is a wide-open, west-facing beach located deep in Monterey Bay. Wave shape is dependent on the sandbars that develop throughout the year, but overall, the peaks here are consistently good. Moss Landing is positioned to work best with a west or northwest swell, though you can find surf here nearly year-round.

In 1853 John Davenport started the first commercial whaling operation in Monterey Bay. The whales were hunted for their blubber, which was then boiled down into oil and used as an energy source. However, in the 1860s and 1870s, more and more people began using kerosene for fuel, and the price of whale oil dropped significantly. By 1886 the whaling industry in the Monterey Bay region was virtually over due to this switch.

In the early 1900s inventions such as the harpoon cannon as well as the development of steam-driven chase boats and processing plants ignited a revival of the whaling industry in the Pacific Ocean. In 1914 the California Sea Products Company chose Moss Landing as the location for a large whaling factory. The company employed a

Ocean in motion down the beach at Moss Landing. Like to paddle much and get caught inside? You'll like this place. Chris Burkard

Norwegian whaling captain by the name of Frederick Dedrick to manage this factory and its two steam-driven chase boats. The whaling plant opened in 1918 and brought in its first whale in 1919. For several months, every time a whale was seen being towed into Moss Landing, a large crowd would gather to watch it being brought in for processing. It's said that the odor of the processing plant was so strong that it caused some of the onlookers to vomit, and that with a southeast wind, it could be smelled all the way to Santa Cruz. The Moss Landing whaling station processed the blubber into oil used to make soap. The meat was cooked for chicken feed, and the bones were ground into bonemeal.

Kayaking in the Elkhorn Slough is a popular activity. It's also a great SUP spot.

Eventually the Moss Landing whaling station found it difficult to catch whales. The population was dwindling, and the whales learned to steer clear of the coastline and chase boats. The factory closed in 1927. Captain Dedrick continued his pursuit of whales by using processing ships in the open ocean instead of plants on the shoreline. Today the only thing left of the Moss Landing whaling station is a pile of boulders on the beach that were once used to anchor the end of the slipway.

Chris Burkard

Marina is a beach break just north of Monterey. From CA 1, take the Reservation Road exit and follow the signs to Marina Beach. This beach is very exposed to northwest wind and gets blown out easily. However, with a waist-high to head-high winter swell and an east wind, it can be a beautiful break. The currents can be strong, and sharks have been sighted here over the years.

Chris Burkard

Lover's Point is a left between Monterey and Pacific Grove. From CA 1, take the Monterey exit and head to the beach. Follow the roads along the cliffs until you see the sign for Lover's Point. Swell wraps into a rocky cove here and can produce a well-shaped but inconsistent left. Lover's Point is best with a midsize winter swell at a medium tide. This is a very beautiful area—a nice place to visit even when it's flat.

Other Information

Local Surf Shops: None, but there are lots of surf shops in Santa Cruz and a few in Carmel/Monterey.

Places to Stay: Moss Landing RV Park, 7905 Sandholdt Rd., Moss Landing; (877) 735-7275. There are several motels in Watsonville and on Reservation Road south of Moss Landing. Red Roof Inn, 1620 W. Beach St., Watsonville; (831) 740-4520.

Places to Eat: The Whole Enchilada, CA 1 and Moss Landing Road, Moss Landing; (831) 633-3038. Phil's Fish Market and Restaurant, 7600 Sandholdt Rd., Moss Landing; (831) 633-2152.

Asilomar

This is a northwest-facing beach near Monterey.

Best tides: Low to medium
Best swell direction: Anything but south
Best wave size: Waist high to slightly overhead
Bottom: Sand and rock
Type of break: Beach break, outside, lefts and rights
Skill level: Novice to advanced
Best boards: Shortboard, funshape, longboard
Best season: Any
Crowds: Can get crowded on weekends
Water quality: Clean
Hazards: Sharks, big surf in winter
Fees and permits: None

Finding the Break

From Monterey: Head south on CA 1. Take the CA 68 exit west toward Pacific Grove and Asilomar. You can park along the road at Asilomar State Park Beach. It's an easy stroll from there to the beach. GPS: N36 37.230 / W121 56.311

Surf Description

There are three main peaks at Asilomar, and at least one of them is usually breaking if there's any type of swell. Roadsides is a right on the north end of the beach. Middles is a peak in the middle of the beach; Reef is a left on the south end. Asilomar

The Monterey Peninsula with heaps of swell as seen from Pacific Grove to 17 Mile Drive. Asilomar is the first beach outside of the bay.   Don Balch

State Beach is fairly exposed to northwest wind, which usually results in blown-out or poorly shaped midday surf. Regardless of surf conditions, however, this break can get crowded on a sunny and warm weekend. On a weekend day in summer when the waves are small, you'll see kids and longboarders all along the beach. And when the waves are bigger, a lot of shortboarders will line up outside.

Asilomar State Beach is located in the quiet town of Pacific Grove just south of Monterey. *Asilomar* is a Spanish word that means "a refuge by the sea." The beach is a picturesque and narrow stretch of sand and rock that's part of the Pacific Grove Fish Garden Refuge and the Monterey Bay National Marine Sanctuary. The adjacent Asilomar Conference Grounds began in 1913 as a camping and gathering site for the YWCA. In 1956 the state of California acquired the 100-acre-plus property; the historic buildings are available for conferences and other events.

Don Balch

Spanish Bay is a right beach break just south of Asilomar on 17 Mile Drive. From CA 1, take the CA 68 exit west toward Pacific Grove and Asilomar. You can park along the road at Asilomar State Park Beach and walk across the beach to Spanish Bay. The break is in front of the Spanish Bay Resort and works best with a waist-high to head-high winter swell.

Don Balch

Mole Point is a right reef break between Monterey and Carmel south of Spanish Bay. From CA 1, take the 17 Mile Drive exit. Mole Point is off 17 Mile Drive just south of Point Joe. This break works with swell from any direction and is best from waist to head high. Mole Point can produce some well-shaped surf and requires skill and experience.

This part of Monterey Bay has several shark stories associated with it, and two reported fatal attacks have occurred here. In 1952 a swimmer was killed by a shark at nearby Lover's Point in Pacific Grove. And in 1955 and 1966, there were shark attacks on free divers not far from Asilomar State Beach. The 1955 attack resulted in minor injuries, but the victim of the 1966 attack sustained major injuries.

The second fatal shark attack in this area occurred in the cove next to Asilomar called Spanish Bay. One morning in 1981, a few days before Christmas, Lewis Boren and some of his friends were surfing the break at Spanish Bay. Lewis reportedly went back in the water by himself after lunch. The next day his shortboard was found with a large chunk missing from it in the shape of a shark bite. Boren's body was then discovered just north of Asilomar State Beach with a matching bite mark. Experts theorized that he was probably paddling outside to catch a larger wave; when his arms were stretched out in front of him, the shark bit through both Lewis and his board. Through analysis of the bite radius, it was determined that the attacker was an 18- to 20-foot-long great white.

The Monterey Bay Aquarium is a great place to learn more about the ocean. And 17 Mile Drive is a beautiful roadway with numerous golf courses, including world-renowned Pebble Beach. (According to Yelp and Wikipedia, there is a nominal fee to drive this road.)

Other Information

Local Surf Shops: On the Beach Surf Shop, 693 Lighthouse Ave., Monterey; (831) 646-9283. Sunshine Freestyle, 443 Lighthouse Ave., Monterey; (831) 375-5015.
Places to Stay: Beachcomber Inn, 1996 Beach Comber Inn, Pacific Grove; (831) 373-4769.
Places to Eat: Hula's, 622 Lighthouse Ave., Monterey; (831) 655-4852. There are numerous restaurants in Pacific Grove and Monterey.

Carmel Beach
This is a protected beach break with well-shaped peaks in Carmel.

Best tides: Medium to high
Best swell direction: South, west, northwest
Best wave size: Waist high to slightly overhead

Bottom: Sand and rock

Type of break: Beach break, lefts and rights

Skill level: Intermediate to advanced

Best boards: Shortboard, funshape

Best seasons: Winter, spring, and fall

Crowds: Can get crowded on weekends

Water quality: Clean

Hazards: Heavy shore pound

Fees and permits: None

Finding the Break

From Monterey: Head south on CA 1. Take the main Carmel exit from CA 1 and turn right. Follow Ocean Avenue all the way to the beach. Ocean Avenue ends at a large parking lot. You can leave your vehicle there and walk up or down the beach to wherever the waves look best. GPS: N36 33.014 / W121 55.747

Surf Description

Carmel Beach is a beautiful half-mile stretch of squeaky white sand with several quality beach-break peaks. The best spots on this beach are at Fourth, Eighth, and 11th Streets. The beach here is somewhat protected from northwest wind, and the wave shape can be excellent. Even when the waves are small, this beach is a great place to hang out on a sunny day.

Carmel used to be a very quaint and mellow village. However, as a result of the Silicon Valley boom, the town has become extremely affluent and is very popular with tourists. There are numerous art galleries, restaurants, and unique little shops in the downtown area; multimillion-dollar homes can be found everywhere you look. If you drive south from Carmel on CA 1, you'll find a beach that's just as beautiful as Carmel Beach but far less crowded.

The coastal section of road just north of Carmel is called 17 Mile Drive and is located within the Del Monte Forest. Starting in 1881, horse-drawn carriages used to take people from the Hotel Del Monte—once located in Monterey—along this road toward Carmel. Visitors would usually stop at Pebble Beach to picnic and simply appreciate the beauty of this gorgeous section of the California coast. In 1916 the property manager of the Del Monte Forest, Samuel Morse, hired Jack Neville and Douglas Grant to design the now-famous Pebble Beach Golf Links. In 1919 the golf course opened to the public, and in 1929 the first national golf tournament was held here. Today there are several golf courses besides Pebble Beach located within the

Del Monte Forest. Although not as well known as Pebble Beach Golf Links, the links at Spanish Bay, Spyglass Hill Golf Course, Cypress Point Club, and Poppy Hills Golf Course are all world-famous.

While there have been no reported shark attacks at Carmel Beach, three have occurred nearby. In 1986 a free diver was attacked, as was a scuba diver in 1990. Both attacks occurred in Carmel Bay and resulted in major injuries. The most recent shark attack that's been reported in this area was in 1995 and involved a diver. The attack occurred at Point Lobos, about 3 miles south of Carmel, and also resulted in major injuries.

Other Information

Local Surf Shops: On the Beach Surf Shop, 693 Lighthouse Ave., Monterey; (831) 646-9283. Sunshine Freestyle, 443 Lighthouse Ave., Monterey; (831) 375-5015.
Places to Stay: Carmel Mission Ranch, 26270 Dolores St., Carmel; (831) 624-6436. There are numerous bed-and-breakfast establishments in Carmel.
Places to Eat: The Hog's Breath Inn, San Carlos Street and Fifth Avenue, Carmel; (831) 625-1044. Baja Cantina, 7166 Carmel Valley Rd., Carmel; (831) 625-2252.

Clear water, clean barrels, and world-class golf nearby at Carmel Beach. Matt Doll

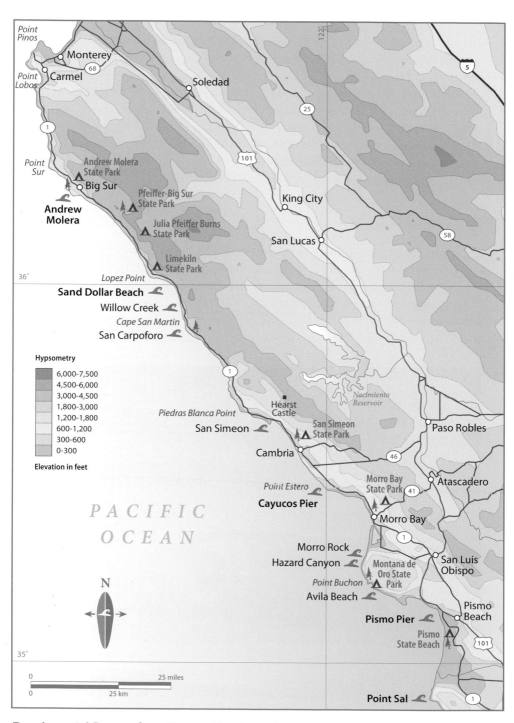

Region 6 (Carmel to Santa Barbara)

REGION 6: CARMEL TO SANTA BARBARA

Technically, Northern California stretches from Oregon to the Golden Gate Bridge, central California comprises the area from the Golden Gate Bridge to Point Conception, and Southern California goes from Point Conception to Mexico.

That's *technically:* Not everyone sees it that way, and for some, central California starts with some indistinct line between Santa Cruz—which definitely considers itself Northern California—and Salinas, where the local TV news station considers itself the voice of the Central Coast.

It's an arbitrary boundary, but let's say the central California coast starts near the rocky southern tip of Big Sur and stretches through vast coastal mountain peaks and sprawling ocean vistas to Santa Barbara—although some may argue that Santa Barbara is more Southern California than central California given its high real-estate values and swanky boutiques. In any case, the vibes in this region are different, ranging from slow and mellow in the north to a more Mediterranean charm in the south. This region is relatively undeveloped compared with the city sprawl of neighboring counties in the south.

The climate on the Central Coast can range from bitterly cold to perfect, depending on the time of year and location. The weather tends to be better in the southern part of central California and less accommodating the farther north you go. Overall the climate is mild. Winter brings moderate rains and greenscape as far as the eye can see, but come late spring through early fall, the landscape is transformed into a sea of dry tumbleweed and trees. The coastlines tend to be less crowded in the north and downright inaccessible in some areas.

There are long stretches of beach between Big Sur and Santa Barbara, but not all of it is accessible—in some remote parts you will flat-out not be welcomed. Unlike other regions in the state, central California is a mix of farmland, large estates, ranches, and tiny towns. One of the most famous points along the long stretch of CA 1—it could be called the region's major tourist attraction—is Hearst Castle in San Simeon. Newspaper mogul William Randolph Hearst built a serious pad on a hilltop in the middle of grazing pastureland.

Overall Surf Description

The surf along the Central Coast sets the deep-blue Pacific against rock and sand cliff walls. Starting farther north, a significant portion of the coastline is simply ocean meeting walls of rock. Winter storms and rainy weather often make the surf conditions unpredictable in winter. When the weather does break in the northern part of the

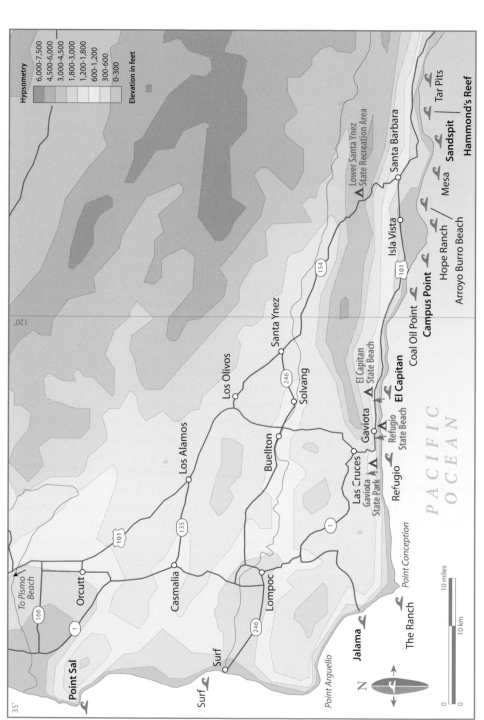

Region 6B (Big Sur to Santa Barbara)

Hypsometry

6,000–7,500
4,500–6,000
3,000–4,500
1,800–3,000
1,200–1,800
600–1,200
300–600
0–300

Elevation in feet

35°

120°

Point Sal

Surf

Surf

Jalama

The Ranch

Point Arguello

Point Conception

PACIFIC OCEAN

To Pismo Beach

166

Orcutt

1

101

Casmalia

135

Lompoc

246

Los Alamos

Buellton

1

Las Cruces

Gaviota State Park

Refugio

Gaviota

Refugio State Beach

Los Olivos

Santa Ynez

Solvang

246

154

El Capitan State Beach

El Capitan

Coal Oil Point

Campus Point

Lower Santa Ynez State Recreation Area

Santa Barbara

Isla Vista

101

Hope Ranch

Arroyo Burro Beach

Mesa

Sandspit

Hammond's Reef

Tar Pits

N

0
0   10 miles
    10 km

Central Coast, it becomes a concoction of beach break after beach break with a few highlighted spots in between. The lower you go past San Luis Obispo, however, the better the surf becomes, and the more tolerable the water temperature. Typically the best conditions are near Santa Barbara, but so are the crowds. As in the far-northern regions of California, you'll need to bring some patience, endurance, strength, rain gear, a wet suit, and an arsenal of boards. You'll find the most locations well south near Santa Barbara, but the people, coastal views, and unsculpted landscape of the Central Coast make it a great place for memorable drives on your way to surf one of California's most stirring regions. The region generally thrives with westerly swells.

Fall Surf

Fall is the best time of year for most of California's Central Coast. After a long, lazy summer, fall usually produces the best conditions of the year, with smooth silky waters that react nicely with larger westerly swells. Surf during this time of year also brings some of the warmest water to the coast, along with crowds. In fall a glance at the surf visible from CA 1 will generally let you know if you've found your spot or not.

Winter Surf

As fall turns into winter, the primo conditions tend to make a turn for the worse as well. Winter is rainy season, and the weather can be downright nasty for surfing. Like an unknown combination burrito from a shady seaside shack, northwest swells, heavy rain, and strong winds don't mix well together. Conditions tend toward poor-to-dismal, and the water temperature drops enough that those with an insatiable itch go out for a paddle. Occasionally large storms will produce some big days along this section of the coast, especially (and more consistently) near Santa Barbara.

Spring Surf

Spring is unpredictable. Overhead surf, tricklers, rain, sunshine, fog, drizzle—you name it, spring will bring it. In general, spring surf is poor along the Central Coast. Only two spots get consistency from wind-driven swells: Santa Barbara and Andrew Molera.

Summer Surf

Summer surf on the Central Coast is like looking out at a windy lake. As the water warms, it brings with it consistent wind from the north and northwest, making surf conditions downright miserable. Shore-break surf is sometimes your best bet; it's the most consistent and predictable. Summertime is also tourist time, so don't be surprised to see beginners right next to you paddling out for the slim pickings.

Average Temperatures for Region (Carmel to Santa Barbara)		
	Air (Morro Bay)	Water (Morro Bay)
Jan	65	54
Feb	66	54
Mar	67	54
Apr	71	54
May	73	54
June	78	55
July	80	56
Aug	82	57
Sept	82	58
Oct	79	57
Nov	72	56
Dec	66	55

Andrew Molera

The scenic Andrew Molera is a great place to surf on the northern tip of the Central Coast. Typically larger and held up nicely by consistent winds, the break produces peaky lefts and rights.

Best tide: Low
Best swell direction: Southwest
Best wave size: Head high to slightly overhead
Bottom: Sand and rock
Type of break: Outside, left and right
Skill level: Intermediate
Best board: Funshape
Best season: Fall
Crowds: Uncrowded
Water quality: Clean
Hazards: Strong currents, rocks at lower tides
Fees and permits: According to Yelp and other sources, a nominal state park parking fee is charged.

Finding the Break

From Monterey: Take CA 1 south until you reach Andrew Molera State Park. The entrance signs are visible from CA 1. Park there and walk in about a mile to the break. It's a long walk with a board but worth the effort. GPS: N36 17.250 / W121 50.623

Surf Description

Located at the southern end of Big Sur and at the end of the Carmel and Monterey area, Andrew Molera State Park sits quietly tucked aside CA 1. Known more for its hiking trails and as a wildlife refuge, Andrew Molera does offer surfers a refuge from the wind-infested waters of the Big Sur coastline. Down the steep hillside and a long walking path, the park has a calm sandy beach. Access is easy, and the facilities are ample for day trips and overnighters. Typically cool year-round, the moderate air

Gone fishin' at the Big Sur River mouth—as the seabirds remain nonplussed at these modern moves on a retro board.   Chris Burkard

temperatures never really feel like they rise above seventy-five, but rarely do they drop below fifty either, unless a cold front is whipping off the Pacific Ocean.

Andrew Molera is windy. Let's face it, the whole northern Central Coast is windy. Consequently, all breaks at Andrew Molera are typically changed by the wind. The best swells come from the southwest, but with prevailing northwesterlies, the break tends to wall up and close out. In the mornings there is usually no wind or a light one, and conditions are better. During this time the wave produces a right that sets up for a nice ride, with any peeling left being a little more mushy. The sand-and-rock bottom holds the wave shape well, but it can close out quickly in larger swells or direct hits from the west. Protected on its northern end, Andrew Molera can offer a refuge from other area surf spots blown out by the wind. It's rarely crowded.

> If you're into scenic beauty with monster views, this is the place. Andrew Molera has tons of hiking trails, which all start and end near the Big Sur River mouth. If you end up camping in the state park, watch the sunset from the headlands that overlook the break.

Even though Andrew Molera sits at the mouth of the Big Sur River, the water is very clean. Big Sur has very little to no development in most areas, so the area has been preserved in its natural state, including the crystal-clear waters of the Pacific. Interesting long wooden pieces often wash up on shore at Andrew Molera; these make nice walking sticks if you plan on exploring any of the area trails. Believe it or not, there is a downside to the strict environmental protection of the marine life. Fish and plant life are abundant, but the river mouth acts as a beacon to the local shark population. Although it's located south of the major shark-producing waters, Andrew Molera can attract its fair share of hungry fin-backed leg nibblers.

Other Information

Local Surf Shops: None along Big Sur Road. A couple back in Carmel/Monterey.

Places to Stay: The only place to stay near Andrew Molera is Andrew Molera State Park, located 20 miles south of Carmel on CA 1, Big Sur; (831) 667-2315; parks.ca.gov.

Places to Eat: Bring something to eat or drink; there isn't much to eat nearby unless you drive to Big Sur. Rocky Point Restaurant, CA 1, Big Sur (between Carmel and Big Sur); (831) 624-2933. The views are spectacular, and the food's decent.

Sand Dollar Beach

The U-shaped cove of Sand Dollar Beach is protected from the wind and strong currents. The waves here are crumbly white lava flows of slow-moving lefts and rights.

Best tide: Medium
Best swell direction: Southwest, west
Best wave size: Head high to slightly overhead
Bottom: Sand
Type of break: Beach break, outside, left and right
Skill level: Intermediate
Best boards: Longboard, shortboard
Best season: Fall
Crowds: Can get crowded on weekends
Water quality: Clean
Hazards: There's a lot of poison oak in this area
Fees and permits: None

Heading out for a solitary session at Sand Dollar Beach.   Elizabeth Pepin Silva

Finding the Break

From Monterey: Take CA 1 south until you reach Sand Dollar Beach. When you spot Willow Creek, you know you're close. Signs will mark the beach area. Parking is available at Sand Dollar Beach or across the street at Plaskett Creek Campground. GPS: N35 55.121 / W121 27.969

Surf Description

Sand Dollar is an extremely popular beach located along the shoreline side of the Santa Lucia Mountains. With its pristine white beaches and gentle sloping sand dune shores, this is a surfer-friendly beach. Easy to find near the Willow Creek and the Plaskett Creek Campground, Sand Dollar offers typical campground amenities like showers, restrooms, and ample parking. The weather is better at Sand Dollar than most areas along the Big Sur coast because it's generally protected by the wind (unless it comes directly onshore from the west).

Just like the stretches of white sand peppering the beach of Sand Dollar, the break has several long sandbars, and these serve up several breaks. The north end of the beach has a small cove-like area, which pushes a right that peters out into the channel. The wave shape is mushy and doesn't offer much shape to crank hard turns. Below the north end, gentle whitewater breakers crowd the shoreline and edges of the beach. A similar break extends down the south end, but it can produce a slightly better wave with more shape. This most often happens when the swell comes in from the west and is overhead. The wave will pick up speed and allow for more vertical turns off the top of the wall.

The local vibe is mellow. Butterflies are plentiful in the right season.

There is plenty of room to spread out here, and the vibe at the beach is pretty mellow. The lack of urban development in this section of the coast creates a relaxed and friendly atmosphere. It's hard not to feel the same vibes you'll pick up at Big Sur—downright surreal at times. You may be waiting for a set to roll in, look out over the water, and see flocks of seagulls or pelicans dive-bombing the water for fish or gliding inches over the ocean's surface. Curious otters will pop their small heads in and out of the water, occasionally breaking the surface and rolling on their bellies with an abalone for a crunchy snack. Be aware of your surroundings, however: As at other beaches in the area, great-white-shark sightings are not uncommon here.

Lucia Griggi

Willow Creek is located just south of Big Sur. Besides its unpredictable break—due to wind, swell direction, and coastline topography—the area is known for great-white-shark sightings. Willow Creek does have a left-hand peak to the north side, but stay clear of the cleanup sets or you'll end up being ping-ponged off the boulders and rocks.

Other Information

Local Surf Shops: None.

Places to Stay: Lucia Lodge, 62400 CA 1, Big Sur; (831) 667-2391. Kirk Creek Campground; (805) 434-1996. There are state campgrounds at Limekiln and Mill Creek.

Places to Eat: Wild Coast Restaurant, 71895 CA 1, Big Sur; (805) 927-2390. Whale Watchers Café, CA 1, Gorda; (805) 927-1590. Nepenthe, 48510 CA 1, Big Sur; (831) 667-2345.

Chris Burkard

San Carpoforo sits at the south end of Big Sur. The break is at the San Carpoforo River mouth. It's a strong break that responds best to low winds and a westerly swell direction. The sandbar can shift during the winter months, creating closeouts, but this tends to be one of the more consistent and powerful spots near San Simeon and often requires a longboard.

SUPDATE: BIG SUR TO SANTA BARBARA

As this surf guide was being updated, three guys from Malibu launched their standup paddleboards at the Andrew Molera/Big Sur river mouth and headed south, taking four and a half days to paddle the Big Sur coast all the way to San Carpoforo Creek. That's a pretty adventurous SUP trip considering they passed Point Sur, where a guy was attacked by a killer whale way back in the 1970s, and covered a lot of coast that is open to wind, fog, and swell. This would be the hard to way to surf F_____ and W_____ C____ and a lot of the secret spots along the Big Sur coast. But they survived and blazed a path others may want to follow.

Another good SUP adventure would be launching from Coast Guard Pier in Monterey and paddling along Cannery Row as far as you want to go: The water is clear and beautiful here, and there is a lot to see by land and sea. If the surf is big, there are a lot of shifting reef breaks along here that might be easier to get on a SUP. And if you really want to get adventurous, go around the point and along the coast of Pebble Beach—just watch out for bad tee shots hooking toward you.

From San Carpoforo Beach to Point Conception, there are miles and miles of empty beaches and distant reef breaks that would be a challenge on a standup paddleboard. You might want to avoid places where elephant seals hang out, as the shark danger in those areas is very real—especially in September and October. And SUP is also a way to get into places where outsiders are historically not welcome. Trespassing into Vandenberg Air Force Base is probably not a good idea, but a SUP would be an adventurous way to access those surf spots from Point Conception and down along the Gaviota Coast—just watch out for those offshore winds that will blow you halfway to the Channel Islands before you know it.

Chris Burkard

San Simeon is a stretch of outside peaks that develop into barreling rights that rarely, if ever, break. True but sad, San Simeon rarely gets Mother Nature to cooperate by aligning all conditions for superior surf. More often than not, the spot produces little surf—and what does come up is mushy, closed out, or generally weak. Your best bet as a visitor is to go check out Hearst Castle or head down to Pico Creek.

Cayucos Pier

Cayucos is fast and hollow, with lefts and rights depending on swell direction. At high tide with a southwest swell, Cayucos rolls in at its best.

Best tide: High
Best swell direction: Southwest
Best wave size: Waist high to head high
Bottom: Sand
Type of break: Outside, beach break, lefts and rights
Skill level: Novice to intermediate
Best board: Shortboard
Best seasons: Fall, spring, and summer
Crowds: Can get crowded on weekends

Water quality: Clean
Hazards: There's a lot of poison oak in this area
Fees and permits: None

Finding the Break

From Monterey: Nestled in Morro Bay, Cayucos is reachable via CA 1. Take CA 1 until you reach Cayucos Drive. Head toward the beach. GPS: N35 26.924 / W120 54.375

Surf Description

Near the northern tip of Morro Bay, Cayucos Pier is an average wave, providing a consistent beach break with inconsistent shape. The name *Cayucos* is, of course, unusual. It comes from the original land grants extending back to the mid-1800s; the term refers to a small fishing boat similar to a kayak.

A big set as seen through a swing set at the Cayucos Pier, probably in winter.
Chris Burkard

Cayucos Pier is the centerpiece of Cayucos Beach. The pier itself is slightly short of 1,000 feet long and marks, for argument's sake, the main section of the beach. Along with surfing, fishing is common at the pier. Cayucos is rarely crowded in the water or out. In the peak of the tourist season in mid- to late summer, you might spot more than the handful of surfers normally in the water. There's plenty of room to hang out on the beach and just as much in the water to find your own spot to surf.

Cayucos Beach has several spots to choose from. Starting with the pier, the wave builds up quickly and tends to close out, allowing for only short rides along a steep face. Occasionally, when a swell comes in from the southwest, particularly in summer, the wave shape will improve, allowing longer turn-carving rides. To the north and south sides of the pier, the sand bottom can create several A-frame peaks that allow for both lefts and rights (depending on the current); these often break slightly farther outside, making for a better ride. The sandbars don't really let you predict where the peak will be best, so the conditions change daily. The waves overall are not difficult, but they're worthwhile. Cayucos Pier can be affected by strong winds from the west and south, which will all but kill any swell.

Cayucos is a typical central California beach town. The area sits on aquamarine Estero Bay. Cayucos is often a destination for relaxation away from the heat and smog

Chris Burkard

There is almost no way to miss Morro Rock. It jumps out of the water like a giant zit on a teenager's forehead. Just off CA 1, Morro is similar to the rest of the coastline, with an uneventful sandbar beach break. The best spot at Morro Rock is farther north, where the ocean landscape creates much bigger swells that take shape into relatively consistent lefts and right. The current and riptide can be strong, so paddle out with a stick you can handle—any size will do.

Chris Burkard

The name should clue you in: Hazard Canyon is not for the weak or faint of heart. Located just south of Morro Bay near San Luis Obispo, it's a strong right-hand reef with a late drop. Paddling out can be difficult and dangerous if you can't hammer through the strong current or bigger surf. A gun or oversize shortboard is your best choice, and it can reward you with some nice barrels.

Chris Burkard

Avila Beach is an outer sandbar break where the San Luis River meets the ocean west of San Luis Obispo. This break can generate well-shaped, two-way peaks, especially after heavy rains have helped create sandbars. Avila Beach works best with a waist- to head-high winter swell at a medium tide.

of the fertile agricultural lands in the Central Valley. Cayucos has a good number of lodging possibilities, including hotels, motels, and bed-and-breakfasts. Day trips to Morro Bay and Morro Rock are close by and offer a unique, scenic view of the Central Coast. Hearst Castle is just a short drive north in San Simeon.

Other Information

Local Surf Shops: Cayucos Surf Company, 95 Cayucos Dr., Cayucos; (805) 995-1000. Good Clean Fun Surf & Sport, 136 Ocean Front Ave., Cayucos; (805) 995-1993.
Places to Stay: Beachwalker Inn, 501 S. Ocean Ave., Cayucos; (805) 995-2133. Cayucos Inn, 20 S. Ocean Ave., Cayucos; (805) 995-3670.
Places to Eat: Hoppe's Garden Bistro & Wine Shop, 78 N. Ocean Ave., Cayucos; (805) 995-1006. Paulski's Northshore Cafe, 155 S. Ocean Ave., Cayucos; (805) 995-1610.

Pismo Pier

This long stretch of beach break split by the Pismo Beach Pier produces peaky lefts and rights, depending on swell direction.

Best tide: High
Best swell direction: Southwest
Best wave size: Waist high to head high
Bottom: Sand
Type of break: Outside, beach break, lefts and rights
Skill level: Novice to intermediate when under head height; advanced when the surf is head high or larger
Best boards: Shortboard, funshape
Best seasons: Fall and summer
Crowds: Uncrowded
Water quality: Clean
Hazards: Hitting a pier piling
Fees and permits: None

Finding the Break

From San Luis Obispo: Head south on CA 1 toward Pismo Beach. Take CA 1 until you reach Point San Luis. Head west and follow the pier signs until you hit the beach. Parking is available near the pier and in surrounding areas. GPS: N35 08.297 / W120 38.684

Surf Description

Located in the heart of San Luis Obispo County, Pismo Beach Pier is a huge sandbar beach with breaks to both the north and south of the pier. Pismo Beach in general provides relief from the summer heat for those who come over from the hot San Joaquin Valley The pier was built in 1924 but underwent significant restoration in 1983 due to storm damage and normal wear and tear. It's 1,370 feet long and has several cantilevered fishing decks, which make it popular among local anglers. The beach and break extend for miles, so there's plenty of room to spread out. The beach mostly faces southwest, favoring a summer swell direction.

The break is consistent and dependable, so if you're not having any luck elsewhere, Pismo is as close to a guaranteed wave as you'll find. Pismo Pier conditions can get windy. The wind is usually stronger in the afternoons and will blow out the surf in summer, particularly during early-evening sessions. Pismo Pier takes a south, west, or combination swell the best. Use the pier as the center point when picking out a break.

Pismo Beach pier. Hitting the lip = good. Hitting the pier = bad.   Chris Burkard

Since Pismo is one giant sandbar, the dunes provide great dune buggy and ATV riding. If the wind is blowing out any swell, this is an easy way to pass the time on the beach.

The south side of the pier is typically better than the north. Pismo sees steady tourism from late spring through early fall, and the beaches tend to be more crowded during this time—but not San Diego– or Orange County–crowded.

Pismo is a very popular beach in summer. When the weather warms along the Central Coast, however, Pismo also attracts some unwanted creatures. Just off Avila Beach in August 2003, a woman swimming on the surface of the water in close proximity to several sea lions feeding near the surface was attacked and killed by a great white shark. The tragic incident paralleled the nearly ninety-three other documented shark attacks in the state of California. She likely became the target of the ambush predator after it was attracted to the nearby sea lions. Surfers and swimmers in wet suits all look the same from below.

Pismo is a good place to surf—just be cautious.

Other Information

Local Surf Shops: Moondoggies Beach Club, 781 Dolliver St., Pismo Beach; (805) 773-1995. Pancho's Surf Shop, 181 Pomeroy Ave., Pismo Beach; (805) 773-7100. Shell Beach Surf Shop, 2665 Shell Beach Rd., Suite K, Pismo Beach; (805) 773-1855. Pismo Beach Surf Shop, 470 Price St., Pismo Beach; (805) 773-2089. Esteem Surf Co., 590 Cypress St., Pismo Beach; (805) 773-2144. Central Coast Surfboards, 855 Marsh St., San Luis Obispo; (805) 541-1129.
Places to Stay: Sandcastle Inn, 100 Stimson Ave., Pismo Beach; (805) 773-2422. Ocean Breeze Inn (formerly Surf Motel), 250 Main St., Pismo Beach; (805) 773-2070.
Places to Eat: Harry's Beach Bar & Nightclub, 690 Cypress St., Pismo Beach; (805) 773-1010. Splash Cafe, 197 Pomeroy St., Pismo Beach; (805) 773-4653.

Point Sal

Just south of Pismo Beach, Point Sal has numerous reef breaks to explore. The most popular peak is a thick, powerful right.

Best tides: Low to medium
Best swell direction: West
Best wave size: Waist high to slightly overhead

Bottom: Rock
Type of break: Outside, right
Skill level: Intermediate to advanced
Best boards: Shortboard, funshape
Best season: All
Crowds: Uncrowded
Water quality: Clean
Hazards: Heavy shore break on a big day
Fees and permits: None

Finding the Break

From San Luis Obispo: Head south on CA 1 toward Santa Maria. Look for signs to the Point Sal Beach Park. GPS: N34 54.182 / W120 40.227

Surf Description

Point Sal is located just southwest of Santa Maria in the northwestern corner of Santa Barbara County. Approximately 13 miles long, the Point Sal Reserve contains 77 acres of marine, plant, and cultural life unique to the Central Coast. Point Sal is largely a giant sand dune along the coast. The beach is almost entirely composed of beach break until the rocky promontory outcropping at the point, which provides a reef break. Point Sal is easy to locate off CA 1. The area is large and relatively isolated so there is little chance for crowds to form anywhere.

Best on a low-to-medium tide where the reef can grab the wave bottom, Point Sal will produce a strong right off the main point that is shapely and hollow in larger conditions. The shape of the wave is best with no wind to little wind. Point Sal is not for beginners. Entering and exiting the point can be difficult when the conditions aren't calm. If you're not a strong paddler or comfortable around rocks, this is not the place for you. Away from the point area, Point Sal's beaches are the typical Central Coast beach break. Point Sal can capture some strong current and heavy surf, making the shore break at high tide on a big day quite hazardous. On lower tides the beach break is mushy when the swell is small and is fast and sometimes hollow when swells are larger.

Point Sal is unparalleled in its natural and cultural resources. Well before today's urban expansion reached the central California coast, Chumash people roamed these shores and settled here. The Purisimento and the Obispeño (hence the city name to the north, San Luis Obispo) used these fertile lands in a once-thriving community. Much thought and time has gone into preserving Point Sal into a natural resource for studying the remains of its original inhabitants and as a sanctuary for marine and plant life. The area has incredible views from many of the unique geological formations along the coast. The sand dunes, combined with large spires of rock and ever-changing terrain, make Point Sal a great place to explore.

According to the photographer, "Point Sal really isn't a surf spot since erosion and earthquakes and things wrecked the original reef there, which was called 'Guta Reef.' My photo was shot on a day when the buoys were reporting a 22-foot west swell, so that should give you some idea of the photo scale. Perhaps on a negative low tide and ultra-clean 4- to 6-foot west swell, Point Sal could shine, but . . . "

Other Information

Local Surf Shops: Moondoggies Beach Club, 781 Dolliver St., Pismo Beach; (805) 773-1995. Pancho's Surf Shop, 181 Pomeroy Ave., Pismo Beach; (805) 773-7100. Shell Beach Surf Shop, 2665 Shell Beach Rd., Suite K, Pismo Beach; (805) 773-1855. Pismo Beach Surf Shop, 470 Price St., Pismo Beach; (805) 773-2089. Esteem Surf Co., 590 Cypress St., Pismo Beach; (805) 773-2144. Central Coast Surfboards, 855 Marsh St., San Luis Obispo; (805) 541-1129.

Places to Stay: Sandcastle Inn, 100 Stimson Ave., Pismo Beach; (805) 773-2422. Ocean Breeze Inn (formerly Surf Motel), 250 Main St., Pismo Beach; (805) 773-2070.

Places to Eat: Harry's Beach Bar & Nightclub, 690 Cypress St., Pismo Beach; (805) 773-1010. Splash Cafe, 197 Pomeroy St., Pismo Beach; (805) 773-4653.

Surf is a long stretch of beach between Point Sal and Lompoc that's home to numerous outer sandbar peaks. From CA 1, head toward the coast just north of Lompoc. The surf works best with a waist- to head-high swell at a medium tide. There have been two fatal shark attacks here, so be warned. Lucia Griggi

Jalama

Jalama has fairly hollow-shaped waves that peak both left and right. Outside swells produce an aggressive wave that good-to-great surfers can tear into.

Best tides: Medium to high

Best swell direction: Southwest, west

Best wave size: Head high to slightly overhead

Bottom: Sand

Type of break: Beach break, outside, lefts and rights

Skill level: Intermediate to advanced

Best boards: Shortboard and gun

Best season: Fall

Crowds: Can get crowded on weekends

Water quality: Clean

Hazards: Watch the current and the paddle-out at Beachbreak

Fees and permits: According to countyofsb.org, there is a nominal fee to park in the campground, including a small surcharge for dogs.

Finding the Break

From Santa Barbara: Take CA 1 north until you reach Jalama Road (between Point Arguello and Point Conception). Take Jalama Road for approximately 15 miles until you reach the beach. Pay to park in the campground; if you park on the road, you'll risk getting a ticket. GPS: N34 30.635 / W120 30.030

Surf Description

Lompoc is home to a large stretch of coastline just north of Santa Barbara. Jalama Beach County Park is one of the many white-sand beaches in the area. It's a popular campground and surf break. Home to more than a hundred campsites, all overlooking the ocean or beachfront, Jalama is a great place to surf, particularly if your budget is tight or you seek the refuge of a campground versus a hotel. The area offers picnic tables, barbecue pits, showers, restrooms, and fresh water. Jalama often fills up in summer, when camping season is at its peak. For a small fee, day use of Jalama Beach is also available.

The spot is composed of three main areas—Beachbreak, Cracks, and Tarantulas. Beachbreak has semi-hollow hammering rides that are close to the campground. The wave is fast and often closes out before any ride is possible. If the wave is rideable, it will be at high tide in a larger swell. Farther down the beach, Cracks and Tarantulas

Jalama is like a box of chocolates. Take that 14-mile detour to the first/last surf spot in central California and you never know what you're going to get. Jalama is exposed to everything, but hopefully you'll get something like this.   Chris Burkard

have peeling fast, peaky swells that are more consistent than Beachbreak. The wave at both Cracks and Tarantulas can get crowded when the swell is larger and breaking. Both locations have nicely shaped waves, allowing for long carving turns and the occasional lip for some aerial practice. Best in high-surf conditions, Jalama is an excellent overall wave.

Jalama is located in the city of Lompoc. The proper pronunciation of the "poc" in Lompoc uses a long *o* sound, as in *smoke*. The name is derived from a Chumash word meaning "lake" or "lagoon." Many Lompoc residents are affiliated with Vandenberg Air Force Base. Located just 7 miles west of town, it's among the nation's most important military and aerospace installations. Lompoc is a popular stop along the drive from San Francisco to Los Angeles. Just off US 101, it has several restaurants and hotels and is the closest major city between Santa Maria and Santa Barbara.

Right, The Ranch is a local break if California still has any local breaks left. Located just north of Santa Barbara and south of Lompoc, the Ranch has several distinct spots to drop in, locals permitting. It faces south so most of the surf tends to be better in summer than in other seasons. The various spots like Little Drakes and Cojo offer up peaky lefts and rights, depending on your location along the Gaviota Coast.

Below, Refugio is an outside right break located a few miles north of Santa Barbara. From US 101, you'll see a sign for the Refugio Beach State Park. Refugio can produce long right lines with well-shaped peaks. This break works best with a waist- to head-high winter swell at a medium to low tide.

Lucia Griggi

Lucia Griggi

Other Information

Local Surf Shops: The Surf Shack, 451 Jalama Rd., Lompoc; (805) 555-5550. One Way Board Shop, 2348 S. Bradley Rd., Santa Maria; (805) 347-3323. Surf Connection, 1307 N. H St., Lompoc; (805) 736-1730.
Places to Stay: Jalama Beach Campground, Jalama Beach State Park; (805) 736-5027.
Places to Eat: Jalama Beach Store & Grill, Jalama Beach State Park; (805) 736-5027.

El Capitan

This is an amazing point break with barrels galore. El Capitan is one place you do not want to get caught inside on a big day.

Best tides: Medium to high
Best swell direction: West
Best wave size: Head high to slightly overhead
Bottom: Rock
Type of break: Point, right
Skill level: Advanced
Best boards: Shortboard, gun
Best seasons: Fall and winter
Crowds: Uncrowded
Water quality: Clean
Hazards: Rocks inside, getting caught inside on a big day
Fees and permits: None

Finding the Break

From Santa Barbara. Head north on CA 1 until you reach the El Capitan State Beach exit. Exit toward the beach under the bridge and you'll reach the park entrance. Leave your vehicle here and walk to the break. GPS: N34 27.585 / W120 01.477

Surf Description

El Capitan State Beach is located in the northern section of Santa Barbara County approximately 17 miles north of Santa Barbara. It has a long stretch of sandy beach and rocky tide pools. The surfing at El Capitan is primarily at the top of the beach, where there's a point break. One of the great and unique aspects of El Capitan is that unlike many beaches where palm trees line the coastline, pockets of sycamore and oaks pepper the shores of the entire state park area. El Capitan is an excellent camping and family beach. Swimming, fishing, and surfing are common among beachgoers. Bike trails abound in the area; the most popular trail connects El Capitan with Refugio State Beach. Access to the beach is very easy off US 101.

El Capitan is another one of California's best point breaks. Producing a long ride moving right along the rocky shore and sand bottom, "El Cap" is an advanced surfer's wave. It drinks up west swells and will even take a combination swell from the south or north. In smaller-size surf more people come to El Capitan; these conditions let people experiment on the smooth, shapely face. The shape is a pure hollow right that allows for any type of maneuvers from hanging ten to floating off the top. As the surf gets bigger, the ride hollows out unless the wind picks up. When it does hollow out, the break requires a bit more skill—the takeoff becomes steeper, and the wave performance picks up. If you've never been in a barrel before, El Capitan is an excellent place to catch your first.

If you're interested in getting in touch with nature—but in a high-end pampering kind of way—the El Capitan Canyon is a great place to stay, even if for one night.

The Gaviota Coast from Gaviota State Park down to Coal Oil Point in Goleta is a remarkably pristine, rural, green, beautiful, undeveloped, and untouched stretch of Southern California coastal pastureland. Along the way are the first of Southern California's classic right points. This is El Capitan showing a bit of its potential.   Chris Burkard

Located near Goleta, the lodge attempts to give each visitor a personal encounter with nature. Staying in one of the one hundred luxury cedar cabins or twenty-six safari-style tents allows each guest to enjoy the terrain of Santa Barbara County while getting spoiled all the way. Whether you stay here or camp elsewhere, however, you need to be aware of where you walk. Rattlesnakes, mountain lions, and especially poison oak can turn any surfing trip into a major bummer fast.

Other Information

Local Surf Shops: None along the Gaviota Coast. Lots in Santa Barbara.
Places to Stay: There is splendid camping at Gaviota, El Capitan, and Refugio State Parks; (805) 968-1033. There are also motels and hotels in Goleta and Santa Barbara. El Capitan Canyon, 11560 Calle Real, Santa Barbara; (866) 352-2729.
Places to Eat: There are numerous restaurants in Buellton, Solvang, Goleta, and Santa Barbara.

Bryce Johnson

Just north of Santa Barbara, Coal Oil Point is exactly what it sounds like. This is a nice point-break wave that works best in larger swells where conditions produce overhead or larger waves. Coal Oil Point is mushier and a slightly easier ride than the neighboring breaks. It tends to be steep at takeoff, so a shortboard or funshape tends to work best.

Campus Point

Campus Point is a right point break found near the Goleta Pier close to the UCSB campus. The wave starts strong with a good wall and slows as it breaks.

Best tide: Medium

Best swell direction: Southwest, west

Best wave size: Head high to slightly overhead

Bottom: Rock

Type of break: Point, right

Skill level: Intermediate

Best boards: Shortboard, funshape, longboard

Best season: Fall

Crowds: Crowded

Water quality: Clean

Hazards: None

Fees and permits: According to lotsafunmaps.com: "Parking here is difficult. There are only a few stalls available for beach access during the week from 7:30 a.m. to 5 p.m. On weekends or after 5 p.m. you can park in any of the stalls. At all times you must pay a pretty hefty parking fee—you use your credit card to pay at the machines and then place the parking pass inside your car by the dashboard. In the evenings and on weekends it's the cheapest . . . "

Finding the Break

From Santa Barbara: Take US 101 north and exit onto CA 217. Take 217 to the UCSB entrance gate. Go left after the entrance and follow the road until you see the UCSB dorms and a parking lot across the street. Paid parking is available in the UCSB lot. GPS: N34 24.535 / W119 50.555

Surf Description

Campus Point gets its name from the University of California–Santa Barbara campus, located a stone's throw away. Crowded at all times due to a flexible class schedule, it's a fun right point-break wave that takes best shape from a southwest-to-westerly swell. It's located close to the Goleta Pier, just opposite the UCSB dormitory buildings. Finding the exact point can be a bit trickier—UCSB is a big campus—but you can ask any security guard, university employee, or student, and they'll point you right where you need to go. If you happen to catch an evening session at Campus Point, head toward Isla Vista—you won't be disappointed.

A small, clean day at Campus Point.   Elizabeth Pepin Silva

Campus Point can be a really nice point break or it can be downright awful. Prevailing wind, swell direction, and tide will completely dictate the break conditions. An above-average point break for the county, the Campus Point swell wells up and makes a fairly solid face that has a wide peak. The wave produces a fast, smooth face that is easily carvable. Near mid- to low tide, the wave ride can increase in length unless the waves are just bombing in from the reef. The longer rides are sectiony and vary from faster on the inside of the break to slow and mushy on the outside. Pretty much any board will do, from short to long. There are sections of the wave for every level of ability.

> **College kids from all over California funnel into Isla Vista for Halloween every year. It used to be out of control, but now there's a tremendous police presence.**

The main surfing crew at Campus Point attend the University of California–Santa Barbara. One of the most picturesque settings for any higher-education institution,

Lucia Griggi

Hope Ranch is a stretch of coast that's home to several reef and beach breaks. It's a very affluent area of Santa Barbara filled with large estates and beautiful homes—people keep thoroughbred horses in their front yards, no kidding. From US 101, take the Las Positas exit and head toward the beach. Turn right onto Cliff Drive and follow it into the Hope Ranch area. Hope Ranch works best with waist- to head-high winter swells at a medium tide.

Elizabeth Pepin Silva

Arroyo Burro Beach is a sand-bottomed beach break just south of the Hope Ranch area of Santa Barbara. From US 101, take the Las Positas exit and head toward the beach. Turn right onto Cliff Drive and then left into the parking lot for Arroyo Burro Beach. This break works best with a waist- to chest-high winter swell at a medium tide.

Mesa is a reef break just north of Leadbetter Beach in an area of Santa Barbara referred to as the Mesa. From US 101, take the Las Positas exit and head toward the beach. Turn left onto Cliff Drive and then right onto one of the streets that has a sign for coastal access. Mesa is a very consistent and somewhat protected spot that works best with a waist- to chest-high winter swell at a medium to high tide.

Lucia Griggi

UCSB is home to approximately 20,000 students. The campus offers nearly 1,000 acres for students to surf, party—and maybe even study. What makes the community at UCSB and Campus Point such a gem is that nearly all the students who attend UCSB are from California. Appreciation for the water and the California coastal environment is born into nearly every student. This is reflected in the academic programming offered at UCSB, which is known as one of leading marine biology schools in the country.

Other Information

Local Surf Shops: Isla Vista Surf Company, 901 Embarcadero Del Norte, Goleta; (805) 968-1145. Surf Country, 5668 Calle Real, Goleta; (805) 683-4450.
Places to Stay: Pilot House Motel, 1 Sandspit Rd., Goleta; (805) 967-2336. Super 8 Motel, 6021 Hollister Ave., Goleta; (805) 967-5591 or (800) USA-HOTELS.
Places to Eat: Blenders in the Grass, 6560 Pardall Rd., Isla Vista; (805) 685-1134. Beachside Bar-Café, 5905 Sandspit Rd., Goleta; (805) 964-7881.

Sandspit

A miracle of modern engineering, this break starts steep and ends with a powerful shore pound. The swell wells up out of nowhere to produce a fast and hollow right.

Best tide: Low
Best swell direction: West
Best wave size: Waist high to head high
Bottom: Sand
Type of break: Beach break, outside right
Skill level: Intermediate
Best board: Shortboard
Best seasons: Fall, spring, and winter
Crowds: Crowded
Water quality: Clean
Hazards: Strong currents, heavy shore break
Fees and permits: None

Finding the Break

From Santa Barbara: Exit Castillo Street off US 101. Take Castillo Street west to Cabrillo Boulevard. From there, make a quick right followed by a left into the harbor area on Harbor Way. There are numerous parking lots in this area. GPS: N34 24.198 / W119 41.597

Surf Description

Sometimes referred to as the American Riviera, Santa Barbara's beautiful beaches and coastline make it a vacation destination for many Californians as well as out-of-state tourists. Santa Barbara is unique among other Central Coast cities in that there are regularly scheduled flights to its airport. By car, it's only a little over 1 hour north of Los Angeles up US 101. Santa Barbara boasts world-class accommodations, a variety of cuisines, and a vibrant cultural and nightlife scene. It isn't just hotels, food, and sightseeing, though. The surfing in the area is good, and it is well used by the local surf talent.

The Channel Islands off the coast of Santa Barbara are worth checking out. You can take a whale-watching boat out of the harbor when the whales are passing through. State Street in downtown Santa Barbara is a fun place to go at night.

Just beyond the reach of downtown Santa Barbara sits Sandspit, a sand-bottomed beach break that works best at low tide but can receive waves in almost any season of the year. As at most beach breaks, the ride tends to be very fast and clean, but it closes fast, leaving room for only a short ride. The wave mostly opens up to a right; in a cross swell it breaks in both directions. Sandspit is a local favorite because the break can be flat-out awesome when the swell direction and tide are just right. Given a low tide and overhead surf, you can find some of the hollowest tubes in the county here, if not the region. You do need to be aware of the breakwater line, however. In stronger currents you can get sucked over or near the breakwater wall. This wall is not kind, and if you're new to Sandspit, you're better off trying to take off and make a right while staying away from the rocks.

In 1602 Sebastián Vizcaino sailed into the deep blue ocean between the Channel Islands and Santa Barbara. Vizcaíno was a religious man. He saw this area around the fourth day of December, which he considered a sacred day, and he named the area in the memory of Saint Barbara. Later in 1848 Mexico signed a treaty with the United States giving land rights to Mexico's northern coastal territory above Tijuana. While California was still a territory, the area was divided among many wealthy landowners, politicians, and entrepreneurs. Santa Barbara was carved out of the California Territory, extending to the northern border that still exists today and as far south as Ventura. Later the territory was further divided to create Santa Barbara and Ventura County. The territory officially became a state in 1850. California's population was growing rapidly, mostly due to the allure of the West and particularly the gold rush.

Aerial of the Santa Barbara Harbor entrance—aka Sandspit. This is a small day that shows how the wave is set up, with sand settling along the outside of the jetty and inside. Sandspit is one of the best man-made-by-mistake waves in California and the world when it's firing. Chris Burkard

Other Information

Local Surf Shops: Surf N Wear's The Beach House, 10 State St., Santa Barbara; (805) 963-1281. Channel Islands Surfboards, 36 Anacapa St., Santa Barbara; (805) 966-7213. Yater Surfboards, 317 N. Milpas St., Santa Barbara; (805) 966-2006.
Places to Stay: There are numerous hotels and motels in Santa Barbara, including Canary Hotel Santa Barbara, 31 W. Carrillo, Santa Barbara; (805) 884-0300 and The Fess Parker Santa Barbara Hotel, 633 E. Cabrillo Blvd., Santa Barbara; (805) 564-4333.
Places to Eat: Harbor Restaurant, Stearns Wharf, Santa Barbara; (805) 963-3311. The Endless Summer Bar-Café, 113 Harbor Way #180, Santa Barbara; (805) 564-1200.

Hammond's Reef

Hammond's can be a great wave with the right conditions. The wave gets better as it moves inside.

Best tide: Low
Best swell direction: Northwest
Best wave size: Waist high to head high
Bottom: Rock
Type of break: Outside, right
Skill level: Intermediate
Best board: Shortboard
Best season: Winter
Crowds: Uncrowded
Water quality: Average
Hazards: None
Fees and permits: None

Finding the Break

From Santa Barbara: Take US 101 south and exit at Olive Mill Road in the town of Montecito. Turn right onto Channel Drive at the stop sign. Park on any of the streets around the Four Seasons Hotel. GPS: N34 25.002 / W119 38.532

Surf Description

Montecito means "little mountain" in Spanish, but the only mountain around here is the mountain of cash you'll need to buy a home. The upscale community of Montecito is home to Oprah Winfrey, Rob Lowe, Danny Kwock, Shaun Tomson, Josh Brolin, and Hammond's Reef. Montecito is among the wealthiest communities in the United States and is home to many high-profile personalities. With only 10,000 residents, Hammond's Reef is a local break if there ever was one. It's normally small and shallow with a lackluster wave, but when it does break, the locals are out surfing it. The break sits at the base of the swanky Four Seasons Hotel. The hotel grounds overlook the entire break area, and there are good views from the grassy knoll just beyond the property line. Parking isn't so easy, as the area doesn't cater to your average surfer, so you'll need to do the valet thing at the hotel or park down the street.

   Hammond's Reef is a rocky outcropping that needs the right conditions to break well. The predominant condition here is small surf with mushy to no shape. When the surf is large, however, the reef pushes up a peak off the reef that builds more

Montecito has a great little village area that's worth checking out. Hammond's was one of surfing legend Tom Curren's surf spots while growing up in the area.

shape as it continues to break. The wave will start with a nice peaked point that allows surfers to drop in along a smooth right wall fairly easily. Be careful not to pearl here—at low tide, you might find the bottom. Best in winter with a west-to-northwest swell direction, the reef is relatively uncrowded. The break often leaves nice long, open areas to make some big turns. As Hammond's Reef increases in wave size, so does the skill required to surf it. Hammond's can be a great spot, because few tourists staying in Montecito are here for the surfing.

The San Ynez Mountains serve as the backdrop to Hammond's Reef and the city of Montecito. These mountains are excellent for hiking and biking along the many roads that switchback along the mountainsides. They're also home to some of Southern California's best wineries, growing predominantly chardonnay and pinot varietals

Hammond's showing some form on a winter west swell—in perfect Santa Barbara weather.   Elizabeth Pepin Silva

due to the temperate and pleasant climate. The Santa Ynez Mountains extend along the south of the county and are bordered to the north by the San Rafael Mountains. Numerous tastings and events are held throughout the year to promote the region's winemakers.

Other Information

Local Surf Shops: Beach House Surf Shop, 10 State St., Santa Barbara; (805) 963-1281. Wilderness Surf Boards, 317 S. Alisos St., Santa Barbara; (805) 962-9518.
Places to Stay: Montecito hotels can be very expensive. Your best value is to head back to Santa Barbara. If you want to stay right at Hammond's Reef, try the Four Seasons Hotel, 1260 Channel Dr., Santa Barbara; (805) 969-2261.
Places to Eat: Palazzio, 1151 Coast Village Rd., Montecito; (805) 969-8565. Pane e Vino, 1482 E. Valley Rd., Montecito; (805) 969-9274.

Lucia Griggi

Tar Pits is a mostly west-facing beach just south of the town of Carpinteria. The bottom here is mostly rock, and with the right conditions, the peaks and waves can be well shaped. Tar Pits can work with swell from almost any direction. However, it's also very exposed and prone to getting blown out.

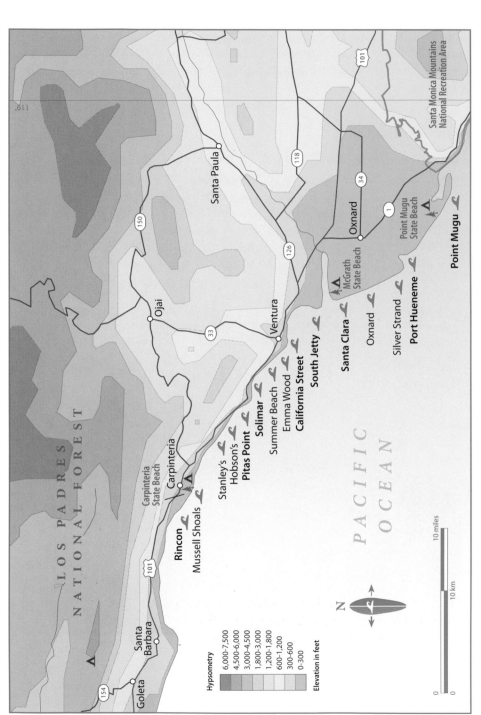

Region 7 (Ventura County)

REGION 7: VENTURA COUNTY

Ventura County starts just south of Santa Barbara in the sleepy town of Carpinteria and stretches its coastal arms to Point Mugu. Along this section of California's coastline sit some of the best stretches of ocean visible from the main freeway artery that feeds Ventura County, US 101. One thing's for certain when visiting this section of California: Ventura County is not Los Angeles County. Looking at cost of living, economy, water temperature, climate, and attitude, Ventura is a great place to explore a more laid-back Southern California vibe. This region is well developed, especially along the coast, as US 101 and CA 1 basically run right along its shores. More roads mean more people on the freeways and in the water.

The climate along Ventura County's coastline is surprisingly mild, if not even cooler than you'd expect. Ventura County tends to be more like Northern California in terms of windy conditions, endless days of marine layers, and cooler water temperatures.

Ventura's coastline is also much more Central Coast than Southern California. In general, the beaches aren't filled with crunchy pebbles of sand, rather, they tend to be rocky flats that slip into the ocean's shore. Ventura never really gets cold or hot, but the best time of the year for good weather is definitely late summer and early fall.

Ventura and Oxnard are the main cities along the Ventura County coast. Apart from the breaks described in this section, most if not all of the beach areas are easily accessible. Out of the water the locals are friendly and helpful. For the most part, the experience in the water is the same as long as you're respectful (duh!). Ventura can easily be reached by major freeway arteries inland as well. If you're a history buff, Simi Valley is the resting place of former president Ronald Reagan. From his burial grounds, you can get a great perspective on both world history and the Ventura County landscape.

Overall Surf Description

Sandwiched between the mellow central California coast to the north and fast-paced Los Angeles County to the south, Ventura County is a mix of what's best and worst about surfing. Fiercely defiant about Ventura's identity the farther south you get, the local vibe can be the polar opposite as you head north. From November through March is when the southern part of the county has its best surf. Summer can be brutal on the region unless a southern swell comes in; then most of the breaks will offer up decent surfing conditions. The water and climate make this county a definite wet-suit-wearing experience. The surf can range from triple overhead all the way down to tiny rollers, so be prepared for all conditions. Crowds range from nonexistent in winter to heavy in summer on weekends.

Fall Surf

The beginning of fall is definitely one of the better times of the year to surf in Ventura County. From there, it quickly deteriorates to a few select spots. Generally, the water is still reasonably warm and the late California summer keeps the air hot and dry until mid-October. You still get some reasonably good swells from the south and west, which portend excellent smaller-surf conditions throughout the county.

A couple of local rogues on the break wall at Silver Strand, taking the measure of an A-frame—perhaps waiting for less wind or the tide to shift . . . who knows what they're waiting for? Chris Burkard

Winter Surf

Winter conditions in Ventura County can still be good, although the outside air temperature is usually at its lowest for the year. Most of the swells will come out of the north, which makes surfing the southern half of the county more appealing. Expect to see the point breaks breaking best—especially right-handed point breaks, given the common winter swell direction.

Spring Surf

If it isn't windy, spring surf can be good; otherwise, find something else to do, because chances are it will be windy. Mornings are the best times to surf in spring; if you're lucky, you'll get late storm swells from the north. If you don't get it just right, though, you're better off shopping.

Summer Surf

Summer surf in Ventura County can be divided into two types: weekend conditions and weekday conditions. We suggest you opt for a weekday, because weekends bring everyone within a 50-mile shot of the coast to the beach. The surf is also relatively flat, with the exception of low tide combined with a small swell at most breaks.

	Average Temperatures for Region (Ventura County)	
	Air (Ventura)	Water (Ventura)
Jan	66	55
Feb	66	57
Mar	65	58
Apr	68	59
May	68	61
June	70	64
July	73	65
Aug	74	67
Sept	74	66
Oct	73	65
Nov	70	60
Dec	66	56

Rincon

Rincon is one of the best right point breaks in California. The cobblestone bottom and sandbar break can easily be seen from the freeway, just south of Santa Barbara. It's a popular spot that can get crowded quickly.

Best tides: Medium to high
Best swell direction: Southwest
Best wave size: Waist high to slightly overhead
Bottom: Sand and rock
Type of break: Point, right
Skill level: Intermediate
Best boards: Funshape, longboard
Best seasons: Fall and winter
Crowds: Crowded
Water quality: Clean
Hazards: None
Fees and permits: None

Finding the Break

From Santa Barbara: Take US 101 south. Look for CARPINTERIA and RINCON signs. Parking is right off US 101—you can't miss it. GPS: N34 24.374 / W119 32.854

Surf Description

Rincon is a legendary California wave because of its length and popularity. The Cove, Indicator, and Rivermouth make up Rincon's 1,000-foot break. It's a very long, sectional wave that's good at almost any height above waist high. Longboards are the preferred riding instrument, although a smaller funshape or minigun can work on large days. If you're in California in fall or winter, this break should not be missed. Parking is hassle-free in one of the nearby lots.

Rincon has been a favorite of Ventura County and Santa Barbara locals for years.

The Cove is probably Rincon's best break. The Cove works its way all the way to the shoreline rocks. The cobblestone bottom allows the wave to hold great shape, from small to overhead. It craves a direct west swell and can be as gentle as a summer breeze or pound out some serious cresting lips that beg to be cranked on. The Cove tends to be the most crowded of the three breaks. Indicator is a much longer ride but lacks the speed and performance of the other breaks. A preferred longboarding wave, Indicator works best in larger surf when you can hitch a long ride all the way across Rincon—figuratively, not literally. The wave allows for relatively easy takeoffs. The wave speed tends to be slower, allowing for multiple turns and cutbacks, even on a big stick. The last break, Rivermouth, links the Cove and Indicator. Sitting at the mouth of the river, the break is easy to locate. The wave performance is probably the worst of the three, but it's often less crowded as well. Similar to the other breaks, Rivermouth likes low tide and a westerly swell. Best in fall and winter, Rincon is a favorite of locals, visitors, and surf junkies.

Rincon has seen its fair share of professional surfers, up-and-coming stars, and board shapers since it became a popular alternative to Malibu in wintertime in the mid-1950s. Surfing legend and Santa Barbara local Tom Curren started pounding the

El Rincon del Mar, Queen of the Coast, Rincon. Whatever you want to call it, when this right point break directly on the Santa Barbara/Ventura county line is firing, it's the best wave in California and one of the best waves in the world.   Chris Burkard

waves at Rincon at an early age. His early work—like that of many before him, including John Severson, Joe Quigg, and Al Merrick—found inspiration from Rincon at one time. Often photographed, this legendary break continues to be a beacon for wide-eyed surfers craving something special and unique along the California coast.

Other Information

Local Surf Shops: Rincon Designs, 659 Linden Ave., Carpinteria; (805) 684-2413. A-Frame Surf Shop, 3785 Santa Claus Lane, Carpinteria; (805) 684-8803.

Places to Stay: The Cliff House Inn, 6602 W. Pacific Coast Hwy., Mussel Shoals; (800) 892-5433. Holiday Inn Express, 5606 Carpinteria Ave., Carpinteria; (805) 566-9499. Best Western Carpinteria Inn, 4558 Carpinteria Ave., Carpinteria; (805) 684-0473.

Places to Eat: Head either north to Santa Barbara or south to Carpinteria. Cajun Kitchen Cafe, 865 Linden Ave., Carpinteria; (805) 684-6010. Sushi Teri, 970 Linden Ave., Carpinteria; (805) 745-1314. The Cliff House Inn, 6602 W. Pacific Coast Hwy., Mussel Shoals; (800) 892-5433.

Mussell Shoals is located just south of Carpinteria and also just south of the famous point break Rincon. It's similar to Rincon but less crowded and less surfed than its more famous counterpart. The rock bottom makes the break slightly less fast than Rincon but just as enjoyable to ride. Bring a long or short board and try to hit it during low to medium tides.

Elizabeth Pepin Silva

Just off US 101 and the Seacliff exit sits a small break called Stanley's. Locals sometimes refer to it as Offramps. Without the right conditions, you wouldn't even know Stanley's was there. With a western swell and at low tide, however, a shortboard can tear through this spot's quick right. If you see it breaking from the road, stop and take advantage of it.

Lucia Griggi

Located in Hobson's County Park, Hobson's is pretty much a dud of a break, but it is a cheap place to stay if you're surfing in the area. Its shores extend outward to a rocky reef that rarely spits out anything remotely worth surfing. Still, in a medium-to-high tide with a strong overhead swell, Hobson's can break—and there usually aren't many others around to crowd your space.

Pitas Point

Pitas Point is a fast right, with super-hollow tubes that spit up mean closeouts.

Best tide: Low
Best swell direction: West, northwest
Best wave size: Head high and above
Bottom: Sand and rock
Type of break: Point, right
Skill level: Intermediate to advanced
Best boards: Shortboard, longboard
Best seasons: Fall and winter
Crowds: Uncrowded
Water quality: Average
Hazards: None
Fees and permits: None

Finding the Break

From Ventura: Take US 101 north to the State Beaches exit. You cannot exit at State Beaches heading south from Santa Barbara. Continue straight past Emma Wood to Faria Park Campground or park along the shoulder of the road where it opens up. GPS: N34 19.108 / W119 23.405

Surf Description

Pitas Point isn't your typical northern Ventura County beach. It doesn't offer up very consistent conditions, and its best wave comes around only a few times a year. It has limited facilities and is really much better as a place to surf for a few hours than somewhere to hang out all day or camp. The shoreline is covered in cobblestones, and the rocky shore is covered with skin-piercing barnacles. Accessing Pitas Point is also difficult, so the crowd factor tends to be nonexistent.

Depending on the conditions, Pitas Point can be a fast hollow wave or, on smaller days, a nice easy trickler that is great for beginners. Pitas really pumps in fall and winter, when the point spits out super-hollow barrels that form great tubes. The wave can get extremely fast at peak low tide and will often close out before you have a chance to bust out the backside of the barrel. The cobblestone and—in some spots—sand bottom lets the wave hold shape throughout the ride. The predominant conditions make for smaller good-quality surf. The reef prefers a western swell direction and requires some skill to surf well. It's a good spot for short- or long-boarders.

At Faria you can walk out of your tent and into the lineup. A camper tests the waters on a fine winter day with overhead west swell lines.

The Carpinteria area offers good local deepwater fishing. Just off the Ventura County shoreline lie the Ventura Flats. The Pacific Ocean is like a nightclub for white sea bass, halibut, and other Pacific fish. Just 15 miles farther west is an underwater mountain range near the Anacapa Islands. The area serves as a breeding ground for fish and other marine life and is often crowded with fishing boats on weekends. If you prefer to stay near shore, try looking for kelp forests. The kelp provides shelter and protection for many species of marine life, but getting lines snagged in the beds can be a problem.

Pitas Point has drawn some heavy comparisons to famous hollow breaks around the world. On unusually low-tide days or during a heavy winter swell, Pitas can unleash some 5-second-plus tube rides.

Other Information

Local Surf Shops: Lots of shops in Santa Barbara and Ventura, but none along here.
Places to Stay: Faria County Beach Park, 4350 W. Pacific Coast Hwy., Ventura; (805) 654-3951.
Places to Eat: Stock up in Santa Barbara if you are heading south, or Ventura if you are heading north.

SUPDATE: VENTURA COUNTY

There are a lot of right point breaks in Ventura County that would be heaven on a standup paddleboard—but these spots are already hellishly crowded, and standup paddleboarders are even hated by longboarders. If you are on your toes and are willing to go midday, midweek, or during bad tides and bad winds, it's possible to get waves at famous spots like Rincon, Pitas Point, and California Street. But if you do the *homo erectus* thing on a firing crowded day, it will be less than fun.

There are surf spots in Ventura that are more SUPpropriate than others. Mondos is the spot at the very inside of Pitas Point—a long, shifting, easy wave that has become popular, and acceptable—for standup paddlers in Ventura County. And if the surf is really pumping, you might want to venture north up along the point toward Pitas and pick off those stray waves that surfers have missed, fallen on, etc. Be clever on a SUP and you can get lots of waves without causing unrest.

That long stretch of open coast between Santa Barbara and Ventura has a lot of opportunities for SUP—from beach breaks that are hard to get to or not interesting to surfers, all the way up to Ventura Overhead—a big shifty wave that would be a lot of fun on a SUP.

Ventura surf spots suffer from crowds during big swells, but SUP offers access to waves that surfers can't get to, so take advantage and you too can find the perfect wave on the perfect day and be alone with the surf and your thoughts.

Solimar

Easily seen from US 101 above is Solimar. A large expanse of beach and rock blankets the stretch of beach break to the Solimar Reef, allowing for lefts and rights.

Best tides: Low to medium

Best swell direction: Southwest, west, northwest

Best wave size: Any

Bottom: Sand and rock

Type of break: Outside, beach break, point lefts and rights

Skill level: Novice to intermediate when under head height; advanced when the surf is head high or larger

Best board: Shortboard

Best seasons: Fall and summer

Crowds: Can get crowded on weekends

Water quality: Average

Hazards: Kelp at lower tides

Fees and permits: None

Finding the Break

From Ventura: Head north on US 101 and look for the State Beaches exit. Look for the fence set back from CA 1. There are dirt lots along Solimar Beach; try to park in the southernmost. GPS: N34 18.469 / W119 21.194

Surf Description

Sandwiched between Emma Wood State Beach Park and Faria Beach Park, Solimar is a southwest-facing beach along northern Ventura County's open coast. The beach area looks out toward Anacapa Island, and the moderate ocean temperature at Solimar Beach makes the area a great place for swimming, surfing, and fishing. There's plenty of parking along Old Highway 1, which runs along the shoreline, but there are no camping facilities, water stations, or showers. The beach is mostly sand, but with some rock and cobblestone mixed in.

Solimar Beach has several breaks, depending on swell conditions. The beach is well spread out, and there's usually plenty of room to pick your spot. The beach break gets driven by wind swells and is somewhat mushy. The sand and rock reefs prefer a west swell, either directly or from the north or south. Farther outside is Solimar Point, which can provide a good left. When it's breaking well, it can be a little crowded, but the wave is worth it, sliding down the line on a longboard. All the way outside is

Soul sister styling sunny Solimar. (Say it three times fast. Surfer is Mary Osborne.)
Elizabeth Pepin Silva

Solimar Reef, which breaks about 1,000 feet offshore. Solimar is easy to see from US 101, so checking out the surf conditions does not require you to drive down to the beach.

Near Solimar, CA 33 takes you inland to the small town of Ojai. Ojai was one of the earliest settlement towns in Ventura County, dating back to the late nineteenth century. The Ojai area was originally settled by farmers and merchants and became an important connector between the gateways of Los Angeles and Los Padres National Forest. Ojai is known for being an artistic community with very progressive political and environmental thinking.

Lucia Griggi

Summer Beach sounds a lot better than it actually is. When it isn't flooding during winter storms or heavy rains, it produces mushy lefts and the occasional right or closeout. For the latter, bring your shortboard; for larger swells that mush, a longboard is a better choice.

Lucia Griggi

Emma Wood sounds like a nice children's beach, but it's nothing like it sounds. There are few breaks in California when the surf is so monstrous. Few folks even have the strength to paddle out and catch one of California's big waves—it's 0.25 mile out. When the tide is low and the swell is beyond pumping out of the west, you'll need a small gun or fast longboard to catch these steep, funneling lefts.

Other Information

Local Surf Shops: Lots of shops in Santa Barbara and Ventura.

Places to Stay: Emma Wood State Beach (North Beach), 900 W. Main St., Ventura; (800) 444-7275. Self-contained vehicle camping only; no tents.

Places to Eat: Solimar has a few spots to grab some food. Also consider Ojai, which is only 20 minutes from the beach. Suzanne's Cuisine, 502 W. Ojai Ave., Ojai; (805) 640-1961.

California Street

Located near the Ventura County Fairgrounds, California Street is a mix of sand and cobblestone. The waves range from solid point breaks to peaky beach-break A-frames.

Best tides: Low to medium

Best swell direction: Southwest, west, northwest

Best wave size: Waist high to slightly overhead

Bottom: Rock and sand

Type of break: Outside, left and right

Skill level: Novice to advanced

Best boards: Shortboard, funshape, longboard

Best seasons: Fall and winter

Crowds: Crowded

Water quality: Clean

Hazards: Locals

Fees and permits: Parking may require a fee.

Finding the Break

From Ventura: Exit US 101 at California Street. Look for SAN BUENAVENTURA BEACH PARK or COUNTY FAIRGROUNDS signs. There's metered and street parking. You can also park at the fairgrounds. GPS: N34 16.519 / W119 17.961

Surf Description

Located just in front of the Ventura County Fairgrounds, California Street is a scenic and convenient break. Years back this was a favorite surfing spot of Ventura locals. Some of the area's best would surf at California Street because of its superior conditions and easy access uninhibited by urban development. Over time, however, the entire California Street area was developed into a seaside recreation area for residents and tourists. Parking isn't a factor now, but the meters are pricey and some have time restrictions. Once you're down at the beach, you can walk along the shoreline path or venture down onto the sand-and-cobblestone shore. Near the pier there are plenty of restaurants and amenities that come with beach modernization.

California Street is a series of breaks, starting with Pipe and working down through Stables and California Street. The breaks are spread out generously, so be prepared to pick your spot. Pipe is the most consistent, but—depending on wave conditions—there are breaks for every ability level and board type. Pipe picks up fall and winter swells the best and will produce a strong right. The wave will wall up better in higher surf and at low to mid-tide. Rumor has it that on perfect days, you can surf from Pipe all the way to California Street, but others will say this is just an unfair Ventura comparison to Rincon.

Below Pipe is Stables. Acting much like a little brother to Pipe, it will hold a wave similar to Pipe, but only if the swell impact zone is headed farther south. On days where the breeze is flowing offshore, you'll quickly smell why they call it Stables.

Ventura County is not lacking for right point breaks. But where Rincon and Pitas Point are generally dormant during the summer because of the Channel Islands, summer swells do leak into the California Street window, making it a year-round surf spot.
Chris Burkard

Below Stables are California Street and Inside Point. Both breaks are mushy rights that are good beginner surfing zones. When the swell comes in a little larger, both California Street and particularly Inside Point well up steep but gentle takeoffs that are great for shortboarding. In any other conditions, you need only your longboard—and watch your dismounts at low tide if you like to ride 'em close to shore. If you're in the area at the beginning of August, the Ventura County Fair is held on the fairgrounds. The area is also referred to as Seaside Park.

Other Information

Local Surf Shops: Ventura Surf Shop, 88 E. Thompson Blvd., Ventura; (805) 643-1062. Wavefront Surf Shop, 154 E. Thompson Blvd., Ventura; (805) 652-1168. Seaward Surf and Sport, 1082 S. Seaward Ave., Ventura; (805) 648-4742. Rip Curl Ventura, 227 S. California St., Ventura; (805) 648-6145.
Places to Stay: Holiday Inn, 450 E. Harbor Blvd., Ventura; (805) 648-7731. Motel 6, 2145 Harbor Blvd., Ventura; (805) 643-7017.
Places to Eat: Jonathan's at Peirano's Mediterranean Cuisine, 204 E. Main St., Ventura; (805) 648-4853.

South Jetty

South Jetty can produce some fun waves with the right conditions—but rarely does. It was better before the breakwater line was extended in the mid-1990s.

Best tide: Low
Best swell direction: Northwest, west
Best wave size: Head high to slightly overhead
Bottom: Sand
Type of break: Outside, left
Skill level: Intermediate to advanced
Best board: Shortboard
Best seasons: Fall and winter
Crowds: Uncrowded
Water quality: Average
Hazards: None
Fees and permits: None

Northeast winds blow offshore at South Jetty, and when there is swell from the west/
southwest, this is the result.   Chris Burkard

Finding the Break

From Ventura: Head south on US 101 to the East Harbor Boulevard exit. Take East
Harbor until you reach the South Jetty. You'll see all the boat masts peeking their
heads above the house rooflines. GPS: N34 14.177 / W119 15.918

Surf Description

South Jetty is a well-maintained sandy beach placed right in front of rows of brightly
colored seaside homes. Parking and access are conveniently located just off US 101.
As you exit the freeway, you can follow East Harbor Boulevard. From there you can
park along the street or find a smaller parking lot near the beach shower and restroom facilities. Once you arrive you'll notice several breakwater walls offshore. You
should be able to easily recognize the South Jetty groin.

South Jetty is a breakwater surf spot that breaks only under specific conditions. A north-to-northwest swell direction needs to come down and bounce or wall up along the jetty wall. This swell direction, along with a low tide, can produce a small, mushy left. It's best when storm swells come down from the north and the wind comes from the east to hold the lackluster shape together. Most of the time South Jetty isn't worth trying. It's another symbol of what modern maritime commerce has done to the surf breaks in Southern California.

Ventura's beaches and harbor are oriented such that waves originating from the west cause sediment to move down the coastline. During most of the year, this natural phenomenon sends clean beach sand from northern county beaches toward southern county beaches. Along the way, most of this sand settles along various beaches, but ocean currents often leave large deposits near the Ventura Harbor, including the South Jetty area. Consequently, the harborways between the jetties are dredged on an annual basis. Dredged material, particularly sand, is clean, but it's a visual nuisance for surfers near the harbor—not to mention the diesel fuel that gets spilled from time to time.

Other Information

Local Surf Shops: Ventura Surf Shop, 88 E. Thompson Blvd., Ventura; (805) 643-1062. Wavefront Surf Shop, 154 E. Thompson Blvd., Ventura; (805) 652-1168. Seaward Surf and Sport, 1082 S. Seaward Ave., Ventura; (805) 648-4742. Rip Curl Ventura, 227 S. California St., Ventura; (805) 648-6145.

Places to Stay: Motel 6, 2145 Harbor Blvd., Ventura; (805) 643-5100. McGrath State Beach Park Campgrounds, 5 miles south of Ventura off US 101 via Harbor Boulevard, Oxnard; (805) 968-1033.

Places to Eat: Pacifico Bar and Restaurant, 2055 Harbor Blvd., Ventura; (805) 643-6000. Vagabond Restaurant, 760 E. Thompson Blvd., Ventura; (805) 643-1390.

Santa Clara

Located right at the river mouth near the Ventura Harbor, Santa Clara is a large sandbar break that produces lefts and rights.

Best tides: Low to medium
Best swell direction: Southwest, west
Best wave size: Any
Bottom: Sand
Type of break: Outside, beach break, left and right
Skill level: Novice to advanced

Best boards: Shortboard
Best seasons: Fall and winter
Crowds: Can get crowded on weekends
Water quality: Poor
Hazards: Poor water quality
Fees and permits: According to yelp.com, there is a nominal parking fee at McGrath State Beach Park.

Finding the Break

From Ventura: Take US 101 south to the Victoria exit. Take Victoria south until you reach Olivas Park Drive. Turn right onto Olivas Park, continue to the T, and go left on East Harbor until you see the river mouth. You can park at McGrath State Beach Park or backtrack a bit, turn left onto Spinnaker Drive, and park at Surfer's Knoll. GPS: N34 13.713 / W119 15.622

Surf Description

Located an easy 1-hour drive north of Los Angeles and in the middle of Ventura County, Santa Clara is an excellent break for surfing. Originally called San Buenaventura, Ventura acts as the central hub for the southern part of the county. Next to the harbor, Santa Clara's shore offers up a long stretch of sandy beach and sandbar breaks. With plenty of beach facilities near the harbor area, Santa Clara is a good family-oriented beach with room to spread out.

Due to its ever-changing bottom, the break will shift depending on wind, rain, and current. Normally, Santa Clara produces fairly average lefts and rights, but when the sandbar lines up, it can be incredible. Santa Clara is best at lower tides and holds up really well when the wind is light to nonexistent. The predictability factor of the shifting sandbar makes for either a great day of surfing or just an average one. Like most of Ventura County, the break favors a westerly swell. Although fall and winter are the most consistent seasons, summer can bring reasonable surf as well.

Beach erosion is a big problem for California beaches, and Ventura County has not been spared. The Santa Clara River runs right down from its headwaters near Acton directly into the Pacific Ocean. Flowing almost directly west for more than 100 miles, the river is augmented by small tributaries from the Santa Susanna Mountains. Since the Santa Clara is a natural river and has not been directed or supported with concrete slabs, the water runs thick with sediment, which is ultimately carried to the coast. A good portion of this sediment comes in the form of sand.

Chris Burkard

Oxnard only gets going during the fall when a southwest swell comes up from down under. Bring the fastest shortboard you have and rip the speedy left down the line. Don't worry about pulling out your biggest aerial tricks; the sand bottom is more forgiving than some of Ventura's other breaks. Just don't take a header at low tide.

Chris Sardelis

Silver Strand *warning:* If you are not surfing with a local and you're not in the water on a weekend when you can blend in with other outsiders, turn back. Silver Strand's wide U-shaped mouth creates one of Ventura's best breaks. The Jetty, Bowl, and Strip all produce great rides, especially in mid-tide with a west-to-northwest swell. The best time to surf here (at your own risk) is fall and winter.

One of the best spots south of the Point Conception line, the Santa Clara River mouth goes both ways—not that there's anything wrong with that.   Chris Burkard

Other Information

Local Surf Shops: Ventura Surf Shop, 88 E. Thompson Blvd., Ventura; (805) 643-1062. Wavefront Surf Shop, 154 E. Thompson Blvd., Ventura; (805) 652-1168. Seaward Surf and Sport, 1082 S. Seaward Ave., Ventura; (805) 648-4742. Rip Curl Ventura, 227 S. California St., Ventura; (805) 648-6145.

Places to Stay: Motel 6, 2145 Harbor Blvd., Ventura; (805) 643-7017. McGrath State Beach Park Campgrounds, 5 miles south of Ventura off US 101 via Harbor Boulevard, Oxnard; (805) 968-1033.

Places to Eat: Pacifico Bar and Restaurant, 2055 Harbor Blvd., Ventura; (805) 643-6000. Vagabond Restaurant, 760 E. Thompson Blvd., Ventura; (805) 643-1390.

Port Hueneme

Port Hueneme is the southernmost beach city in Ventura County. It's composed of a pier and a long stretch of sand that runs north until it reaches the port jetty walls.

Best tide: Medium

Best swell direction: West, southwest

Best wave size: Any
Bottom: Sand
Type of break: Beach break, outside, lefts and rights
Skill level: Intermediate to advanced
Best boards: Shortboard
Best seasons: Fall and summer
Crowds: Uncrowded
Water quality: Average
Hazards: None
Fees and permits: None

Finding the Break

From Oxnard: Take CA 1 south and exit at East Hueneme Road. Head west toward the beach and military bases. Turn left onto North Ventura Road and keep going on South Ventura Road until it ends at the beach. Parking is easy—just pick your spot. GPS: N34 08.583 / W119 11.665

A lot of choices for watermen on a wind swell day at Port Hueneme. Elizabeth Pepin Silva

Surf Description

Port Hueneme's surf break is located along the 50-acre Hueneme Beach Park. The beach park is relatively easy to access from CA 1 or US 101. At the south end of Ventura County, Port Hueneme is the last major city along the Ventura County coastline. Near the park the surfing is consistent and varied from shore break to pier-piling performance waves. The area is quiet, but there is ample parking right along the beach, as well as restaurants and lodging. Along the beach you'll find some shower facilities and lifeguard stations.

> **The local vibe in Port Hueneme used to be strong and aggressive. The area made surfing-world news a few years back when a local surfer head-butted and broke the ribs of an out-of-towner. Be on your best behavior.**

Port Hueneme has a few different breaks. Those along the beach area will deliver short lefts and rights, depending on the swell direction. Farther from the main pier area, there's plenty of room to spread out. The break improves in summer, but it can also hold a good winter swell from the north or northwest. Swells from the northwest can sometimes get blocked a little by the Channel Islands, but this is rare; the break all along the shoreline can catch almost any swell. Near the pier the ride tends to well up a little better, with conditions being best at mid-tide.

Crowds are rarely a factor, and the pier area can be a particularly good place for beginners when the water temperature is up and the swell is from the south.

The port of Hueneme is the last and only deepwater harbor between Los Angeles and San Francisco. Even though it's not centrally located, it is the main point of entry for California's central and Ventura coasts. If you come to California and rent a car, chances are that car arrived via Port Hueneme—automobiles are one of the port's main imported products. If you surf the port area, especially on the north end of the beach, do not be surprised to see large container vessels and cargo ships slip on by throughout the daylight hours.

Other Information

Local Surf Shops: Anacapa Surf 'n Sport, 260 S. Surfside Dr., Port Hueneme; (805) 488-2702. Ventura Surf Shop, 88 E. Thompson Blvd., Ventura; (805) 643-1062. Beach Break Surf Shop, 1559 Spinnaker Dr. #108, Ventura; (805) 650-6641.
Places to Stay: Country Inn, 350 E. Hueneme Rd., Port Hueneme; (805) 986-5353.
Places to Eat: Antonio's Mexican, 423 Port Hueneme Rd., Port Hueneme; (805) 488-1405.

Point Mugu

Point Mugu is an isolated break near the Point Mugu Military Base. The break is a fast closeout that can be gentler if a nice easterly wind blows.

Best tides: Low to medium

Best swell direction: West

Best wave size: Waist high to slightly overhead

Bottom: Sand

Type of break: Outside, left and right

Skill level: Intermediate to advanced

Best board: Shortboard

Best seasons: Fall and winter

Crowds: Uncrowded

Water quality: Clean

Hazards: None

Fees and permits: None

Finding the Break

From Oxnard: Take CA 1 south until you see signs for Point Mugu. Don't park anywhere near the base—your car will be towed. GPS: N34 05.134 / W119 03.656

Surf Description

Along the beach side of the Santa Monica Mountain Range, Point Mugu State Park is located about 15 miles south of Oxnard on CA 1. Point Mugu features approximately 5 miles of open ocean shoreline. Access is limited to one main entry point between the rock outcropping marking Point Mugu and the military base. The shoreline consists of rocky bluffs mixed in with sandy beaches, some sand dunes, and a steep hillside backdrop along the inland side.

Surfing here is limited to the stretch of beach between Point Mugu's giant pointed rock outcropping and the Point Mugu Military Base. The surf in front of the base is now closed, and we can only imagine how the break is for those enlisted in the military. Point Mugu is a sandbar break that washes up onto a long sand-and-rock beach. Mostly producing peaky beach breaks, the wave tends to close out and isn't worth the haul in small-surf conditions. This doesn't happen often, but it will break better in larger swells from overhead to double overhead. Surfing in front of the point at Point Mugu is difficult because of limited access points, fishing lines from above, and better surf elsewhere along the beach.

The Santa Monica Mountains National Recreation Area serves as the backdrop to Point Mugu. The park area is a joint effort among federal, state, and local park agencies. These agencies work with private landowners who have grandfathered land rights to protect the natural ecosystem and seashore. Even during Southern California downpours, the seashore doesn't experience toxic runoff like other areas. Most of the vegetation is under a constant Mediterranean-like climate, which promotes the growth of wild grasses as well as sycamore, oak, and walnut trees. There are many hiking trails; information is readily available at the national park visitor center in Thousand Oaks.

Other Information

Local Surf Shops: Anacapa Surf 'n Sport, 260 S. Surfside Dr., Port Hueneme; (805) 488-2702. Ventura Surf Shop, 88 E. Thompson Blvd., Ventura; (805) 643-1062. Beach Break Surf Shop, 1559 Spinnaker Dr. #108, Ventura; (805) 650-6641.
Places to Stay: Country Inn, 350 E. Hueneme Rd., Port Hueneme; (805) 986-5353.
Places to Eat: Antonio's Mexican, 123 Port Hueneme Rd., Port Hueneme; (805) 488-1405.

Off-limits Point Mugu quality, worth getting chased by the military police, going to Leavenworth, and just wrecking your life over in general.   Chris Sardelis

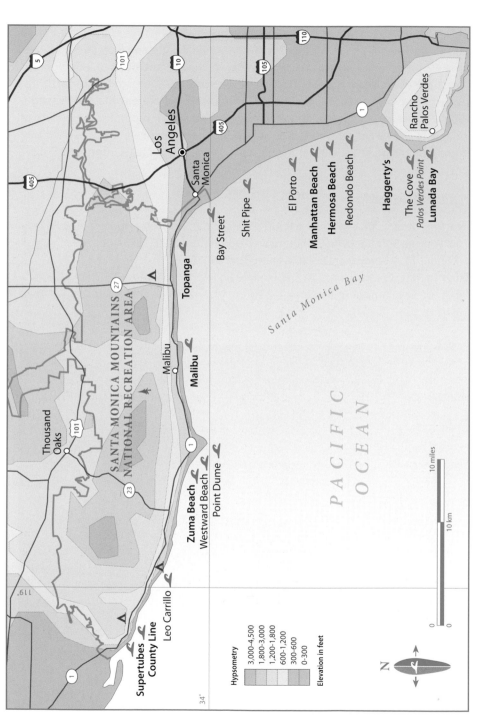

Region 8 (Los Angeles County)

REGION 8: LOS ANGELES COUNTY

Los Angeles County surfing is exactly what you'd imagine it to be. Some of the world's most legendary surf spots, like Malibu, reside here, but ironically, most of Los Angeles County sits in a giant sideways J-shaped bay that collects the pollution and river runoff of its nearly ten million residents. Los Angeles County starts just south of Point Mugu and works its way along CA 1 to the rocky cliff shores of Palos Verdes. Starting in north LA County, most of the breaks can be seen from CA 1. South of Leo Carrillo, along the coast, CA 1 snakes along the shoreline to one side and multimillion-dollar estates to the other. As you move east and south into the more populous Los Angeles Basin past Topanga, the beaches become more crowded and the water goes from blue to brown. Los Angeles is one of the most developed counties in the United States. Farther south past Will Rogers State Beach, LA's swanky coast morphs from spread out to cramped, with housing and apartments packed so tight, you barely have room for parking.

The Los Angeles County coastline is exactly what you'd imagine it to be: mild if not sunny winters followed by pure blue-sky springs and hot summers. The coast typically stays cooler than inland locations by ten to fifteen degrees. Don't be surprised in May and June if the entire coast is covered with a thin marine layer that the locals refer to as June Gloom. Los Angeles can get windy in the afternoons, which wreaks havoc on surf conditions. Beaches tend to fill with nice grainy sand, except for the breaks north of Topanga; here you'll find a combination of sand and rock reef. There really isn't a bad time of year in Los Angeles, although most locals freak out when the temperature outside drops below sixty.

Malibu, Santa Monica, Marina Del Rey, Venice, Manhattan, Hermosa, Redondo, and Palos Verdes are the main cities along the Los Angeles coastline. All the surf breaks described in this section are easily accessible by car or by foot, but it will take you a long time to get there and a long time to park. This is LA, which means traffic 24 hours a day, seven days a week. As for the local talent, it is LA, for God's sake. There are so many actors-by-day/waitstaff-by-night here, you're bound to find whatever you want whenever you want it. There isn't much of a local vibe except at the end of the county. The northern section of Los Angeles County is very mellow, picturesque, and pleasant. The farther south you go, the more LA it becomes, until it transitions again in Palos Verdes, where the houses get big and so does the vibe in some spots. Los Angeles can be reached by almost any freeway. If you fly in to Los Angeles International Airport, airplanes do take off right over the beach, so you'll be close to just about everything.

Ben Marcus

Yoga guru Alex "Aflex" Westmore strikes a poised pose during golden hour on a winter afternoon between the Malibu Pier and First Point at Surfrider Beach.

Overall Surf Description

The first thing you should know about Los Angeles surfing is that it's not like the movies. No matter where you go, there will be crowds, and the water temperature is pretty cool. Unless you have a thick skin, you'll need a wet suit and a variety of surf-boards. Due to the different directional breaks, the region can be divided into two areas: Los Angeles Basin breaks (Bay Street to Lunada Bay) and North County breaks (Topanga to Supertubes). It's pretty simple, really: Los Angeles Basin breaks work best with westerly swells, while North County breaks work best with swells coming from the south. The good news about the region is that you can find surf here year-round, depending on swell direction and size. Santa Ana winds can destroy even the best swell, however, and it's not a good idea to surf after it rains. Every drainpipe and runoff flows toward the beach; things can get downright toxic after a heavy rain. Crowds are always a factor, but the best time is weekdays from late morning to early afternoon.

Fall Surf

It doesn't take a genius to figure out why fall is the best time of year to surf here. The air temperature is perfect, the water temperature is nice, and the swell direction is usually coming in perfectly for the entire region. You still get some reasonably strong Santa Ana winds and the crowd factor is high, but you can longboard in Malibu all day or go to Disneyland for the day and surf at dusk.

Winter Surf

Winter produces the best surf, but the temperature drops outside as well as in the water. Most of the winter swells will come out of the north or west, which makes surfing in any part of the county appealing. North County point breaks can be movie-like, but the runoff can be brutal. If you do surf after it rains, make sure you've had all your shots.

Spring Surf

Spring surf in the region is determined by wind and swell direction. For the most part, it's fair and small. If you're lucky enough to get a monster South Pacific swell, you will not be disappointed—nearly all breaks will be booming, up to double overhead in certain spots.

Summer Surf

Summer surf here isn't much better than spring, but the temperature rises both in and out of the water, making for some nice scenery at the beach. More often than not, summer brings afternoon winds, so your best bet if you find a break you like is to surf it in the morning and take the afternoon off to go sightseeing.

Average Temperatures for Region (Los Angeles County)		
	Air (Los Angeles)	Water (Los Angeles)
Jan	68	58
Feb	70	58
Mar	73	60
Apr	73	61
May	75	61
June	80	64
July	84	66
Aug	85	68
Sept	83	67
Oct	79	66
Nov	73	64
Dec	69	60

Supertubes

Supertubes is a remote break just off CA 1. It can produce fast, solid, hollowed-out rights under medium to large swells and a low tide. Otherwise it's flat but scenic.

Best tide: Low

Best swell direction: Northwest

Best wave size: Waist high to slightly overhead

Bottom: Sand and rock

Type of break: Point, right

Skill level: Advanced

Best board: Shortboard

Best season: Winter

Crowds: Uncrowded

Water quality: Clean

Hazards: Exposed rock outcroppings at low tide

Fees and permits: None

A rare secret spot somewhere on the LA side of Mugu Rock. Rare because secret spots in Southern California are rare, and rare because it breaks only rarely.   Chris Sardelis

Finding the Break

From Los Angeles: Head north on CA 1. Supertubes is off CA 1 at the northernmost point of Los Angeles County. Take CA 1 until you see a small rock outcropping before Point Mugu. Parking is only available along CA 1 or on a few of the dirt shoulders. GPS: N34 05.073 / W119 03.077

Surf Description

I is the best letter to describe Supertubes. *Isolated, inconsistent,* but *incredible* are all perfect adjectives to define the break here. Located just north of the Los Angeles County line, Supertubes sits at the bottom of the giant rock outcropping known as Point Mugu. The area is isolated from any part of Los Angeles or Ventura County. It's a good 20-minute drive in either direction to get to any reasonable semblance of a convenience store, supermarket, or gas station. All of this bodes very well for the crowd factor: There isn't much of one.

Being located well away from any housing runoffs or traffic makes Supertubes' water clean, unless it has just rained. Timing is everything at Supertubes. If you catch the right swell direction from the northwest and the swell size is chest high to double overhead, you will get one of the best-shaped rights with hollow tubes in all California. Supertubes then has just what the name implies: fast, hollow rights that blast off the underwater rock reef forming the point at Point Mugu. Under any other conditions, though, Supertubes doesn't do much. The occasional west or southwest cross swell will bump up a mushy crumbler, but it's not worth the trek. If you're lucky enough to be in the area when it breaks, pray you have your board on your roof rack and your wet suit in the car.

> There are several hiking trails and recreation areas near Supertubes. Go to Thornhill Broome State Beach, park or camp, and hit some of the trails in Sycamore Arroyo Verde Canyons.

Due to its isolated location, marine life in the area thrives, which is great if you're standing on the shore looking for dolphins—but note that the area has also seen some limited shark activity. Although there have been few reported shark attacks in Los Angeles County and only one fatality in the last twenty years off the Malibu area, sharks are not uncommon here.

Other Information

Local Surf Shops: Zuma Jay's, 22775 Pacific Coast Hwy., Malibu; (310) 456-8044. Becker's Malibu, 23755 Malibu Rd., Malibu; (310) 456-7155. Malibu Surf Shack, 22935 Pacific Coast Hwy., Malibu; (310) 456-8508. Drill Surf & Skate, 30765 Pacific Coast Hwy., Malibu; (310) 457-7715. Clout Rideshop, 29575 Pacific Coast Hwy., Malibu; (310) 457-1151.

Places to Stay: Hotels are expensive in Malibu. Even the RV parks are expensive in Malibu. Malibu Beach RV Park, 25801 Pacific Coast Hwy., Malibu; (310) 456-6052. Point Mugu State Park, 9000 W. Pacific Coast Hwy., Malibu; (818) 880-0350. Better to look for a cheaper hotel over the hill in Thousand Oaks or the Valley.

Places to Eat: Neptune's Net, 42505 Pacific Coast Hwy., Malibu; (310) 457-3095. Malibu Kitchen, 3900 Cross Creek Rd., Malibu; (310) 456-7845. Nobu, 22706 Pacific Coast Hwy., Malibu; (310) 317-9140.

County Line

County Line is a small rock-and-sand outside break that rolls in around a point of land just to the north of the main beach. Small in terms of beach area, the break will hold almost any wave, big or small.

Best tide: Medium
Best swell direction: South, southwest
Best wave size: Waist high to slightly overhead
Bottom: Sand and rock
Type of break: Beach break, point, left and right
Skill level: Novice to intermediate
Best boards: Longboard, shortboard, funshape
Best season: Fall
Crowds: Can get crowded on weekends
Water quality: Average
Hazards: None
Fees and permits: None

Finding the Break

From Los Angeles: Head north on CA 1 until you see the Los Angeles–Ventura County Line signs. Look for Neptune's Net restaurant; the break is directly across. There's plenty of parking near the break right off CA 1. GPS: N34 03.159 / W118 57.744

In Los Angeles you will never be lonely on a wave with the County Line crowd.
Chris Burkard

Surf Description

County Line explains your exact geographic location in relation to Ventura and Los Angeles Counties. The first thing anyone will notice about the break—after its precise name—is that it's almost like not being in LA County at all. There are no stores, strip malls, restaurants, or Botox parlors. County Line represents the quiet side of northern Los Angeles County, where the water becomes cleaner, the air is unpolluted, and the pace of life slows dramatically. A lot like Leo Carrillo, the break at County Line tends to be less crowded and less-often surfed than most of the breaks nearby. There aren't many amenities around the beach—with the exception of Neptune's Net, a small restaurant and pub that always has its fair share of motorcycle patrons.

County Line is a fairly consistent break that has three main areas. The cobblestone shore, rock outcroppings, and kelp beds are consistent in all areas of County Line. To the north lies a right filled with kelp beds that offers the best wave. Off the point the break spreads out and pitches a bunch of different wave shapes and sizes. There are a few other quirky spots at County Line, but they require some local knowledge and can put a hurting on you, so they are not recommended. In summer the beach-break area gets more consistent. County Line is a good place to learn how to surf as well. Farther inside the break line on weekends, many Valley dwellers and Angelenos will head here for instruction on how to surf. County Line can break in almost any type of swell, but be careful of the kelp beds if it's breaking farther outside.

Due to its location at the northern end of Los Angeles County, County Line sits amid rolling grass and shrub-lined hillsides with little to no housing development for miles. This is unusual for Los Angeles County, which has decimated the natural beauty of the coastline farther south. You can see from the beaches, water, and many points along CA 1 why so many people who came to California never left. Keep your eyes peeled as you wait for a nice set to come in. It's not unusual to see pods of dolphins

Leo Carrillo is located pretty much on the line between Ventura and LA Counties. It's a right point break that can be seen from CA 1. It tends to be less crowded and less-often surfed than most of the breaks in this section, but it's a nice, shapely wave. Bring a longboard, and watch out for beginners on weekends. Chris Burkard

or the occasional whale swimming only a few hundred feet offshore near Leo Carrillo, County Line, and Supertubes.

Other Information

Local Surf Shops: Zuma Jay's, 22775 Pacific Coast Hwy., Malibu; (310) 456-8044. Becker's Malibu, 23755 Malibu Rd., Malibu; (310) 456-7155. Malibu Surf Shack, 22935 Pacific Coast Hwy., Malibu; (310) 456-8508. Drill Surf & Skate, 30765 Pacific Coast Hwy., Malibu; (310) 457 7715. Clout Rideshop, 29575 Pacific Coast Hwy., Malibu; (310) 457-1151.

Places to Stay: Hotels are expensive in Malibu. Even the RV parks are expensive in Malibu. Malibu Beach RV Park, 25801 Pacific Coast Hwy., Malibu; (310) 456-6052. Point Mugu State Park, 9000 W. Pacific Coast Hwy., Malibu, (818) 880-0350. Better to look for a cheaper hotel over the hill in Thousand Oaks or the Valley.

Places to Eat: Neptune's Net, 42505 Pacific Coast Hwy., Malibu; (310) 457-3095. Malibu Kitchen, 3900 Cross Creek Rd., Malibu, (310) 456-7845. Nobu, 22706 Pacific Coast Hwy., Malibu; (310) 317-9140.

Zuma Beach

Zuma Beach is a popular beach with mostly a hollow closeout break. There's a solid left that breaks fast. When there's a cross swell and winds blow east to offshore, Zuma can line up well.

Best tide: Medium
Best swell direction: West, southwest, south
Best wave size: Any
Bottom: Sand
Type of break: Beach break, left
Skill level: Intermediate to advanced
Best boards: Shortboard, funshape
Best seasons: Fall, spring, and summer
Crowds: Crowded
Water quality: Average
Hazards: None
Fees and permits: None

Finding the Break

From Los Angeles: Head north on CA 1. Zuma Beach is about halfway between Malibu and the Ventura–Los Angeles County line. There is plenty of parking off CA 1 or in several Zuma Beach parking lots. GPS: N34 01.361 / W118 49.872

Surf Description

Located at the northern end of Malibu in Los Angeles County, Zuma Beach is an extremely long, flat valley of beach break that extends for almost 2 miles. The beach area itself is open and sandy. Parking is easy in one of the many lots that line CA 1, and there's plenty of free parking along the road as well. Restrooms, showers, and lifeguard towers are nearly everywhere, making Zuma an excellent place to bring

Not an A+ day by any means, but this is what you'll see when driving by Zuma Beach most days: a peak with more or less shape, with more or less people on it. Zuma has over a mile of this and is a good place to get some space and waves for yourself. Chris Burkard

the whole family for the day. Zuma has a unique Southern California landscape with clear water and great waves that draw crowds from inland just over the mountains in Encino and the valley.

Nestled between two of Malibu's many rolling hills, the break is mostly a closeout that attracts strong winds. Zuma is best with a westerly swell or variation of one. At each end there are a few lefts and rights rolling off the landscape where the sea meets the shoreline, but for the most part the rides along Zuma are short and fast. Wave shapes range from peaky A-frames to total closeouts. The peaks produce a fast left that can close out abruptly on the beach. In smaller surf Zuma is a great beginner spot, but the size must be no more than 2 feet. There's plenty of room to spread out at Zuma, but during the summer the beach can get as crowded as the 405 freeway near LAX. A blackball policy exists at Zuma when the crowds are heavy, so watch for the posted flags. The south end of Zuma has a very strong beach break called Drainpipes, which can be dangerous.

> **Every fall Zuma Beach hosts the Nautica Triathlon, which attracts many of LA's celebrated triathletes—that girl in the one-piece who looks like JLo? That's JLo.**

One of the downsides of Los Angeles County beaches is the water quality. Zuma's water is significantly cleaner than that at most other beaches in the county, like Shit Pipe or even Malibu. Being slightly more north and out of the main Los Angeles Basin, however, the water temperature starts to drop faster than other beaches in the region. It's a small price to pay when you think about the brown and red foam of Zuma's southern cousins.

Other Information

Local Surf Shops: Zuma Jay's, 22775 Pacific Coast Hwy., Malibu; (310) 456-8044. Becker's Malibu, 23755 Malibu Rd., Malibu; (310) 456-7155. Malibu Surf Shack, 22935 Pacific Coast Hwy., Malibu; (310) 456-8508. Drill Surf & Skate, 30765 Pacific Coast Hwy., Malibu; (310) 457-7715. Clout Rideshop, 29575 Pacific Coast Hwy., Malibu; (310) 457-1151.

Places to Stay: Hotels are expensive in Malibu. Even the RV parks are expensive in Malibu. Malibu Beach RV Park, 25801 Pacific Coast Hwy., Malibu; (310) 456-6052. Point Mugu State Park, 9000 W. Pacific Coast Hwy., Malibu; (818) 880-0350. Better to look for a cheaper hotel over the hill in Thousand Oaks or the Valley.

Places to Eat: Neptune's Net, 42505 Pacific Coast Hwy., Malibu; (310) 457-3095. Malibu Kitchen, 3900 Cross Creek Rd., Malibu; (310) 456-7845. Nobu, 22706 Pacific Coast Hwy., Malibu; (310) 317-9140.

Lucia Griggi

Westward Beach is a beach break just north of Point Dume; there are signs off US 101. It can generate very hollow, tubing waves and works best with a waist-high to slightly overhead swell at medium tide. This break can capture swell from virtually any direction but is most consistent in winter. Westward Beach can be a heavy beach break that requires skill and experience.

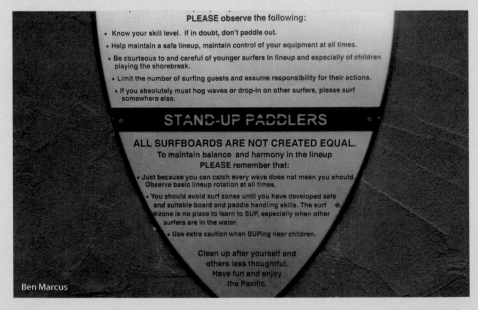

PLEASE observe the following:

- Know your skill level. If in doubt, don't paddle out.
- Help maintain a safe lineup, maintain control of your equipment at all times.
- Be courteous to and careful of younger surfers in lineup and especially of children playing the shorebreak.
- Limit the number of surfing guests and assume responsibility for their actions.
- If you absolutely must hog waves or drop-in on other surfers, please surf somewhere else.

STAND-UP PADDLERS

ALL SURFBOARDS ARE NOT CREATED EQUAL.
To maintain balance and harmony in the lineup
PLEASE remember that:

- Just because you can catch every wave does not mean you should. Observe basic lineup rotation at all times.
- You should avoid surf zones until you have developed safe and suitable board and paddle handling skills. The surf zone is no place to learn to SUP, especially when other surfers are in the water.
- Use extra caution when SUPing near children.

Clean up after yourself and
others less thoughtful.
Have fun and enjoy
the Pacific.

Ben Marcus

Point Dume is a point break north of Malibu. The best way to access Point Dume is to park at Westward Beach and walk south. There are numerous quality peaks at this spot that catch swell year-round. Most of the breaks work best with a waist- to head-high swell at a low to medium tide.

SUPDATE: LOS ANGELES COUNTY

Like Santa Cruz and most other places in the populated areas of California, there are beaches and surf spots where standup paddlers are welcome and some where they're not. In Los Angeles County the Point Dume area has had its problems with standup paddlers. This semiprivate stretch of coast is still protected by locals in a kind of old-school localism.

The surfers at Dume don't really like outsiders at all, so when standup paddlers began showing up in ones and threes and by the dozen, it caused friction. It's a problem because Dume is a shifting, rolling wave that backs off and moves around, and that makes it pretty good for SUP, which can cover a lot of distance.

In the Malibu area Latigo Point is a popular, less troublesome spot for standup paddlers. It is also a shifting, kind of flat-faced wave that surfers have trouble catching and riding sometimes, but standup paddlers love it. Just be sure to wear a good leash because if you lose your board at high tide here, it's history.

At Surfrider Beach standup paddlers avoid the shortboard waves at Second and Third Points, and those that dare go into the surf stick to First Point. That's not a problem on small days, but a SUPista at First Point on a big day is trouble brewing. An adventurous standup paddler could find a wave alone at Zuma or at a lot of the hidden breaks along the Malibu coast that are hard to get to, and hard to see, but are there for someone who wants to go looking.

The long stretch of beach from Santa Monica to Torrance has lots of opportunities for standup paddlers who want to get away from crowds and get waves to themselves. Along the Palos Verdes Peninsula, SUP are not going to be welcome at competitive shortboard spots like Haggerty's and Lunada Bay. Carrying your board down the cliffs to PV Cove is an option but again: Use your SUP as an exploratory tool and you'll be able to find some waves along the peninsula with no one riding them.

For inland paddlers, Marina Del Rey can be a lot of fun. Launch from wherever, check out all the luxury yachts and cruise all the way out to the ocean for a bit of exercise.

Malibu

Malibu is one of the world's most famous long, lazy point breaks. It's a wave that holds nearly any size swell. The break starts just off the point near the lifeguard station.

Best tide: Medium

Best swell direction: Southwest, west, south

Best wave size: Any

Bottom: Sand

Type of break: Point, right

Skill level: Intermediate to advanced

Best boards: Longboard, shortboard

Best seasons: Fall, spring, and summer

Crowds: Crowded

Water quality: Poor

Hazards: Crowds

Fees and permits: None

Finding the Break

From Los Angeles: Head north on CA 1. Look for signs that say Malibu or just look for the Malibu Pier from the road. Park in one of the many lots off CA 1—but note that they fill up fast. GPS: N34 02.230 / W118 40.604

Surf Description

Malibu is one of the world's most famous breaks. Hollywood films, magazine pictorials, and an entire generation of America grew up with Malibu as the focal point for California surfing culture. Malibu was arguably the epicenter of 1950s and 1960s surf culture. Surfing legends like Miki Dora surfed Malibu, but ultimately it was all about a girl named Gidget. Her real name was Kathy Kohner—now Kathy Zuckerman—and she brought more notoriety to surfing than any other female in the sport's history. Today Malibu, or 'Bu, is still considered a surfer's rite of passage—or right of passage.

Consisting of several sections, Malibu has both points and inside sandbar breaks. First Point is the inside break, followed by Second Point in a faster middle section, and finally Third Point, which is faster yet. Getting out to the break at low tide can be painful on the feet, because there are small rocks and boulders everywhere along the shore—and urchins from Second to Third. Watch the dismount if you take a long left all the way in. Malibu holds all types of swell sizes, but 3 to 6 feet seems to work best for wave shape. Malibu tends to be crowded because of the name, and the water quality isn't what it used to be in the old picture shows. Closer to the pier the rides aren't as long and conditions get worse, but it is less crowded if it's breaking.

This isn't a guarantee by any means, but if you're looking to combine celebrity-watching and surfing, Malibu is as good a place as any. Malibu is home to many of Hollywood's biggest stars. Along the Malibu coast you'll find many homes belonging to celebrities. Not surprisingly, even Hollywoodites get bitten by the surf bug from time to time. Brad Pitt and Mel Gibson aren't going to drop in on your wave, but you might see them at Duke's or Malibu Kitchen.

If you want to spot a celebrity, hang out at Malibu Kitchen, a favorite of Jerry Seinfeld, Gary Busey, Garry Shandling, and a thousand other stars.

Looking over and through the Malibu Pier, a longboarder shoots the curl at First Point and two shortboarders split a peak at Third Point.   Chris Sardelis

Other Information

Local Surf Shops: Zuma Jay's, 22775 Pacific Coast Hwy., Malibu; (310) 456-8044. Becker's Malibu, 23755 Malibu Rd., Malibu; (310) 456-7155. Malibu Surf Shack, 22935 Pacific Coast Hwy., Malibu; (310) 456-8508. Drill Surf & Skate, 30765 Pacific Coast Hwy., Malibu; (310) 457-7715. Clout Rideshop, 29575 Pacific Coast Hwy., Malibu; (310) 457-1151.

Places to Stay: Malibu Beach RV Park, 25801 Pacific Coast Hwy., Malibu; (310) 456-6052. Point Mugu State Park, 9000 W. Pacific Coast Hwy., Malibu; (818) 880-0350. Malibu Beach Inn, 22878 Pacific Coast Hwy., Malibu; (310) 456-6444. Malibu Creek State Park, located 4 miles south of US 101 on Las Virgenes/Malibu Canyon Road, Malibu; call for fee info at (818) 880-0367.

Places to Eat: Neptune's Net, 42505 Pacific Coast Hwy., Malibu; (310) 457-3095. Malibu Kitchen, 3900 Cross Creek Rd., Malibu; (310) 456-7845. Nobu, 22706 Pacific Coast Hwy., Malibu; (310) 317-9140. Duke's Malibu, 21150 Pacific Coast Hwy., Malibu; (310) 317-0777. Malibu Seafood, 25653 Pacific Coast Hwy., Malibu; (310) 456-3430.

Topanga

Another long right point break, Topanga starts with a long building swell that's fairly easy to drop into. It shapes out smoothly into a long right that can hollow out on larger days.

Best tide: Medium
Best swell direction: West, northwest
Best wave size: Any
Bottom: Rock and sand
Type of break: Point, right
Skill level: Intermediate to advanced
Best boards: Shortboard, longboard
Best seasons: Fall and summer
Crowds: Crowded
Water quality: Poor
Hazards: Rocks at low tide on the inside
Fees and permits: None

A so-so day at Topanga, but this is what the spot looks like, unless there is a giant south or west swell rolling into this corner of the Santa Monica Bay.   Elizabeth Pepin Silva

Finding the Break

From Los Angeles: From where the 10 meets Pacific Coast Highway, head six miles north on CA 1 to Topanga Canyon. You can park in the Topanga Canyon lot at the break. GPS: N34 02.417 / W118 34.772

Surf Description

Topanga Beach sits at the base of the Malibu hills just on the southwest side of CA 1. There are several lifeguard stations, showers, restrooms, and parking areas along the Topanga Beach area. Nestled among the ultraexpensive homes of Malibu, Topanga is an old-school longboarder wave. Topanga sits at the bottom of Topanga Canyon. This is important because Topanga Canyon acts as both a wind protector and a wind hazard. Blowing east, the wind gets funneled along the beach and obliterates any wave; if the Santa Anas are blowing west, however, they hold up the wave and can create an epic, long, hollow right.

The wave is best when the swells come down from the north or west. The break can have several sections at times. The best conditions are no wind to a slight breeze with the surf coming in at just a few feet high. Topanga will allow rides of varying length, but the best rides come on a 10-foot-plus longboard in a small to medium swell. The entry to the water is covered by cobblestones and rock, so use caution when entering the water. It's easy to turn an ankle on the entry or exit, which can ruin your day quickly. It's a spot well surfed by locals and inland board junkies. Some of the earliest pioneers of surfing and most vocal critics of Los Angeles urban sprawl and its effect on the ocean waters came from this area.

> **If you have strong legs, rent a bike at the base of Topanga Canyon and ride to the top to enjoy some of the California coast's best views.**

One of these locals was Bill Cleary. Known to surf Topanga frequently, Cleary went on to impact the surfing world through the Surfrider Foundation's political and environmental work. He was one of the original founders of the organization. His early efforts helped preserve the quality of our beaches and ocean, especially in California. Bill also served as the associate editor of *Surfer* magazine for several years. Along with David Stern, he wrote one of California's earliest surfing guides, *Surfing Guide to Southern California*.

Other Information

Local Surf Shops: Zuma Jay's, 22775 Pacific Coast Hwy., Malibu; (310) 456-8044. Becker's Malibu, 23755 Malibu Rd., Malibu; (310) 456-7155. Malibu Surf Shack, 22935 Pacific Coast Hwy., Malibu; (310) 456-8508. Drill Surf & Skate, 30765 Pacific Coast Hwy., Malibu; (310) 457-7715. Clout Rideshop, 29575 Pacific Coast Hwy., Malibu; (310) 457-1151.

Places to Stay: Malibu Beach RV Park, 25801 Pacific Coast Hwy., Malibu; (310) 456-6052. Point Mugu State Park, 9000 W. Pacific Coast Hwy., Malibu; (818) 880-0350. Malibu Beach Inn, 22878 Pacific Coast Hwy., Malibu; (310) 456-6444. Malibu Creek State Park, located 4 miles south of US 101 on Las Virgenes/Malibu Canyon Road, Malibu; call for fee info at (818) 880-0367.

Places to Eat: Chart House, 18412 Pacific Coast Hwy., Malibu; (310) 454-9321. Gladstones, 17300 Pacific Coast Hwy., Pacific Palisades; (310) GLA-FISH.

Chris Burkard

As the Northern County merges into the greater Los Angeles Basin, the surfing gets bad quick. Along with a few small, wacky spots mostly formed by breakwaters, Bay Street is a reasonable place to catch waves when there's a small south swell. It doesn't get surfed very often, except by those who don't know that the largest concentration of runoff spillways comes right through here.

Lucia Griggi

As you fly out of LAX, ever wonder why no one is out surfing? The name should clue you in: Shit Pipe is exactly that, a large sewer pipe running out to the ocean in front of Los Angeles International Airport. This is nasty polluted water, even when it isn't raining. Unless there's a mondo northwesterly rocking down the coast, you're better off somewhere else.

Mike Durand, courtesy of swellmagnet.com

El Porto is a winter swell beach that favors a north, northwest, or cross swell. Like Shit Pipe, the water is bad, so unless you couldn't care less about your health, this is not the place to surf. When it does break well, the sandbar shifts to form pretty fast-moving lefts and rights that close out unless you can pick the right spot. You will know you have arrived at El Porto when you see the giant Chevron oil refinery—or tanker ships moored offshore.

Manhattan Beach

Manhattan Beach is a sandbar break that can produce some high surf conditions in winter and some dismal surf in summer. It's best in larger surf conditions, when the wave is a fast closeout—can you choose wisely, Grasshopper?

Best tide: Low
Best swell direction: Any
Best wave size: Waist high to head high
Bottom: Sand
Type of break: Outside, left and right
Skill level: Novice to intermediate
Best boards: Shortboard, longboard
Best seasons: Fall and winter
Crowds: Can get crowded on weekends

Water quality: Poor

Hazards: Pier pilings, poor water quality

Fees and permits: Parking may require a fee.

Finding the Break

From Los Angeles: Take I-405 to any of the beach city exits. For quicker access to Manhattan Beach, take the Artesia Boulevard exit all the way down to the beach. There's plenty of parking all along Manhattan Beach and near the pier. GPS: N33 53.007 / W118 24.862

Surf Description

Would anyone really decide anything significant through a coin flip? Well, that's precisely how Manhattan Beach got its name. Originally, it was a small section of a 10-mile stretch of sandy beach called Rancho Sausal Redondo. Later, Manhattan Beach landowner George Peck called the area Shore Acres. Then Stewart Merrill bought the southern stretch of Rancho Sausal Redondo and called his section Manhattan, after his old hometown. Eventually the two decided to flip a coin in a winner-name-all contest, and Manhattan West was born.

Manhattan Beach is a sandbar break that changes depending on the swell conditions and wind direction. The sandbar breaks far enough offshore that you can catch a ride that's reasonably decent, but by no means long. It breaks best at low tide and produces both left and right breaks from the typical swell hitting the peak of the sandbar and peeling off. The wave shape is a crumbling mess under smaller surf and at mid- to high tides. At lower tides or during bigger swells, particularly from the west and northwest in winter, it's a fast closeout unless there are shoulders that can provide some lippy waves for some good aerial practice. Parking can be a hassle, but it is fairly plentiful. Meters abound all over the place near the pier and along the finger streets connecting the beach to CA 1.

> **Manhattan Beach is the favorite beach spot for the west side's beach nightlife. Manhattan hosts several professional beach volleyball events throughout the summer.**

Even though the South Bay doesn't sport the superior conditions of Malibu or Huntington Beach, it has had a significant impact on surfing history. In fact, the city bordering Manhattan Beach to the south is Redondo Beach. And along the Redondo Beach boardwalk sits a small statue of George Freeth. Most people, surfologists

Firing Manhattan Beach, but where's the crowd? Must be a Lakers game on.
Scott Valor - BurningPier.com

included, simply pass by the spot without realizing who George Freeth was. During the early years of the twentieth century, several Southern California entrepreneurs were trying to find ways to bring Los Angeles residents to the beach. Freeth was hired to perform a surfing demonstration at Redondo Beach. Although we don't know how much he was paid, it was surely far less than the fees given today to surfing's top athletes for performing at contests around the world!

Other Information

Local Surf Shops: ET Surfboards, 904 Aviation Blvd., Hermosa Beach; (310) 379-7660. Pier Surf, 21 Pier Ave., Hermosa Beach; (310) 372-2012. El Porto Surfboards, 3804 Highland Ave., Manhattan Beach; (310) 545-9626. Becker Surfboards, 301 Pier Ave., Hermosa Beach; (310) 372-6554. Spyder II, 65 Pier Ave., Hermosa Beach; (310)

374-2494. Surf Concepts, 2001 N. Sepulveda Blvd., Manhattan Beach; (310) 545-7397.
Places to Stay: Manhattan Beach Marriott, 1400 Park View Ave., Manhattan Beach; (310) 546-7511. Residence Inn, 1700 N. Sepulveda Blvd., Manhattan Beach; (310) 421-3100.
Places to Eat: Back Home in Lahaina, 916 N. Sepulveda Blvd., Manhattan Beach; (310) 374-0111. Blue Agave Grill, 1019 Manhattan Beach Blvd., Manhattan Beach; (310) 545-7331.

Hermosa Beach

Hermosa Beach is a sandbar break that breaks best at low tide and produces both left and right mushy peaks.

Best tides: Low
Best swell direction: Any
Best wave size: Waist high to head high
Bottom: Sand
Type of break: Outside, left and right
Skill level: Novice to intermediate
Best boards: Shortboard, longboard
Best seasons: Fall and winter
Crowds: Can get crowded on weekends
Water quality: Poor
Hazards: Pier pilings, poor water quality
Fees and permits: None

Finding the Break

From Los Angeles: Take I-405 to any of the beach city exits. Look for the signs to Hermosa Beach and park anywhere along the beach. GPS: N33 51.725 / W118 24.097

Surf Description

Hermosa Beach is the last of the South Bay coastline's major beach cities. *Hermosa* translated from Spanish means "beautiful," and the city today offers a well-manicured stretch of creamy-colored sand with a boardwalk-style atmosphere. The average temperature here is seventy degrees in summer and fifty-five in winter—a lot cooler than most people imagine a California summer to be. Most of this is due to the marine layer that covers the area for much of early summer. Hermosa Beach is located in a

Looking south along Hermosa Beach from the pier. Looks like a winter day. What's the clue? Santa Claus going straight! And the kid who burned Santa on that wave might have gotten a good little pocket ride, but he'll be bumming on Christmas morning.
Jim Everett

smaller geographic area than most other South Los Angeles County beaches, giving it a unique feel.

Similar to Redondo and Manhattan, Hermosa is a sandbar break that changes depending on the swell conditions and wind direction. It breaks best at low tide and produces both left and right breaks with a crumbling shape. Surf near the pier is slightly better, but look out for the fishing hooks. Hermosa's best season for surfing is winter or even late fall due to its west-to-northwest-facing beaches. An unfortunate aspect of this spot is that—while rain is rare here in winter and fall—when it does come down, Hermosa's waters can get downright dirty and unsurfable.

One of the pioneers who helped shape the sport and culture of surfing hailed from Hermosa Beach. Surfing photographer Leroy Grannis was raised steps from the beach. Learning to surf at a young age, Grannis translated his childhood experiences into the camera lens. During the 1960s he helped popularize the sport with a photographic style that embodied California surf culture. Grannis passed on to that darkroom in the sky in February of 2011—but his iconic images will live forever.

Other Information

Local Surf Shops: ET Surfboards, 904 Aviation Blvd., Hermosa Beach; (310) 379-7660. Pier Surf, 21 Pier Ave., Hermosa Beach; (310) 372-2012. El Porto Surfboards, 3804 Highland Ave., Manhattan Beach; (310) 545-9626. Becker Surfboards, 301 Pier Ave., Hermosa Beach; (310) 372-6554. Spyder II, 65 Pier Ave., Hermosa Beach; (310) 374-2494. Surf Concepts, 2001 N. Sepulveda Blvd., Manhattan Beach; (310) 545-7397.

Places to Stay: Quality Inn, 901 Aviation Blvd., Hermosa Beach; (310) 374-2666. Hotel Hermosa, 2515 Pacific Coast Hwy., Hermosa Beach; (310) 318-6000.

Places to Eat: Aloha Sharkeez, 52 Pier Ave., Hermosa Beach; (310) 374-7823. FFF Fishack, 53 Pier Ave., Hermosa Beach; (310) 379-5550.

Lucia Griggi

Redondo Beach is the last of LA's three favorite hangouts for the younger crowd: Manhattan, Hermosa, and Redondo. At the south end of the beach sits a large breakwater wall that serves up some of the LA Basin's larger, faster waves. Swells coming from directions other than south hit the breakwater wall and spit out some fast-moving lefts that crumble to the beach. In smaller surf the crowds can make this spot resemble an LA freeway; avoid the summer water traffic.

Haggerty's

Located on the northwest side of Palos Verdes, Haggerty's is a rocky point break that shoots out hard lefts, especially in fall and winter.

Best tide: Varies

Best swell direction: West, northwest

Best wave size: Head high and bigger

Bottom: Rock

Type of break: Point, left

Skill level: Advanced

Best boards: Shortboard, gun

Best seasons: Fall and winter

Crowds: Crowded

Water quality: Average

Hazards: Rocks at Upper Hags

Fees and permits: None

Finding the Break

From Los Angeles: Take CA 1 south until you see the hilly point jutting out over the Pacific called Palos Verdes. Look for Malaga Cove School and park along the street. Parking is tough here, and so is access: You have to scale the rock cliffs down to the beach. GPS: N33 48.081 / W118 23.708

Surf Description

Located at the top northwest side of the Palos Verdes Peninsula, Haggerty's is the first break along a rising, cliff-side coastline. It's relatively easy to get to compared with nearby spots like Indicator and the Cove. Haggerty's, however, is a performance wave and not to be confused with the Cove, which is a longboarding wave. With tidal changes and rock reefs, this break requires some skills and respect, especially when the swell is over 8 feet. This is an extremely nice-shaped wave and breaks differently from most Southern California waves because it likes a west and especially a northwest swell. Consequently, it's made to order for those looking for winter surf in California.

Haggerty's—aka Hags—can handle all swells and explodes in larger conditions. It's composed of Lower, Middle, and Upper Haggerty's. Lower is mushy and tends to be small. It sits on the border of Torrance and Palos Verdes and spits out small lefts that are rideable but not really desirable. Hags and Upper Haggerty's—aka Middles—are more aggressive and larger. Be careful of the rocky outcropping and shallow rock reef areas at low tide. One of the better-known breaks in the Los Angeles Basin, Haggerty's tends to be crowded. It's often surfed by locals looking to avoid the heavier vibes at Lunada Bay and the Cove.

Apart from the break, the area offers one of the best views of Santa Catalina Island (now known simply as Catalina Island) from the west- and southwest facing shores. Transportation and day trips are available through the nearby port of Long Beach or down in Newport Harbor. High-speed boats can zip you across the 20-mile-plus channel in record time. Avalon, the main landing city on Catalina, is a good day trip for most, offering shopping, walking tours, and pristine beaches. It is a great way to see one of California's best-kept island secrets.

> **If for some reason the surf isn't breaking at Haggerty's, try golfing at American Golf's Rancho Palos Verdes Golf Course. These links overlook some coastal sections of blue and are a bargain for the price.**

California is abundant in many ways, but left points are not one of the facets of its abundance. Haggerty's, on the inside of the Palos Verdes peninsula, is an exception to that—a for-real left point that can look like Bali on a big winter swell—and is very popular with the huddled masses of the Los Angeles Basin. George Konstantouros

Other Information

Local Surf Shops: Roland Surfboards, 1205 S. Pacific Coast Hwy., Redondo Beach; (310) 316-7803. Vanguard Surf and Skate, 5205 Pacific Coast Hwy., Torrance; (310) 373-2501. O.O. Surf, 1217 S. Pacific Coast Hwy., Redondo Beach; (424) 603-0946. Soul Performance, 2215 Artesia Blvd., Redondo Beach; (310) 370-1428.

Places to Stay: Head into Torrance—there aren't many places to stay near Haggerty's. Palos Verdes Inn, 1700 S. Pacific Coast Hwy., Redondo Beach; (310) 316-4211. Torrance Palos Verdes Courtyard, 2633 W. Sepulveda Blvd., Torrance; (310) 533-8000.

Places to Eat: Admiral Risty, 31250 Palos Verdes Dr. W., Rancho Palos Verdes; (310) 377-0050. Pacific Fish Center and Restaurant, 131 Fisherman's Wharf, Redondo Beach; (310) 374-8420.

nickbotner.com

The Cove is a great uncrowded outside break sitting in the middle of beautiful Palos Verdes. It attracts some of the oldest surfing crew in the southern LA Basin due to its location in an area of older single-family homes and its favorable longboard waves. The Cove has some rock reef that can get exposed at low tide; the currents can be strong. This is not a beginner break, and respecting the lineup is compulsory.

Lunada Bay

Lunada Bay lies near the center point of Palos Verdes. Its location and outer reef allow it to capture all the large northern swells. It can hold very big surf and has an average wave in smaller conditions.

Best tides: Medium to high

Best swell direction: North, northwest

Best wave size: Head high and bigger

Bottom: Rock

Type of break: Point, right

Skill level: Advanced

Best board: Gun

Best season: Winter

Crowds: Uncrowded

Water quality: Poor

Hazards: Locals

Fees and permits: None

Finding the Break

From Los Angeles: Take I-110 toward San Pedro. Follow the signs toward Palos Verdes and look for Paseo Lunada. You can park on Paseo Lunada and then head down the cliffs. GPS: N33 46.264 / W118 25.322

Surf Description

Palos Verdes is surrounded by the majestic Pacific Ocean on three sides. The peninsula is a collection of just under 30 square miles of housing-filled hillsides, quietly set apart from Los Angeles in the southwest corner of the county. If you like huge surf, this is the place: Lunada Bay is one of the few breaks in California that is a true big-wave ride. Located off Paseo Del Mar, in Palos Verdes Estates, it's a difficult break and beach to access. Steep trails lead down the bluff to the rocky shoreline. Chances are, if you're reading this, you do not live in Palos Verdes. It's very wise to have someone drop you off or park your car as far from the access path as possible.

Lunada Bay breaks best in huge swells and walls up with hollow, fast rights. It breaks biggest in winter, when the swells come down from Alaska. Unlike any other break in Southern California, it will hold extremely large surf. You need some skills to surf Lunada when it's breaking. A big performance wave, it requires the right equipment as well: a gun or mini–gun board. There are no lifeguards on duty. Unless it's big, Lunada may not be worth the access; when the surf is less than 6 feet, Lunada just doesn't break.

The sense of community or ownership of the surf here is strong, to say the least. The land shape and isolation reflects the vibe you will get at Lunada and from nearly all its residents. Unfortunately, this is made very clear in the water, on the way to the water, on surfing bulletin boards, on websites, and on and on. Cars are consistently vandalized near Lunada Bay, and surfers are heckled and often provoked into fights or at least physical confrontations. It's sad that such a beautiful section of Los Angeles County has some of the worst attitude in the state.

Palos Verdes and Rancho Palos Verdes make up the Palos Verdes Peninsula. There are several lookout points—in winter months you may even spot some whales migrating down to Baja California.

Lunada Bay is infamous for protective locals—and this overview of a winter day explains why. Chris Sardelis

Other Information

Local Surf Shops: Roland Surfboards, 1205 S. Pacific Coast Hwy., Redondo Beach; (310) 316-7803. Vanguard Surf and Skate, 5205 Pacific Coast Hwy., Torrance; (310) 373-2501. O.O. Surf, 1217 S. Pacific Coast Hwy., Redondo Beach; (424) 603-0946. Soul Performance, 2215 Artesia Blvd., Redondo Beach; (310) 370-1428.

Places to Stay: Try heading back to Torrance or into San Pedro. Palos Verdes Inn, 1700 S. Pacific Coast Hwy., Redondo Beach; (310) 316-4211. Torrance Palos Verdes Courtyard, 2633 W. Sepulveda Blvd., Torrance; (310) 533-8000.

Places to Eat: Admiral Risty, 31250 Palos Verdes Dr. W., Rancho Palos Verdes; (310) 377-0050. Pacific Fish Center and Restaurant, 131 Fisherman's Wharf, Redondo Beach; (310) 374-8420.

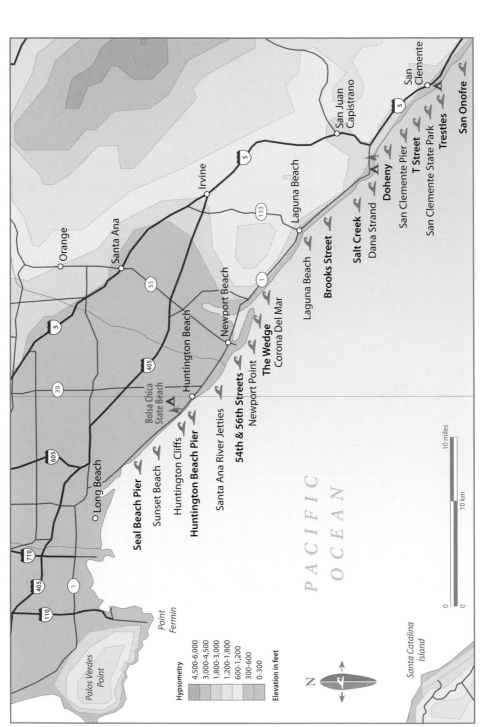

Region 9 (Orange County)

REGION 9: ORANGE COUNTY

Orange County borders the southern end of Los Angeles County starting with Seal Beach. From Seal Beach down to San Clemente, you can find some of the most interesting, wealthy, conservative cities and surf breaks in all of Southern California. Orange County used to be a large agricultural community that primarily produced oranges—hence the name. The county still has a small base of farms, but you won't see any of them near the coast. In fact, this is one of the few spots around where you can view expensive housing developments. It's easy to make your way around the area: Just find CA 1 and go south or north, depending on your destination.

The Orange County coastline is fairly flat from Seal Beach to Newport Beach. Once you pass Newport Beach and enter Corona Del Mar, the landscape changes from flat marshlands to rolling hills and steep cliff sides until it flattens out again at the bottom of Dana Point. This area is home to some of California's most consistent and beautiful weather. Winter, of course, is the coolest time of the year, but even then the average low is around seventy degrees. As in many parts of the state, a drawback here is June Gloom, which can come as early as May and stay into late June. Orange County can also get notoriously windy in the afternoons as the Santa Anas come barreling through the inland mountains, bringing along hot desert air. The beaches in some spots are legendary, and the region is home to Surf City USA, otherwise known as Huntington Beach. Rarely does a weekend go by that there isn't a surf contest somewhere along the Orange County coastline.

Huntington Beach, Newport Beach, Laguna Beach, and San Clemente are the main cities; just north of the county line, however, is Long Beach, which some folks consider an unofficial part of Orange County (technically it's in Los Angeles County). All the surf breaks described in this section are easily accessible by car or by foot. Most have state parks or large parking areas to accommodate the beach crowd, making Orange County one of the friendliest surf counties in California. Overall, the vibe is pretty mellow, since it requires a six-figure income to live near the beach in most places. Nightlife is also excellent, with the main cities having the most to offer in the way of entertainment and local talent. Orange County can be accessed by any of the main Los Angeles or San Diego freeways. If you're arriving from out of state, flying in to John Wayne Orange County Airport or Long Beach Airport tends to be the easiest. Don't be surprised to see mouse ears on your flight—Orange County is home to Disneyland and other amusement parks.

Overall Surf Description

Orange County's surf scene stretches for more than 40 miles. The breaks primarily favor a south swell, but—unlike Los Angeles and Ventura Counties—Orange will serve up surf every day of the week regardless of how miserable the conditions might be. The majority of the coastline, with the exception of the shores between Corona Del Mar and Laguna Beach, is made up of sandbars. These sandbars produce endless surfing spots where you can rip it up with the best locals or hang out by yourself on a nice left or right. As in most of Southern California, you'll need a wet suit, but come June some of the brave just wear board shorts as water temperatures creep above seventy degrees. Orange County hosts one of the world's best longboard waves at San Onofre and is also home to the US Open of Surfing championship in Huntington Beach. Shortboards, longboards, mini-guns, funshapes, even whacked-out hybrids for the Wedge are all useful in Orange County; you simply have to pick your spot. Mornings are usually the best time here—if you can, after 9:00 a.m., when most people have gone to work. The one drawback is wind. When it blows hard in the afternoon, the wind can cripple the consistent surf of Orange County. The water is relatively clean—although watch out for river mouths and harbor mouths—and crowds are always a factor in summer and on weekends. Surf is usually best in late spring, summer, and early fall.

Santa Ana winds, a west swell, and the web address on the lifeguard tower—www.surf city.org—pretty much say it all about Huntington Beach. Chris Sardelis

Fall Surf

Fall surf in Orange County is as good as any other region. As the late-season south-facing swells continue to push onto the shores of the coast, nearly all the beaches put out knee- to head-high surf every day. Fall tends to be less crowded as well, and Indian summers are known to extend all the way into early November.

Winter Surf

Winter surf in Orange County is great or horrible. Storms coming down from the north often are big enough even to spit out nicely shaped A frames over the sandbars from Seal Beach to San O. Most of the point breaks in the area continue to fire in winter, and some of the beaches pick up west and northwesterly swells. The water can drop down into the high fifties, but outside temperatures rarely drop below sixty.

Spring Surf

Spring is a mix of swell directions in Orange County, but the good news is that the sandbars and point breaks can all take it. Regardless of direction, spring surf is usually decent. An early southern swell is not uncommon in April. The only downer about spring surf in the area is that it tends to get windy in the afternoons; also, the gray marine layer called June Gloom can set in as early as May.

Summer Surf

Summer surf in Orange County is as good as it gets. Old Man Winter has gone down under, and when he throws a strong storm up north, all of Orange County rejoices. The water temperature rises into the seventies, the air temperature hits the eighties, and summer surfing is just about perfect. Summer also brings the crowds, so there is plenty of scenery to look at, too.

Average Temperatures for Region (Orange County)		
	Air (Huntington Beach)	Water (Newport Beach)
Jan	69	58
Feb	70	60
Mar	71	60
Apr	74	61
May	75	64
June	79	66
July	83	69
Aug	84	70
Sept	83	69
Oct	80	68
Nov	74	64
Dec	70	61

Seal Beach Pier

Seal Beach is mainly a pier break surrounded by sandbar reef. The wave will break in all types of conditions but is best under a south swell. The south side is favored by bodyboarders, the north side by surfers.

Best tide: Medium

Best swell direction: South, southwest

Best wave size: Waist high to slightly overhead

Bottom: Sand

Type of break: Beach break, left and right

Skill level: Novice to intermediate

Best board: Shortboard

Best season: Winter

Crowds: Can get crowded on weekends

Water quality: Poor

Hazards: Rain can make water quality poor, stingrays

Fees and permits: According to pierfishing.com, there is a nominal fee for parking near the Seal Beach Pier.

Finding the Break

From Los Angeles: Take I-405 to the Seal Beach Boulevard exit. Take Seal Beach Boulevard about 2 miles to CA 1, turn right, and make a left onto Main Street. There's plenty of metered parking around the pier or on local streets. GPS: N33 44.295 / W118 06.425

Surf Description

One of the less visited spots in the northernmost tip of Orange County is Seal Beach Pier. Located just north of tiny Sunset Beach and just south of the Los Angeles County line is the quiet town of Seal Beach. Unlike Huntington Beach or Bolsa Chica, if you're not careful, you can miss Seal Beach pretty quickly from CA 1, which cuts slightly inland around the downtown. Once you're in the surf, though, you'll know when you're at Seal Beach: Glance over the water and you'll see massive container ships waiting to be towed into the port of Long Beach.

Seal Beach is a lot like Huntington Beach Pier in that it can produce some really good waves when the swell comes out of the south or southwest. The sandbars will hold the wave and gradually wall up, producing a good longboard wave in smaller swells and a solid funshape or shortboard ride in larger surf. Waves break on both sides of the pier, but the north side is typically better, building up quick walls with peaky drops under south or southwest swells. The south side of the pier breaks best in winter when the swells come down from the north. The wave is especially good when offshore winds blow.

There are two unusual landmarks to note on Seal Beach Boulevard. Leisure World, the first, is a gated senior citizen community of approximately 10,000 people. Then there's the Seal Beach Naval Weapons Station. Indeed, Uncle Sam picked up some prime real estate here: Almost two-thirds of Seal Beach is owned and operated by the US government—which makes it feel roomy and nice, unlike a lot of Orange County.

Smoke on the water on the south side of Seal Beach Pier—with the heavy metal thunder of Long Beach in the distance.   Chris Sardelis

Chris Sardelis

Just south of Seal Beach is the small, funky town of Sunset Beach. Look for the giant water tower converted into a house and you'll know you've hit town. Sunset has a long, sandy coastline filled with one huge stretch of beach break. Better at lower to mid-tide, the break is enhanced by a south swell. Parking can be difficult on the side access streets all along CA 1.

Chris Sardelis

Huntington Cliffs is just south of the Bolsa Chica Reserve. Easily identified by its cliffs on the ocean side of CA 1 and the oil transfer station inland, Huntington Cliffs has a consistent sand reef break that can hold nearly any size swell but performs best at low to medium tide with a south swell. Huntington Cliffs is also known as Dog Beach since it's the only stretch of beach in Orange County where dogs can run free and off-leash.

Other Information

Local Surf Shops: Drop Surf Shop, 905 Ocean Ave., Seal Beach; (562) 430-7090. Inflight Surf & Sail, 1250 Pacific Coast Hwy., Seal Beach; (562) 493-3661. Katin Surf Shop, 16250 Pacific Coast Hwy., Huntington Beach; (562) 592-2052. Bruce Jones Surfboards, 16927 Pacific Coast Hwy., Huntington Beach; (888) 592-2314.

Places to Stay: Seaport Marina Hotel, 6400 E. Pacific Coast Hwy., Seal Beach; (562) 434-8451. Seal Beach Inn & Gardens, 212 Fifth St., Seal Beach; (562) 493-2416.

Places to Eat: Seaside Grill, 101 Main St., Seal Beach; (562) 430-0006. Mahe, 1400 Pacific Coast Hwy., Seal Beach; (562) 431-3022.

Huntington Beach Pier

The western boundary of Huntington Beach is several miles of beach breaks, with the pier being the center point. Good most of the year, the pier is better in winter when the swells pump out double overhead A-frames. The waves can be peaky and fast and often close out, but there's always a good spot.

Best tides: Low to medium
Best swell direction: Northwest, southwest
Best wave size: Waist high to slightly overhead
Bottom: Sand
Type of break: Beach break, outside, left and right
Skill level: Novice to advanced
Best boards: Longboard, shortboard, funshape
Best season: Any
Crowds: Crowded
Water quality: Average
Hazards: Pier pilings, other surfers
Fees and permits: None

Finding the Break

From Los Angeles: Take I-405 to Beach Boulevard. Exit and head west a few miles until you reach CA 1. When you see the Hyatt Hotel resort, make a right and head 1 mile to the Huntington Beach Pier. There's plenty of parking near the pier, on CA 1, and in the lots. N33 39.375 / W118 00.167

Surf Description

Surf City USA, aka Huntington Beach: To many folks, this is the place where California surf culture begins and ends. With its 7-mile stretch of beach break extending from Bolsa Chica down to the Santa Ana River mouth, Huntington Beach is one of the largest and most accessible surf breaks in all California.

The town was originally a coastal oil community. William Huntington built a railroad in the early 1900s to bring more Orange County residents to the beach. In the process Huntington Beach grew into the thriving surf mecca it is today.

Huntington Beach is host to all types of breaks. Each can vary greatly on the same day at different tides and in different spots. Starting south of the Huntington Beach

Overview of both sides of the Huntington Pier, which puts some shape and corners into miles of beach break.   Chris Sardelis

Pier, the sandbars will hold a consistent off-shore break from almost any swell direction. The break tends to close out more and closer to the shoreline. The main break is located at the pier, where the sandbar holds waves of any size from small tricklers to double over-head. The wave both left and right of the pier will turn into a nice performance wave in larger swells. To the north, extending to Dog Beach or Huntington Cliffs, you can pick any spot, but note that the wave shape here favors longboarders in smaller surf.

Huntington is home to the International Surf Museum, located just off Main Street. Every Friday the pier hosts a farmers' market filled with good eats and stuff to buy.

Huntington Beach has embraced surf culture possibly more completely than any other coastal city. Playing host to the US Open of Surfing, Huntington attracts the best surfers from around the world to the south side of the pier in midsummer. More than 200,000 spectators take in this annual event, and more surfing contests have been added as the popularity of the sport grows. After you've surfed Huntington, there are two must-visit places during your stay. The International Surf Museum, just off Main Street, houses some great information about the sport's history and the legends who've popularized it. And just a few hundred feet away lies a place to fuel up before or after surfing: the Sugar Shack. A huge supporter of the local surfing talent, the Sugar Shack is just as much a part of the local surfing scene as the surf itself.

Other Information

Local Surf Shops: Huntington Surf & Sport, 300 Pacific Coast Hwy., Huntington Beach; (714) 374-2373. Sakal Surfboards, 201 Main St. #C, Huntington Beach; (714) 536-0505. Katin Surf Shop, 16250 Pacific Coast Hwy., Huntington Beach; (562) 592-2052. Bruce Jones Surfboards, 16927 Pacific Coast Hwy., Huntington Beach; (888) 592-2314. Rockin' Figs Surf Headquarters, 316 Main St., Huntington Beach; (714) 536-1058. Jacks Surfboards, 101 Main St., Huntington Beach; (714) 536-4516.
Places to Stay: Hilton Waterfront Beach Resort, 21100 Pacific Coast Hwy., Huntington Beach; (714) 845-8000. Best Western Huntington Beach Inn, 800 Pacific Coast Hwy., Huntington Beach; (714) 536-7500.
Places to Eat: Sugar Shack Cafe, 213 Main St., Huntington Beach; (714) 536-0355. No Ka Oi, 215 Main St., Huntington Beach; (714) 960-8300.

Chris Burkard

Santa Ana River Jetties: Located between Huntington Beach and Newport Beach, the Santa Ana River runs right into the Pacific Ocean, creating some quick lefts and rights over the ever-changing sandbar. Do not surf here after it rains—you're more likely to get stuck by a syringe needle than anything else. Without wind, the break runs from 1 foot to head high; when there is wind, forget about it.

54th and 56th Streets

In Newport Beach the best-known spots among the numbered finger streets are the crowded 54th and 56th Street breaks. The waves here break quickly into mushy lefts and rights depending on your location next to the rock jetties.

Best tide: Medium
Best swell direction: Anything but west
Best wave size: Head high to slightly overhead
Bottom: Sand and rock
Type of break: Point, lefts and rights
Skill level: Novice to advanced
Best board: Shortboard

Best seasons: Fall and summer
Crowds: Crowded
Water quality: Poor
Hazards: Jetty rocks, locals
Fees and permits: There may be a fee for parking.

Finding the Break

From Los Angeles: Take I-405 to CA 55, then head south on the 55 toward Newport Beach/Costa Mesa. CA 55 ends and turns into Newport Boulevard. Take Newport to CA 1 and go left at Balboa Boulevard. There are plenty of meters on the streets, but don't block a driveway—you'll get towed. GPS: N33 36.745 / W117 55.814

The hottest hundred yards are still pretty hot. A local rogue boosting between the Newport Jetties. Chris Sardelis

Surf Description

Along the apartment-building-lined streets of Newport Beach at its northernmost end lie 54th and 56th Streets. Here you'll find the younger side of Orange County surfing. Many of the locals who surf these streets live right in the neighborhood or down the street on the Balboa Peninsula. These surf spots are human-made rock jetty breaks. The breaks go both left and right, depending on the side of the jetty. South and north swells produce the best waves, and they tend to be fast. On smaller-swell days, the waves can be mushy, but anything over 3 feet and the wave starts to build in performance.

54th and 56th Streets are on the north side of Newport Beach. Take a walk along the pier and check out the local scene. This area of Newport has a great cement strand running along the beach for about 5 miles.

Parking can be miserable, because most of the spaces are already taken up by residents in one of the hundreds of mini–apartment complexes all around Newport. Trying to find a place to park in summer is nearly impossible, and the parking enforcement is downright brutal. You will be towed if you park even 6 inches in front of a resident's driveway. The break can also get as crowded as any break in Orange County. Unfortunately, the local surf crew doesn't take kindly to outsiders (which is funny because most of them aren't from Newport Beach anyway). If the vibe goes south, which can happen fast in summer, walk a few blocks south from 56th down to the pier. The area offers up a lot in the way of restaurants, bars, and beach scene.

Around mid- to late September each year, there are two events to see if you find yourself at 54th and 56th Streets. The city of Newport Beach hosts both a surf championship and the Taste of Newport—a three-day food festival that draws around 75,000 locals and visitors. More than thirty restaurants and fifteen wineries serve up a sample of what edibles Newport Beach has to offer.

Other Information

Local Surf Shops: Frog House, 6908 Pacific Coast Hwy., Newport Beach; (949) 642-5690. Green Room, 6480 Pacific Coast Hwy., Newport Beach; (949) 548-9944.
Places to Stay: Balboa Inn, 105 Main St., Balboa; (949) 675-3412. Best Western Newport Beach Inn, 6208 W. Pacific Coast Hwy., Newport Beach; (949) 642-8252.
Places to Eat: Ho Sum Bistro, 3112 Newport Blvd., Newport Beach; (949) 675-0896. Mutt Lynch, 23 Ocean Front, Newport Beach; (949) 675-1556.

Chris Sardelis

Sandwiched between the Newport and Balboa Piers, Newport Point is mostly a closeout and good for bodysurfing, not surfing. The exception is times when there's a storm coming up from Baja California; this creates a south-southeast swell and "Pipeline comes to Newport."

The Wedge

The Wedge is less a surf break than a natural phenomenon. It's a bodysurfing break where waves crash off the Newport Jetty wall and collide with the normal wave swell to create a huge closeout face.

Best tide: Varies

Best swell direction: Southwest, south

Best wave size: Head high and above

Bottom: Sand

Type of break: Beach break, left

Skill level: Advanced

Best board: Shortboard

Best season: Summer

Crowds: Can get crowded on weekends

Water quality: Clean

Hazards: Extremely powerful shore pound

Fees and permits: None

Finding the Break

From Los Angeles: Take I-405 to CA 55, then head south on the 55 toward Newport Beach/Costa Mesa. CA 55 ends and turns into Newport Boulevard. In turn, Newport Boulevard turns into Balboa Boulevard; look for the Balboa Pier. You can park in the pier parking lot or at street meters. GPS: N33 36.022 / W117 54.014

A big day at the dirty old Wedge is a major media event.   Chris Sardelis

Surf Description

Ever been given a wedgie? The Wedge is the wave equivalent of a giant upward thrusting movement that will put a hurting on your backside if you aren't careful. This is a bodyboarding or bodysurfing wave. Although some rare, fine examples of not-so-intellectually motivated thrill seekers have attempted to surf the Wedge, it is not advisable.

The Wedge is best in early mornings and early evenings during a south swell. It's more commonly a gigantic bodysurfing death trap of a wave that hits hard on the Newport Jetty wall, bounces off, and merges with another wave to create a suicide bomb.

The Wedge isn't the easiest place to find for the novice driving around Newport Beach. It sits just beyond the reach of multimillion-dollar beachfront homes at the edge of the Balboa Island Jetty and the end of East Balboa Boulevard. Walk toward the

Chris Sardelis

If you've ever seen TV's *The OC*, you'll remember its opening shot of giant houses along the shore. Well, that's Corona Del Mar. Unlike the show, however, there's rarely any surf near the real Corona Del Mar Jetty or along Crystal Cove State Park. You're better off grabbing your scuba gear or golf clubs and playing the ultraexclusive Pelican Hills Golf Course. As at Newport Point, only a unique and large swell will ever break in Corona Del Mar.

Chris Sardelis

Known for its upscale boutique shopping, the art-friendly community of Laguna Beach has some reasonable surf near the main stretch under the right conditions. A south swell and low tide are usually required for there to be any surf. An easy way to see if the conditions are good is to simply drive CA 1 until you reach the base of Laguna Beach, or stop by the Las Brisas restaurant and check out the view from above.

small park located at the junction of the jetty and the beach. Finding parking at the Wedge can be downright brutal, but if you search a few streets inland on the Balboa Peninsula, you can no doubt find a spot.

Try the Balboa Fun Zone on the opposite side of the Balboa Pier. You'll find restaurants, amusements, rides, and a ferry (running every 10 minutes) that can shuttle you over to Balboa Island.

The Wedge is a well-photographed surf break. Many jetties have been built along the California coastline, but what makes the Wedge unique is that under ideal conditions, the most spectacular-looking waves are created off a human-made structure. Most artificial structures, like the harbor built in Dana Point, have ruined surf breaks and caused significant beach erosion. In this case—and really by dumb luck—this unnatural wave phenomenon was born. When the Wedge is pumping full steam, local camera crews, surfing photographers, and spectators will gather around to see the waves break, but more often they are there to see the wipeouts.

Other Information

Local Surf Shops: Frog House, 6908 Pacific Coast Hwy., Newport Beach; (949) 642-5690. Green Room, 6480 Pacific Coast Hwy., Newport Beach; (949) 548-9944.
Places to Stay: Balboa Inn, 105 Main St., Balboa; (949) 675-3412. Best Western Newport Beach Inn, 6208 W. Pacific Coast Hwy., Newport Beach; (949) 642-8252.
Places to Eat: Ho Sum Bistro, 3112 Newport Blvd., Newport Beach; (949) 675-0896. Mutt Lynch, 23 Ocean Front, Newport Beach; (949) 675-1556.

Brooks Street

Brooks Street is a rock reef that breaks in three main spots. It's a temperamental break, so make sure the swell direction is from the south or southwest.

Best tide: Medium
Best swell direction: South
Best wave size: Head high and above
Bottom: Rock
Type of break: Outside, left
Skill level: Advanced
Best board: Shortboard

Best season: Summer
Crowds: Crowded
Water quality: Clean
Hazards: Watch for outcropping of rocks at lower tides
Fees and permits: None

Finding the Break

From Los Angeles: Take I-405 50 miles to Laguna Canyon Road, or take CA 1 to Laguna Beach. Parking can be very difficult. Park anywhere you can find a spot. GPS: N33 32.508 / W117 47.091

Surf Description

Brooks Street can be really good with the right conditions; otherwise it can be a total bust. Brooks Street really requires a southern hurricane out of Baja California, but it will take other swells. It's mostly in summer and into fall that stronger south swells cause a good-size bump where the reef meets the swell. There are three rock reefs off Brooks Street that—depending on wave size—put out a smooth right with rocks in between. If this is your first time at Brooks Street, surf only at low tide. The spot is sheltered by a kelp bed and some large rock outcroppings and shelves. There are some exposed rocks on the far east side of the beach, but most of the reefs in Laguna Beach run parallel with the shore.

Brooks Street can be hard to find, so make sure you look for the sign where the street ends at the beach. You'll find a park bench, and that's it. Unlike Doheny or Salt Creek, there are no bathrooms, no showers, and almost no parking. Walk down the concrete steps to the beach and paddle out. The sand-and-rock beach area is very narrow along this section of coast. Parking can also be a problem because the meters are expensive and allow a maximum of only 2 hours. There is also a small alleyway on both sides of Brooks Street, but it's often full after the early-morning hours or late in the afternoon. Park illegally and you will get a ticket, guaranteed.

Brooks Street sits in the famous Laguna Beach. Beyond the surf, Laguna is one of the nicest places around if you're looking for some great grinds and an artistic culture

Laguna Beach is an artists' refuge in Southern California. This town is home to some of the finest collections of artwork in the state. Take a walk around the local shops or stop by the Laguna Beach Art Museum.

Two reefs, not enough parking, lots of boils, occasional surf stars, occasional closeouts, crowded on a south swell, scenic beauty, good places to eat for after. Brooks Street in Laguna, on a cold-blue winter day. Lucia Griggi

second to none in Orange County. The beach has also hosted several famous surfing entrepreneurs and their adventures. Hobie Alter, father of the foam-and-fiberglass surfboard, had a family house in Laguna Beach; he later went on to create one of the most popular ocean watercraft, the Hobie Cat. Tom Morey, creator of Morey boogie boards, Morey-Pope Surfboards, and innovative fins, also spent significant time in Laguna Beach. The same for Gordon Clark, the founder of Clark Foam.

Other Information

Local Surf Shops: Hobie Surf Shop, 294 Forest Ave., Laguna Beach; (949) 497-3304. Toes on the Nose, 276 S. Pacific Coast Hwy., Laguna Beach; (949) 494-4988. Thalia Surf Shop, 915 S. Coast Hwy, Laguna Beach; (949) 497-3292. Costa Azul, 689 S. Coast Hwy.,

Laguna Beach; (949) 497-1423. Laguna Surf and Sport, 1088 S. Coast Hwy., Laguna Beach; (949) 497-7000.

Places to Stay: Laguna Beach Motor Inn, 985 N. Pacific Coast Hwy., Laguna Beach; (949) 494-5294. Laguna Reef Inn–Best Western, 30806 S. Pacific Coast Hwy., Laguna Beach; (949) 499-2227. Surf and Sand Hotel, 1555 S. Pacific Coast Hwy., Laguna Beach; (949) 497-4477.

Places to Eat: Las Brisas, 361 Cliff Dr., Laguna Beach; (949) 497-5434.

Salt Creek

Salt Creek is a picturesque sandy beach located in Monarch Beach north of Dana Point. It has three different breaks: a sharp left point break at the south end, a middle break that breaks in all conditions, and a quick beach break.

Best tide: Medium

Best swell direction: Southwest, west, northwest

Best wave size: Waist high to slightly overhead

Bottom: Sand and rock

Type of break: Beach break, point, left

Skill level: Novice to advanced

Best board: Shortboard

Best seasons: Fall and summer

Crowds: Crowded

Water quality: Clean

Hazards: Exposed rocks near the point at lower tides

Fees and permits: None

Finding the Break

From Los Angeles: Take I-5 to the Doheny Beach exit/CA 1. Go north about 2 miles until you see the signs for Salt Creek or the giant Ritz-Carlton. You can also access Salt Creek by heading south on CA 1. Park above Salt Creek Beach in the giant parking lot and walk down to the shore. GPS: N33 28.891 / W117 43.479

Surf Description

Nestled under the Salt Creek Beach Park, the clear blue waters of Salt Creek welcome surfers looking for a reasonable wave with plenty of scenery and a mellow vibe. Located just north of Dana Point and south of Laguna Beach, Salt Creek sits at the

Wallet permitting, try the Ritz-Carlton bar-patio at dusk. Sit down and have a drink or something to eat on the large elevated outdoor dining area. The sunsets are unreal, and the setting is just about as good as it gets.

base of two major hotel chain properties. The stone walls of the Ritz-Carlton Hotel and the front nine holes of the St. Regis Monarch Beach golf course greet the sand beaches of Salt Creek. The beach stretches out over an elongated sandy cove. Parking is easy in a large lot just south of the Ritz-Carlton. Once you're parked, take the long walk down the hill to the beach.

Salt Creek Beach Park offers three different breaks: the Point, Middles, and Gravels. The Point, at the south end, doesn't break in small surf, but on larger days it produces reasonable rides. The most common ride is a sharp left point break. Quickly following the Point is a middle break called (not surprisingly) Middles, which breaks in all conditions. Middles is where most surfers at Salt Creek stay throughout the day. Finally, a quick beach break called Gravels skims across the shoreline. This is a sandy beach break under most conditions, though if the swell is waist high or larger, the break becomes more rideable.

Salt Creek as seen from the parking lot. Time to trot on down there and get some of Orange County's finest. Chris Sardelis

Chris Burkard

Located just north of San Clemente and below Salt Creek, Dana Strand is a small break that works best in a low to medium tide and with a strong southern swell. Like many other south-facing beaches in Orange County, Dana Strand has a peaky swell that breaks both left and right. At higher tides and in small surf, you're better off renting a sailboat from Dana Point Harbor than surfing.

Along the bluff above Salt Creek Beach during late summer to early fall, you can witness the gray-whale migration down the California coast. The best place to watch is a grass bluff along the southern perimeter of the Salt Creek Beach Park area. The park has many benches for seating, a concession stand, and an expansive, unobstructed view of the Pacific. It's not uncommon for calves to come in extremely close to shore—often within a few hundred feet. If you're on a surfboard, don't try to paddle out to catch a closer look. Gray whales are protected animals, and there is almost no way to catch up with one on a surfboard.

Other Information

Local Surf Shops: Girl in the Curl Surf Shop, 34116 Pacific Coast Hwy., Dana Point; (949) 661-4475. Killer Dana, 24621 Del Prado, Dana Point; (949) 489-8380. OC Surf and

Sport, 34255 Pacific Coast Hwy. #112, Dana Point; (949) 481-3386. Infinity Surfboards, 24382 Del Prado, Dana Point; (949) 661-6699. Hobie Sports Dana Point, 34174 Pacific Coast Hwy., Dana Point; (949) 496-0117.
Places to Stay: DoubleTree Guest Suites, 34402 Pacific Coast Hwy., Dana Point; (949) 661-1100. Holiday Inn Express, 34280 S. Pacific Coast Hwy., Dana Point; (949) 248-1000.
Places to Eat: Salt Creek Grille, 32802 Pacific Coast Hwy., Dana Point; (949) 661-7799. Bubba Kahuna's, 34320 Pacific Coast Hwy., Dana Point; (949) 496-0119.

Doheny

Located on the south side of the Dana Point Harbor, Doheny State Beach will only take southern swells and produces a very gentle, crumbling wave that breaks slowly and collapses before reaching the shore.

Best tide: Medium
Best swell direction: South
Best wave size: Waist high to head high
Bottom: Sand and rock
Type of break: Outside, beach break, right
Skill level: Novice
Best board: Longboard
Best season: Summer
Crowds: Can get crowded on weekends
Water quality: Poor
Hazards: Beginners, poor water quality
Fees and permits: None

Finding the Break

From Los Angeles: Take I-5 south to the Doheny Beach exit/CA 1. Go north about 0.25 mile; Doheny is on the left. Park in the lot located in front of the beach. GPS: N33 27.733 / W117 40.889

Surf Description

Doheny is located at Doheny State Beach at the base of the cliff side in Dana Point. Surfers knew Doheny originally as Dana Point, Killer Dana, or Dana's Point, but now the only area of surfable water is simply known as Doheny. Doheny has become mostly a beginner wave since it was destroyed in the 1970s by the harbor and jetty built in its place. Years ago it was one of the longest longboard waves in Southern California—comparable to Malibu or Rincon. Nowadays it's usually a peeling wave that breaks right and fades away as it gets closer to shore. It will only catch a swell from the south and creates a very small and gentle wave, ideal for longboarding.

Before 1966 many folks considered Dana Point the best break in all Southern California, if not the entire West Coast. It had one of the longest right point-break waves ever ridden by early California surfing pioneers. Imagine surfing history's best—Corky Carroll, Greg Noll, Billy Hamilton, Bruce Brown, and others—all lining up in one spot, Dana Point. In the name of progress, however, Dana Point became a harbor housing the affluent folks' sailboats, yachts, and powerboats along what is now called Orange County's Gold Coast.

Doheny is a great beach to hang out at if you're with the family or friends. It has several areas to barbecue as well as ample restroom and shower facilities. The beach offers plenty of room to spread out and relax.

Continued on Page 298

The Doheny equation = one guy hanging five to impress three chicks while another envious guy pushes three fins in his way as two guys paddling out take notes and the guy on the inside is about to get washed into shore. Must be summer. Jean Paul Molynieux

SUPDATE: ORANGE COUNTY

Doheny Beach and San Onofre were two of the first places in the world to legislate/limit the use of standup paddleboards in the surf zone. This suggests there has been some friction between SUPpers and surfers, going back a few years.

In the *Orange County Register* for June 1, 2010, Brittany Levine detailed the problem under the title "Beach Restrictions Ruffle Standup Paddlers":

"It all started in 2008 when the US Coast Guard and the California Department of Boating and Waterways declared stand-up paddleboards to be vessels, putting them in the same category as kayaks and wave skis. That definition, adopted last year by state beaches in Orange County, has led to restrictions on where stand-up paddleboarders can be at some beaches and, consequently, to conflicts between traditional surfers and paddleboard surfers."

The squabbles between surfers and standup paddlers at Malibu had also been happening at San Onofre and Doheny, and in April of 2010 the Orange Coast District of the California Department of Park and Recreation laid down rules and put up signs segregating standup paddlers and surfers at Sano and down Doheny way.

Beginning April Fool's Day 2010, the launching of paddle-assisted vessels was allowed only at Thor's Hammer, marked by a jetty that separates the swimming beach from the lagoon area about 1000 yards south of Dana Point Harbor. Standup paddleboards were allowed from Thor's Hammer south to the border of Capistrano Beach but were not allowed in the 1,000 yards of popular surfing area to the west—all the way to the jetty of Dana Point Harbor.

San Onofre is one of the most popular beaches in southern California. In the summer there is a line of RVs and other vehicles that wait an hour or more to drive down to the sand's edge and ride the easy, gentle, Waikiki-esque waves that break over rocks and sandy beach.

San Onofre is like Waikiki in that it's a perfect wave for beginning standup paddlers to learn their strokes and ride waves, but the influx of *surfers erectus* caused the State of California to issue order 925-96-024:

> In accordance with the provisions of Section 4326, California Code of Regulations, the water area extending from the high water mark waterward 1,000 feet, along the entire length of beach known as San Onofre Surf Beach, from the northwest boundary of the Military Enlisted Men's Beach extending southeast to the "Dog Patch" surf break, is declared a prohibited area to all vessels, (ref Definition harbors & Navigation Code Sec, 651 and 651.1), except law enforcement, lifeguard, research and commercial fishing vessels, while in the performance of their official duties. The prohibition will continue indefinitely.

Standup paddlers in Orange County need to obey those laws or risk fines from the cops and recriminations from surfers. But despite how crowded Orange County is, there are still lots of opportunities for standup paddlers to find the perfect wave and be alone with their thoughts. From the Santa Ana River to Huntington Cliffs are many, many miles of beach breaks, which shift from set to set, hour to hour, tide to tide, and day to day. With the mobility of a SUP, it shouldn't be hard to find a peak to yourself and get all the waves you can handle without pissing anyone off.

On flat days Dana Point Harbor provides a scenic circuit for getting some exercise, and Alamitos Bay near Seal Beach would also be a fun place to stroke around and get a wetlands experience in the midst of all that population. And cruising the Laguna coast on a SUP with a mask and snorkel would also be fun—especially during lobster season.

Cotton's on a giant day would be fun on a SUP, because it's a shifty wave that lends itself to the visibility and mobility advantages of a standup paddleboard.

Lots of SUPportunities behind the Orange Curtain—it's just a shame Killer Dana is no more, because movies of it from back in the day show that it would have been a great wave for standup paddlesurfing.

Doheny State Beachpark came to be in 1931 when real estate mogul Edward Doheny donated the land for public use. Doheny State Beach is separated into two sections. Campgrounds are located in the southern area, with a few campsites only steps away from the beach. The day-use area is in the north, with a large parking lot, 5-acre lawn, picnic facilities, and volleyball courts. Doheny is located at the mouth of San Juan Creek, and it has thus become one of the most polluted beaches in all of Orange County.

Other Information

Local Surf Shops: Girl in the Curl Surf Shop, 34116 Pacific Coast Hwy., Dana Point; (949) 661-4475. Killer Dana, 24621 Del Prado, Dana Point; (949) 489-8380. OC Surf and Sport, 34255 Pacific Coast Hwy. #112, Dana Point; (949) 481-3386. Infinity Surfboards, 24382 Del Prado, Dana Point; (949) 661-6699. Hobie Sports Dana Point, 34174 Pacific

Lucia Griggi

San Clemente Pier is the last pier in Orange County, located at its southern tip. Like most pier breaks, San Clemente creates a fast-moving wave that works best in a southern swell direction but can handle some cross swells, wind swells, and northern swells. Depending on swell direction, both sides of the pier can be surfed and create small, somewhat hollowed-out lefts and rights that mush up and can close out.

Coast Hwy., Dana Point; (949) 496-0117. Hole in the Fence, 34215 Doheny Park Rd., Capistrano Beach; (949) 429-2323.

Places to Stay: DoubleTree Guest Suites, 34402 Pacific Coast Hwy., Dana Point; (949) 661-1100. Holiday Inn Express, 34280 S. Pacific Coast Hwy., Dana Point; (949) 248-1000.

Places to Eat: Salt Creek Grille, 32802 Pacific Coast Hwy., Dana Point; (949) 661-7799. Bubba Kahuna's, 34320 Pacific Coast Hwy., Dana Point; (949) 496-0119.

T Street

San Clemente's T Street has three breaks. It's typically a small wave that produces mellow lefts and rights on either side of the pier.

Best tide: Low

Best swell direction: South, northwest

Best wave size: Waist high to head high

Bottom: Sand and rock

Type of break: Outside, beach break, left and right

Skill level: Novice to advanced

Best boards: Shortboard, longboard

Best seasons: Summer and winter

Crowds: Crowded

Water quality: Average

Hazards: Exposed rocks at lower tides

Fees and permits: According to funorangecountyparks.com, there's a nominal fee for meters, and annual permits are available for San Clemente residents as well as nonresidents.

Finding the Break

From Los Angeles: Take I-5 south to the Pico Avenue exit. Take Pico west through downtown, turning onto Trafalgar Street. There's parking at the base of Trafalgar Street in the parking lot or at a meter. GPS: N33 24.990 / W117 37.024

Surf Description

The easiest way to know you've reached San Clemente's T Street is by looking at the street signs. If you're on Trafalgar Street and you're looking at the ocean, chances are this is T Street. The break is located close to downtown, so there's plenty of parking; the meters are usually your best bet.

T Street is broken up into three breaks that always seem to have a wave even under the poorest of conditions. Each break ties in with changes San Clemente has undergone over the years—they're all named after some restaurant, shack, or structure that was torn down. The first break here is Cropley's, which busts fast peaky rights, but often only in winter. Beach House is a sandbar break on the south side of T Street. It typically will hold slightly larger swells better and produces both lefts and rights. T Street can get crowded on weekends and can see knee-high to head-high waves. It's also a very popular spot for bodyboarders, so be prepared to share the space. On bigger swells the outer reef point produces the best peaks.

The San Clemente Pier and T Street are important to surfing history. Onetime resident John Severson, founder of *Surfer* magazine, spent time here and certainly helped shape today's modern surfing culture.

The once quiet and relatively unknown surfside town of San Clemente has seen steady growth and transformation since the 1980s. Surfing in San Clemente has also undergone changes that parallel its housing and population boom. T Street, however, has remained a bastion of consistency. Some very influential surfing talents have passed through its water, including hard-pounding speed and aerial extremists Matt Archbold and Martin Potter. The influence of T Street has made its way out of the ocean and into the streets and parks of San Clemente as well, where skateboarding tricks mimic what you see at the pier.

T Street on a typical day: blue skies and sunshine, a bit of surf, palm trees. Southern California at its best. Lucia Griggi

Other Information

Local Surf Shops: Rocky's Surf City, 100 S. El Camino Real, San Clemente; (949) 361-2946. Stewart Surfboards, 2102 S. El Camino Real, San Clemente; (949) 492-1085. Trestles Surf Outlet, 3011 S. El Camino Real, San Clemente; (949) 498-7474. T Patterson Surfboards, 1407 N. El Camino Real, San Clemente; (949) 366-2022. Jed Noll Surfboards, 1709 N. El Camino Real, San Clemente; (949) 369-6500. Terry Senate Surfboards, 208 Calle de los Molinos, San Clemente; (949) 361-1740.
Places to Stay: Comfort Suites, 3701 S. El Camino Real, San Clemente; (949) 361-6600. Hampton Inn Suites, 2481 S. El Camino Real, San Clemente; (949) 366-1000.
Places to Eat: Cafe Rae, 1421 N. El Camino Real, San Clemente; (949) 492-8480. Z Pizza, 1021 Avenue Pico #C, San Clemente; (949) 498-3505. There are two Pedro's Tacos on El Camino Real in San Clemente—try them both.

Chris Burkard

San Clemente State Park is a long stretch of sand-and-rockyoutcropping beach just to the north of the county line. Unlike other Orange County breaks, San Clemente State Park is a versatile place to ride some of the county's more mellow longboarding surf—and in spots some peaky, fast-breaking sand reef breaks. The state park area is easily accessed off I-5. It can get crowded in summer, so arrive early if you plan to surf here.

Trestles

At the southern end of San Clemente sits Trestles. Perched behind a large housing complex and relatively obscure from the road, Trestles produces some of the best and most consistent surf in Orange County.

Best tide: Medium
Best swell direction: South, southwest, northwest
Best wave size: Head high and bigger
Bottom: Rock and sand
Type of break: Outside, left and right
Skill level: Novice to advanced
Best boards: Shortboard, funshape, longboard
Best season: Any
Crowds: Crowded
Water quality: Average
Hazards: Exposed rocks at lower tides
Fees and permits: None

Finding the Break

From Los Angeles: Take I-5 to the Cristianitos exit. Take Cristianitos down to the San Mateo Campground and parking-lot area. Drop off your vehicle here, and walk to any spot that looks good. Another option is to turn left at the Cristianitos overpass and park along the street on the east side of the freeway; then walk down the bike path and cross the train tracks by foot; watch out for trains. GPS: N33 23.744 / W117 35.517

Surf Description

Trestles is one of the best breaks in Orange County. Unlike other county breaks, Trestles isn't easily accessible, which makes it a favorite of locals. Surf addicts will swear that on the right day under the right conditions, Trestles produces some of the best surf anywhere in the world. Upper(s) and Lower(s) are the most often surfed breaks, followed by Cotton's and Church's. Each break changes depending on swell, wind, and wave conditions, but they all spit out wave shapes for every skill level.

Starting with Upper Trestles, carefully make your way into the water past the rocky ankle-breaking shoreline. Best between tides, Uppers has a multiple of spots to plant yourself for left and right takeoffs from peaky A-frames. Lower Trestles is similar to Uppers, but better. The caliber of surfing at Lowers is strong, so don't get in when it's crowded if you're a pizzy.

The break at Lowers holds a strong, smooth right line that allows for big turns, big air, and big photo opportunities—and the left is where Christian Fletcher experimented with aerial surfing.

Cotton's is located just above Upper Trestles. The wave isn't as good as Uppers', but it still produces a fairly consistent left and lacks the crowds at Uppers and Lowers.

Church's—if you consider it part of Trestles—is the last of the four breaks in the area. When it's breaking well, Church's is predominantly a right point break. In bigger surf Church's wave shape is much better than smaller swells, but swell direction has more to do with wave shape here than swell size; north or west is best.

If you're new to the world of surfing, the best youth-oriented event in the United States is held at Trestles. The National Scholastic Surfing Association (NSSA) is dedicated to building the future of America's top surfing prospects. The NSSA holds its annual contest at Lower Trestles because of location and surf conditions—the same reasons that make Trestles one of Orange County's favorite performance waves. The competition has been held here since 1992 and is a great place to view tomorrow's professional surfers.

There's a visual metaphor here—or maybe it's just a bad pun. This is Lower Trestles on a solid day. It's a stretch to call it a "freight training right." A little better might be "passenger training right" because Lowers always has a lot of riders.   Nathan French

Other Information

Local Surf Shops: Rocky's Surf City, 100 S. El Camino Real, San Clemente; (949) 361-2946. Stewart Surfboards, 2102 S. El Camino Real, San Clemente; (949) 492-1085. Trestles Surf Outlet, 3011 S. El Camino Real, San Clemente; (949) 498-7474. T Patterson Surfboards, 1409 N. El Camino Real, San Clemente; (949) 366-2022. Jed Noll Surfboards, 1709 N. El Camino Real, San Clemente; (949) 369-6500. Terry Senate Surfboards, 208 Calle de los Molinos, San Clemente; (949) 361-1740.
Places to Stay: San Clemente Inn, 2600 Avenida Del Presidente, San Clemente; (949) 492-6103.
Places to Eat: Molly Bloom's Irish Bar & Restaurant, 2391 S. El Camino Real, San Clemente; (949) 218-0120. Pipes Cafe, 2017 S. El Camino Real, San Clemente; (949) 498-5002.

San Onofre

If you ever wanted to learn to surf, San Onofre is the place. Locally called San O, the wave is a rock and sand reef break. The break at San O is spread out, so it's easy to pick your spot and surf all day.

Best tide: Medium
Best swell direction: Southwest
Best wave size: Waist high to head high
Bottom: Rock and sand
Type of break: Outside, left and right
Skill level: Novice to advanced
Best board: Longboard
Best season: Summer
Crowds: Crowded
Water quality: Clean
Hazards: Sharks
Fees and permits: According to sanofoundation.org, there is a day-use fee and an annual use pass is available.

Finding the Break

From Los Angeles: Take I-5 south to the San Onofre Beach exit. Look for the giant power plant domes. Pay your fee at the San Onofre Beach road access booth and park on the beach's shore. GPS: N33 23.050 / W117 35.010

Four girls for every guy on the beach at San Onofre. Old Man's breaks off in the distance, as these gals wait for the young women's heat to begin.   Elizabeth Pepin Silva

Surf Description

San O is a dream wave for longboarders and all levels of surfers from beginner to ripper. Not easy to see from I-5, San Onofre can be viewed from a mass transit parking lot next to the giant nuclear power station domes. The bluff overlooking the shoreline gives a full view of the entire break at San Onofre. Another nice thing about the parking lot is that it lets you check out the surf conditions without paying the California state parking fee. If you show up on a summer weekend and the line to get by the parking-fee collection booth is long, turn around—you'll be waiting forever.

San Onofre is a crumbling, long easy wave that breaks in three spots: Dogpatch, Old Man's, and the Point. All break just about the same but cater to different age demographics. The reason they all break pretty much equally is that San Onofre is a combination of sand and rock reef bottom. It's gradual in almost every section of the beach. The best swell direction for San Onofre is a direct hit from the south, but it will hold a variety of swell directions and is extremely reliable for some surf even when other spots are flat.

San Onofre is laid-back, and the demographic in the water is representative of the surfing style here. Both young and old crowd the waters at San O, but the vibe is nearly always mellow. It's probably one of the best places in Orange County to learn how to surf from a friend, instructor, or parent. Dogpatch, as the name implies, is a place where a dog could learn how to surf. The wave breaks slow and easy. The Point is also a longboard wave, but in higher surf conditions it can provide both lefts and rights that a funshaper or shortboarder can ride with relative ease. You probably can figure out the wave shape from the name "Old Man's." Look for the thatch-roofed hut as your marker.

Other Information

Local Surf Shops: Rocky's Surf City, 100 S. El Camino Real, San Clemente; (949) 361-2946. Stewart Surfboards, 2102 S. El Camino Real, San Clemente; (949) 492-1085. Trestles Surf Outlet, 3011 S. El Camino Real, San Clemente; (949) 498-7474. T Patterson Surfboards, 1409 N. El Camino Real, San Clemente; (949) 366-2022. Jed Noll Surfboards, 1709 N. El Camino Real, San Clemente; (949) 369-6500. Terry Senate Surfboards, 208 Calle de los Molinos, San Clemente; (949) 361-1740.

Places to Stay: San Clemente Inn, 2600 Avenida Del Presidente, San Clemente; (949) 492-6103.

Places to Eat: Molly Bloom's Irish Bar & Restaurant, 2391 S. El Camino Real, San Clemente; (949) 218-0120. Pipes Cafe, 2017 S. El Camino Real, San Clemente; (949) 498-5002.

REGION 10: SAN DIEGO COUNTY

San Diego County is as far south as you can get in the state of California. Bordering Orange County to the north and Mexico to the south, San Diego has a wonderful mix of culture and great surf. This is a sailing and surfing county. Slightly milder in temperature both in and out of the water than its northern counterpart, Orange County, San Diego is beautiful all year round. It's also very easy to get around here. For the purposes of this book, you just need to use I-5 and CA 1, and the only airport to fly into is San Diego International. All the surf breaks described in this section (with the exception of Black's) are easily accessible by car or by foot.

San Diego's landscape is generally dry but filled with sharp green pine trees and low-lying shrubs that change color from dry brown to lush green between seasons. Unlike other Southern California regions, there are no significant offshore islands. San Diegans are the recipients of very consistent surf. Winter, of course, is the coolest time of the year, but the average low even in winter is around sixty-six degrees. The county sees a touch of the late-spring and early-summer marine layer. It can also get windy, but more often than not the winds come in the afternoon when the temperature rises. The beaches in San Diego are packed in Pacific Beach and La Jolla; most of the other spots, however, are large enough that a crowd never forms.

The county starts just north of Oceanside and includes places like Cotton's, Trestles, and San Onofre—which a lot of people think of as Orange County spots. However, the best way to tell you are heading south into San Diego down I-5 is the giant nuclear power plant structures near the water's edge. Past here you will run into a vast stretch of incredible surf—all of it off-limits. This is Camp Pendleton, and it's owned by Uncle Sam; if you try to surf here, a marine MP might arrest you under the Patriot Act. While it's flat in Oceanside, from Encinitas to La Jolla the San Diego County coastline quickly slopes into a fantastic vista of rolling hills and cliff sides.

Oceanside, Del Mar, La Jolla, and San Diego are the main cities along the San Diego County coastline. Bordering San Diego County to the south are Baja California and the city of Tijuana. If you're interested in seeing something Mexican besides a touristy border town, Ensenada and Rosarito are reachable by car from San Diego. North of the border in San Diego County there are several state parks, and the area is very friendly to outdoor and surf culture. Nightlife is also excellent, with Pacific Beach, Del Playa, and downtown in the Gaslight District having the most to offer; you can also take in the wealthy swank of La Jolla and Del Mar.

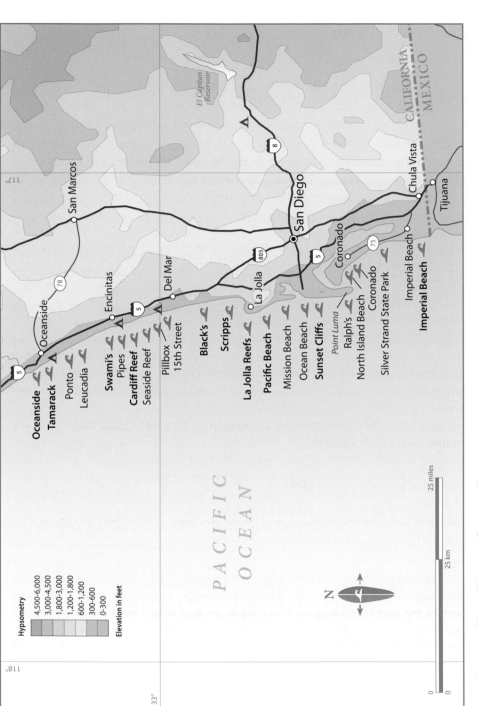

Hypsometry

4,500–6,000
3,000–4,500
1,800–3,000
1,200–1,800
600–1,200
300–600
0–300

Elevation in feet

118°

117°

33°

El Capitan
Reservoir

San Marcos

78

Oceanside

5

Oceanside

Tamarack

Ponto

Leucadia

Encinitas

Swami's

Pipes

Cardiff Reef

Seaside Reef

5

Del Mar

Pillbox

15th Street

Black's

Scripps

La Jolla Reefs

La Jolla

Pacific Beach

Mission Beach

Ocean Beach

Sunset Cliffs

Point Luma

Ralph's

North Island Beach

Coronado

Silver Strand State Park

Coronado

75

805

5

San Diego

8

Chula Vista

Imperial Beach

Imperial Beach

Tijuana

CALIFORNIA
MEXICO

PACIFIC
OCEAN

N

0   25 km

0   25 miles

Region 10 (San Diego County)

Overall Surf Description

San Diego County is the southernmost section of the California coastline, extending to the border of Mexico. It offers typical California surf, producing four types of breaks: beach, sand reef, rock reef, and point. San Diego produces its best wave conditions when there is a direct westerly swell or a variation from the south or north. The coastline is mostly sandbars. These sandbars produce endless surfing spots on open stretches of beaches visible from the roadside. There are a few cliff-side surf breaks near Point Loma and a few harder-to-access locations like Black's, but for the most part San Diego County has very surfing-friendly topography. A wet suit is recommended throughout the year, but in late summer it can be shed for a rash guard and board shorts. San Diego is home to some very scenic shoreline, especially from Black's to La Jolla Reefs. Shortboards, longboards, and funshapes are the best equipment, unless a storm comes directly out of Hawaii and lands monsters along the shore. Like most of California, mornings are the best time to surf in San Diego County; still, the area attracts a young transient population, so the best surf spots can get crowded at times. The water is clean and very clear at many breaks, but an occasional Tijuana sewage dump can wreak havoc. Surf is usually best in the late fall, winter, and early spring, while summer tends to be poorer.

Fall Surf
Fall surf in San Diego County is as good as most of the other popular California locations. Most of the autumn swell comes from the west, southwest, or northwest. The swell direction, combined with reasonable size, creates good waves across the coastline. Late in the fall season, the water temperature will start to drop, so a wet suit is recommended past September.

Winter Surf
One of the only colder times of the year—if you can call it cold in San Diego—is winter. Winter surfing is reasonably good to fair. Swell direction from the north brings cold water, lower air temperatures, and thicker wet suits. Only breaks that can capture swell from the west or northwest do well in winter.

Spring Surf
Spring surfing in San Diego is generally good weather-wise, but it's hit or miss surf-conditions-wise. Locals relish the warming of the air and water temperatures, and most of the surfing celebration takes place on southwest-, west-, and northwest-facing shores. There tend to be fewer crowds than in summer, but it is the time of year when the hard-core crew of winter has to welcome back the softies who hibernated during the colder months.

It's a bit of work to make it down the cliffs to Black's Beach, but it can be so worth it.
Lucia Griggi

	Average Temperatures for Region **(San Diego County)**	
	Air (San Diego)	**Water (San Diego)**
Jan	66	58
Feb	66	58
Mar	66	58
Apr	69	60
May	69	63
June	72	65
July	76	66
Aug	78	68
Sept	77	66
Oct	74	65
Nov	70	61
Dec	66	59

Summer Surf

Summer is great for crowds and parties in San Diego, but the surfing can be unpredictable. Unlike its northern border county, San Diego doesn't do that well in summer. The swell direction from the south doesn't cooperate well with the sandbars, reefs, or point breaks along the coast. Knee-high junk to head-high mush at best dominates the summer surfing scene—though it's hard to complain given nearly seventy-degree water temperatures and warm summer days.

Oceanside

Oceanside is a sand reef break located in the northern part of San Diego County.

Best tide: Medium
Best swell direction: Any
Best wave size: Waist high to slightly overhead
Bottom: Sand
Type of break: Outside, beach break, left and right
Skill level: Novice to advanced
Best boards: Shortboard, longboard
Best season: Any
Crowds: Can get crowded on weekends
Water quality: Poor
Hazards: None
Fees and permits: None

Finding the Break

From Los Angeles: Take I-5 south to the Mission Avenue exit. Head west toward the beach. Turn left or right onto Pacific Street, depending on which area you'd like to surf. Parking is available near the harbor area and farther south just off Pacific Street. GPS: N33 11.154 / W117 22.645

Surf Description

Sitting at the northernmost tip of San Diego County, Oceanside boasts a relatively low cost of living compared with other California coastal cities. It has a very steady economic base thanks to Uncle Sam, who has strategically positioned Camp Pendleton Military Base on its northernmost beaches. For national security reasons, unless you are a member of the armed forces stationed at Camp Pendleton, you'll be sticking to

Oceanside is open to swell from all angles, a lot of wind = a lot of variables. But sometimes the equation equals this. Bryce Johnson

the surf outside the boundaries of Camp Pendleton—trespassing could lead to arrest or even death.

Oceanside Beach is a long stretch of sand reef that dishes up miles and miles of consistent breaks all along its shores. Starting from the north end, there are harbor breaks on either side of the jetty walls. The left and right well up quickly off the wall and produce nice carving waves. Farther south you can pick your spot. There are long stretches of beach. Some of the area's better surfing talent heads toward the pier, which—like other sand reef pier breaks—spits up lefts and rights depending on swell direction and conditions. Farther south down Oceanside Beach, the wave tends to be a little mushier on small days and favors a midsize to long board.

Oceanside is also home to the California Surf Museum (surfmuseum.org). Considering the huge impact California has had on the world of surfing, the museum offers an excellent historical perspective on the impact of surf culture on California. According to its literature, the museum presents standing displays of surfing equipment and photographs. Every six months it introduces a new feature exhibit highlighting one of the pioneering legends of the surfing world. Approximately 20,000 people visit the museum annually.

Other Information

Local Surf Shops: Surf Ride Board Shop, 1909 S. Coast Hwy., Oceanside; (760) 433-4020. Action Beach, 310 Mission Ave., Oceanside; (760) 722-7101. Asylum Surf, 310 Mission Ave., Oceanside; (760) 722-7101. Real Surf Shop, 1101 S. Coast Hwy., Oceanside; (760) 754-0670. Sun Diego Boardshops, 5620 Paseo Del Norte, Carlsbad; (760) 607-1220.

Places to Stay: There are a lot of tiny hotels and motels in Oceanside. Marina Comfort Suites, 888 N. Coast Hwy., Oceanside; (888) 574-7462. Southern California Beach Club, 121 S. Pacific St., Oceanside; (877) 477-7368.

Places to Eat: Johnny Manana's, 308 Mission Ave., Oceanside; (760) 721-9999. The Beach Break Cafe, 1902 S. Coast Hwy., Oceanside; (760) 439-6355. Lemon Grass Thai Restaurant, 1813 S. Coast Hwy., Oceanside; (760) 433-1783. Azafran Cuban Cuisine, 1001 S. Coast Hwy., Oceanside; (760) 435 0005.

Tamarack

Tamarack is a sandbar reef break just south of Oceanside in Carlsbad. The break creates a lippy wave and allows rides into the shoreline.

Best tides: Low to medium
Best swell direction: Anything but north
Best wave size: Waist high
Bottom: Sand
Type of break: Beach break, left and right
Skill level: Novice to advanced
Best boards: Longboard, shortboard, funshape
Best seasons: Fall, winter, and spring
Crowds: Can get crowded on weekends
Water quality: Average
Hazards: None
Fees and permits: According to news.carlsbadca.gov, there is a nominal fee to park.

Finding the Break

From Los Angeles: Take I-5 south to the Tamarack Avenue exit. Exit Tamarack and head west almost 1 mile. Parking is right off the beach at Tamarack State Beach. GPS: N33 08.768 / W117 20.681

Surf Description

Tamarack is part of the Carlsbad State Beach area. The park has three main areas: Tamarack, Warm Water Jetty, and Terramar. Tamarack is another long stretch of beach split by the Tamarack River mouth. The river mouth's sandbar creates an outside break between the two jetties. The break consists of a lippy wave and allows rides into the shoreline at most tides. Tamarack and the other beach areas are relatively easy to identify from CA 1.

Tamarack's conditions can vary greatly depending on the weather. As a general rule, if there's little to no wind, Tamarack will have something to surf on regardless of the swell size and direction. It typically holds a south swell better than other beaches in the county, but it can produce peaky A-frames breaking both left and right. The takeoff is mushy in smaller surf and can get steep and quick when there's a strong south swell at low tide.

Carlsbad, like many other northern San Diego County cities, has undergone its share of transformation since the 1990s. Once known as an agricultural community, Carlsbad was simply a city between Orange County and San Diego. Today it's very different. Golf courses, ultraexclusive hotels, and urban housing developments have turned this once-"ag-surfing" town into an upscale community. Fortunately, the beaches and breaks have not been impacted by San Diego's urban sprawl over the

Walking the track to Tamarack—getting there a little bit before the tide, but it will get better as it's coming up. vincebodie.com

Anthony Ghiglia

Located in South Carlsbad and just in front of the Batiquitos Lagoon, Ponto is a fairly good-size and consistent break that peels off both lefts and rights, depending on swell direction. Ponto holds any westerly swell best, but the sandy bottom at a low tide can be really low, so watch your dismount. Watch the lagoon runoff after a rain, too, as it can collect some undesirable materials that ultimately flush right into the break.

Chris Burkard

Just south of Ponto is Leucadia, a long stretch of beach, rock, kelp, and sand. It's relatively easy to access, but most points require the use of long stairways up and down the cliff shores. Longboarders as well as shortboarders can handle several sections of Leucadia, depending on swell direction and size.

years. A prime example of the unusual growth Carlsbad has seen are two recogniz-able American icons of industry. Golf club manufacturer Calloway makes its home in Carlsbad, while childhood toy staple LEGO is the focus of an entire theme park just a few miles inland off I-5.

Other Information

Local Surf Shops: Raw Skin Surf 'n Sport, 2796 Carlsbad Blvd., Carlsbad; (760) 434-1122. Offshore Surf Shop, 3179 Carlsbad Blvd., Carlsbad; (760) 729-4934. Sun Diego Boardshops, 5620 Paseo Del Norte, Carlsbad; (760) 607-1220.
Places to Stay: South Carlsbad State Beach Campground, 7201 Carlsbad Blvd., Carlsbad; (760) 438-3143 or (800) 444-PARK.
Places to Eat: The Armenian Cafe, 3126 Carlsbad Blvd., Carlsbad; (760) 720-CAFE. Spirito's Italian Restaurant, 300 Carlsbad Village Dr. #208, Carlsbad; (760) 720-1132.

Swami's

Swami's is a small sandy beach located just below the cliffs of Encinitas. It's a nice point break that creates shapely hollow rights.

Best tides: Low to medium
Best swell direction: West, northwest
Best wave size: Slightly overhead
Bottom: Sand
Type of break: Outside, left and right
Skill level: Novice to advanced
Best boards: Shortboard, longboard, funshape
Best season: Winter
Crowds: Crowded
Water quality: Clean
Hazards: Crowds
Fees and permits: None

Finding the Break

From Los Angeles: Take I-5 and exit at Encinitas Boulevard. Take Encinitas to CA 1 and turn left. Look for the gold-colored domes on the Self Realization Fellowship's walls and park at Swami's' entrance past K Street. If the lot is full (it's tiny), you can park just off CA 1 to the south. GPS: N33 02.245 / W117 17.681

Surf Description

How does a surf break get a name like Swami's? It comes from a spiritual center located right near the break. Swami's is located at the southern end of Encinitas. There is no possible way to miss it while driving down CA 1 because unless you're looking for South Bend, Indiana—which we hope you are not—the only golden domes around here belong to the Self Realization Center. What exactly is a Self Realization Center? It's a place where San Diego County residents study Eastern and East Asian philosophies.

Swami's gets its name from the Self Realization Fellowship, which built two golden domes in honor of the Swami Paramahansa Yogananda in 1937.

Like the golden domes, the vibe at Swami's is enlightening and mellow. Many locals swear this is the best break in San Diego County—and it very well might be, if you're a longboarder. On crowded days,

Don Balch

Pipes is a sand reef break sitting just below the main downtown section of Encinitas. Several campgrounds surround Pipes, including San Elijo, which is easily accessible just off CA 1. Pipes receives a westerly swell direction best. The break serves up both lefts and rights from anywhere on the beach, and the conditions are usually best at low tide.

Day of Dreams at Swami's, January 7, 2003. High pressure over Nevada created a high-pressure system and Santa Ana winds, which met in swift collision with a very west swell. According to Surfline's "20 Perfect Storms: The 20 Best Swells Since 1985" (surfline .com), a small, complex low-pressure system from southwest of Japan combined with a "complex low" in the Gulf of Alaska. The resulting swell came from 265 to 290 degrees and lit up Swami's as good as it gets. According to the photographer, "The winds weren't as bad as the crowd." Kevin Roche

especially on weekends, the spiritual vibe lessens to more tolerance than anything. Swami's is a consistent wave regardless of conditions, with several waves within the break zone. It gets better with size and starts outside with a mellow takeoff followed by a small holed break until it peters out at the channel's edge. Low tide will make the inside break more surfable. Any size board can be used at Swami's, but longboarders rule the majority of the waves.

The parking lot just above Swami's offers great views if you'd like to check out the break before walking down the cliff side to paddle into a few. The entire area at one point belonged to the Noonan family. Encinitas used to be a fairly reasonable place to live on the California coast—well, so did almost all of California at some point. But imagine this while you're perched along the railing overlooking Swami's: The Noonan family bought the land back in the late 1800s because of the majestic views. The purchase price was right around $1,000. Just think if all our ancestors had real estate instincts like that!

Other Information

Local Surf Shops: K-Five Surf & Sport, 280 N. El Camino Real, Encinitas; (760) 436-6613. Longboard Grotto Surf Shop, 978 N. Coast Highway 101, Encinitas; (760) 634-1920. Hansen Surfboards and Surf Shop, 1105 S. Coast Highway 101, Encinitas, (760) 753-6595.

Places to Stay: San Elijo State Beach Campground, Cardiff-by-the-Sea; (800) 444-7275. South Carlsbad State Beach Campground, 7201 Carlsbad Ave., Carlsbad; (800) 444-7275. Rodeway Inn, 1444 N. Coast Highway 101, Encinitas; (800) 546-1598. Portofino Inn, 186 N. Coast Highway 101, Encinitas; (760) 944-0301.

Places to Eat: Jamroc 101 Caribbean Grill, 101 N. Coast Highway 101, Encinitas; (760) 436-3162. St. Tropez Bistro & Bakery, 947 S. Coast Highway 101, Encinitas; (760) 633-0084.

Cardiff Reef

Cardiff Reef is a long stretch of beach that sits between two small hillsides bordering the ocean. It's popular with longboarders due to its sand bottom and slow, mushy wave.

Best tides: Low to medium
Best swell direction: Northwest, west
Best wave size: Waist high to slightly overhead
Bottom: Sand
Type of break: Point, right
Skill level: Intermediate to advanced
Best boards: Longboard, shortboard
Best season: Winter
Crowds: Can get crowded on weekends
Water quality: Poor
Hazards: Poor water quality
Fees and permits: According to yelp.com, there is a nominal fee to park at Cardiff State Beach.

Finding the Break

From San Diego: Take I-5 and exit at Manchester. Take Manchester west toward the beach. Turn onto the coast highway until you reach Cardiff Reef. There's a parking lot at the beach for a fee, or you can park along the beach access roads. GPS: N33 01.135 / W117 16.970

Surf Description

The rocky reefs along Cardiff can handle anything from little tricklers to double over-head. Cardiff Reef produces both lefts and rights that will wall up, creating a steeper approach that peels off nicely. Cardiff Reef is a long right point break best suited for longboards. The wave starts out mushy and hollows out into a small barrel right that picks up speed as it goes. Farther left near the San Elijo Lagoon is Suckouts, a small, short, hollow break that pushes right into Cardiff Reef once it's closed out.

Georges is the popular name for Cardiff State Beach. Georges stretches out in front of the San Elijo Lagoon. There is little sand on this beach; most of the shoreline is made of small stones that are difficult to walk on, let alone hang out on. The state of California from time to time will pump sand in to create more beach area due to the harsh Pacific surf that seems to drink sand along Cardiff's shores. For many locals and those without good balance, it's far easier to see the beach from one of the many restaurants along CA 1 and the coast. It should not be a surprise that most surfers and families will go a bit farther to Pipes or San Elijo for camping and easier access.

One of the area's more famous residents is Rob Machado, who—after a short childhood stint in Australia—was raised close to Cardiff Reef in Cardiff-by-the-Sea. Machado grew up surfing the San Diego County waves and launched himself into a pro career in his late teens. Like many surfers in the area, he comes from a family

Sometimes you can get too much of a good thing. Cardiff Reef on a west swell and strong Santa Ana winds. Challenging.   Kevin Roche

that moved here from somewhere else, allowing offspring to perfect their craft in the sunny Southern California surf. In Machado's case, San Diego County became his playground.

SUPDATE: SAN DIEGO COUNTY

From Colton's Point to the Mexican border, San Diego County is 70 miles of SUP Heaven: oodles of adventures for standup paddlers. If you want to try something really dumb, paddle into Camp Pendleton from the San Onofre side or the Oceanside side, and get all the waves you want until someone points an automatic weapon at you—just kidding, *don't* try it.

But you don't have to trespass on federal property to get waves to yourself in San Diego County. Cardiff Reef is a popular spot for SUP because the waves are shifty and rolling and flat-faced, and SUPs are perfect for chasing them down and making the most of them.

If you don't dig the walk down the cliffs to Black's Beach, try launching at Scripps Pier and paddling north along the beach—grab waves that no one else can get to, but avoid the packs of surfers unless you enjoy stinkeye and salty language.

The same goes for Sunset Cliffs: Launch from the north side and cherry-pick waves as you move south. No need to get in the way of any surfers. There are lots of waves going unridden along here. And you can do the same at La Jolla: Launch at the north end and go all the way around to Pacific Beach Point—another perfect spot for SUP.

On and on: Del Mar, Carlsbad, Seaside Reef, and all along the beach from Coronado to Imperial Beach—but you might want to avoid the training area for the Navy SEALs south of Coronado, unless you want to confront a pissed-off guy in a Draeger Rebreather pointing an underwater Glock at you.

Has anyone surfed giant Tijuana Sloughs on a SUP? Another opportunity for the truly adventurous.

And for non-open-ocean thrills, all those lagoons and waterways in north San Diego County would be fun to paddle, and you could spend a lot of time paddling around San Diego Harbor—just stay away from aircraft carriers, or that SEAL with the Rebreather might be all over you.

Other Information

Local Surf Shops: Patagonia Surf Shop, 2185 San Elijo Ave., Cardiff-by-the-Sea; (760) 634-9886. Nirvana Surfboards, 111 Chesterfield Dr. #115, Cardiff; (760) 274-4622. Envirosurfer Eco-Friendly Surf Shop, 2463 Newport Ave., Cardiff; (888) 901-0114.
Places to Stay: Comfort Inn Cardiff-by-the-Sea, 1661 Villa Cardiff Dr., Cardiff-by-the-Sea; (760) 944-0427. Cardiff-by-the-Sea Lodge, 142 Chesterfield, Cardiff-by-the-Sea; (760) 944-6474. Cardiff-by-the-Sea Campgrounds, 2051 San Elijo Ave., Cardiff-by-the-Sea; (760) 436-0431.
Places to Eat: Pipes Cafe, 121 Liverpool Dr., Cardiff-by-the-Sea; (760) 632-0056. Las Olas, 2655 US 101, Cardiff-by-the-Sea; (760) 942-1860.

Kevin Roche

Between two peaks on the Solano Beach coastline sits a long, sandy section of the coast called Seaside Reef. It's a small break good for above-average surfers all the way up to the best local talent. Its sandy bottom typically keeps the waves small and creates a good left that allows you to rip some turns. Seaside Reef breaks best at lower tides and in smaller to medium swells. Parking is easy; a lot sits right in front of the beach off CA 1.

Anthony Ghiglia

Located between Cardiff Reef and the river mouth, Pillbox is a sand reef break that has a few spots of rocky shelf. Part of an 8-mile stretch through Encinitas and Solano Beach, Pillbox works best on low tide. The break also favors a south-to-southwest swell and produces a small to large wave, depending on conditions. The wave drops in quickly and can leave solid open faces for some excellent turns.

Don Balch

Found in upscale Del Mar, 15th Street has both a rock reef and a sand reef break. Depending on your location, 15th Street works in almost all types of conditions. Low tide works best near or on the reef and can produce a small, relatively fast wave with a quick drop. Farther outside the main rock reef, sandbars take over, and mid- to high tide works best with San Diego's traditionally mushier waves.

Black's

Black's is a hard-to-reach yet unforgettable break. Rarely crowded, it has several peaky areas along its shore that allow for some hollow, fast-moving lefts and rights.

Best tides: Low to medium
Best swell direction: West, northwest, southwest
Best wave size: Head high and above
Bottom: Sand
Type of break: Beach, right
Skill level: Advanced
Best boards: Shortboard, gun
Best season: Winter
Crowds: Crowded
Water quality: Clean
Hazards: None
Fees and permits: None

This is what a surfer wants to see while huffing it down the cliffs to Black's.   Lucia Griggi

Finding the Break

From San Diego: Take I-5 north to Ardath Road. Take a right onto La Jolla Shores Drive. Turn left onto Calle Frescota until you come to the free public parking lot at La Jolla Shores. This lot includes 350 spaces, including eight parking spaces for people with disabilities. Walk north 1 mile. Use caution regarding the unstable cliffs above and tidal conditions, which may obstruct passage. GPS: N32 51.461 / W117 15.382

Surf Description

If you're a native of San Diego or have ever lived here, no doubt you know about Black's Beach. Strange but true: Two very different cultures meet on the trails and beaches of Black's nearly every day, but one couldn't be less interested in the other Besides its amazing surf, Black's is home to many nudists seeking a little rest and relaxation at the beach. Although not officially sanctioned, nudism is allowed.

Your best bet to see San Diego's wildlife is at the San Diego Zoo, but at Black's you are almost guaranteed to see San Diego's human form of wildlife.

Black's is a picturesque collage of ocean swell meeting sandbar. Nestled along the steep hillsides of northern La Jolla and just north of the Scripps Pier, this is arguably the best beach break in California. Black's has several peaks in the break, depending on conditions, but overall the wave is fast, has a steeper-than-average takeoff, and busts down with nicely paced walls that can take larger swells as well. On bigger days you must be a strong paddler to get out at Black's; if you're not, watch from the hillside. There are rarely lifeguards on duty, so don't surf here if this is even a consideration. Also, access can be difficult—the cliffs of Black's Beach are unstable, and slides can occur without warning, so it's best to stay well away from them.

> **Black's is known for its former "clothing optional" status. But don't be surprised if you find "rule breakers" on the beach.**

Black's Beach is a sandy, 2 mile-long stretch of beach formally known as Torrey Pines City Beach and Torrey Pines State Beach. The beach is jointly owned by the city of San Diego and the state of California. Making Black's even more unusual is a glider port atop the cliffs overlooking the beach; here, hang gliders and paragliders fly over the shoreline.

Other Information

Local Surf Shops: Mitch's Surf Shop, 631 Pearl St., La Jolla; (858) 459-5933. La Jolla Surf Company, 721 Pearl St., La Jolla; (858) 454-4547. World Core, 7863 Girard Ave., La Jolla;

(858) 456-6699. Bessell Surfboards, 515 Westbourne St., San Diego; (858) 456-2591. Roxy La Jolla, 1111 Prospect St., La Jolla; (858) 459-1460.

Places to Stay: La Jolla Beach Travelodge, 6750 La Jolla Blvd., La Jolla; (800) 454-4361.

Places to Eat: El Pescador, 627 Pearl St., La Jolla; (858) 456-2526. Cody's La Jolla, 8030 Girard Ave., La Jolla; (858) 459-0040. Fugu's Sushi and Wok, 915 Pearl St., La Jolla; (858) 456-1414.

Scripps

Sometimes known as Scripps Pier or Scripps Ranch, Scripps is a right break that generates powerful surf in larger swells, and holds smaller waves as well.

Best tide: Medium

Best swell direction: West, northwest

Best wave size: Head high and above

Bottom: Sand

Type of break: Beach break, right

Skill level: Novice to intermediate

Best boards: Shortboard, longboard

Best season: Winter

Crowds: Crowded

Water quality: Poor

Hazards: None

Fees and permits: None

Finding the Break

From San Diego: Take I-5 and exit at La Jolla Village Drive. Head west down the long hill until you reach the bottom. Turn right onto La Jolla Shores Drive and head toward the Scripps Pier. At Torrey Pines Road, turn left. There's plenty of parking in the lots surrounding the beach and pier. GPS: N32 50.998 / W117 16.263

Surf Description

Ever lend some money to a brother, friend, or surfing buddy and think, *Nothing good will come of this?* In 1878 Edward W. Scripps borrowed $23 from his brother and founded the Penny Press in Cleveland. Years later Scripps launched United Press and built a publishing and media empire. One of the many places in San Diego County named after the Scripps family is the Scripps Institution of Oceanography. Now part of the University of California–San Diego, it's one of the oldest, largest, and most important centers for marine science research, training, and public service in the world.

Although no known surfers borrowed any money from the Scripps family, this break still bears the Scripps name. It's a large sandbar break that attracts huge crowds. Scripps in general is a dominating right that can handle most sizes of swells; still, it works best in smaller waters, where it produces an easy-entry takeoff into a barreling right that holds on for a long time before closing out.

Scripps can readily accommodate everyone from beginners to advanced surfers. Beginners should stay away from the pier and the pier pilings and stick near the shoreline to ride the re-formed waves. Even better for beginners is to move farther south toward La Jolla and try some of the smaller swells that form mushy waves just off the various sandbars. At the pier the crowd factor can be high, especially on summer weekends. Here you will find consistently good surfing conditions for advanced surfers, more often than not busting aerials off hard-charging lefts.

Birch Aquarium is a great place to check out some of the local sea and plant life. If you know little about kelp and sea lions, it is a good way to pass the time on cold or blown-out days. Birch Aquarium is located at 2300 Expedition Way.

The lab is open for deep-ocean research at Scripps Pier. anthonyghiglia.com

Other Information

Local Surf Shops: Mitch's Surf Shop, 631 Pearl St., La Jolla; (858) 459-5933. La Jolla Surf Company, 721 Pearl St., La Jolla; (858) 454-4547. World Core, 7863 Girard Ave., La Jolla; (858) 456-6699. Bessell Surfboards, 515 Westbourne St., San Diego; (858) 456-2591. Roxy La Jolla, 1111 Prospect St., La Jolla; (858) 459-1460.
Places to Stay: La Jolla Beach Travelodge, 6750 La Jolla Blvd., La Jolla; (800) 454-4361.
Places to Eat: Jose's Court Room, 1037 Prospect St., La Jolla; (858) 454-7655. Busy Bee's, 6861 La Jolla Blvd, La Jolla; (858) 456-2738.

La Jolla Reefs

La Jolla Reefs is composed of several breaks, each of which can accommodate smaller surf as well as large swells.

Best tides: Low to medium
Best swell direction: Southwest, west, northwest
Best wave size: Head high and above
Bottom: Sand
Type of break: Beach break, right
Skill level: Intermediate to advanced
Best boards: Shortboard, longboard
Best seasons: Fall and winter
Crowds: Crowded
Water quality: Clean
Hazards: Exposed rock areas
Fees and permits: None

Finding the Break

From San Diego: Take I-5 and exit at La Jolla Village Drive. Head west down the long hill until you reach the bottom. Continue straight ahead until you reach La Jolla Village. Turn right at the T-intersection, then left at the coastline. Pick your spot along the stretch of breaks if you can find parking, especially on weekends. GPS: N32 50.530 / W117 16.868

Surf Description

The name *La Jolla* comes from Spanish and means "the jewel." Everything about La Jolla—from its seaside homes to the crystal-clear water and incredible surf—is indeed

Lots of wind, lots of sea and a shack with a view at one of California's most exalted surf spots on an emotional winter day at Windansea.   Don Balch

a precious gem not to be missed. La Jolla has also been home to some of surfing's best surf clubs, board shapers, and surfing characters. From historical surf icon Bob Simmons at Windansea to Pat Curren's youth surf playground and board shaper Rusty Preisendorfer, La Jolla Reefs have been instrumental in shaping both the Southern California and global surf culture.

La Jolla Reefs is composed of three main areas: Big Rock, La Jolla Cove, and Windansea. Big Rock's reef break is a strong left with a quick takeoff and a lot of force. It requires some local knowledge when it's firing, so if you're a first-timer, go when the conditions aren't ideal to get acquainted. The wave is better in smaller surf, but it's an aggressive wave and requires skill. La Jolla Cove tends to be a bit smaller year-round and also has a fast, peaky break both left and right. However, it isn't well known for small stuff. Ideal in winter and during very high surf, La Jolla Cove is where the most of La Jolla's past and present surfers are indoctrinated into the world of big-wave surfing. Big-wave conditions don't come often, but when they do, if you have the mustard, it's worth a try. Otherwise watch from the rocky shore.

Windansea served for many years as the preferred hangout and home to San Diego's best surfers. A mushy longboardable wave with fewer crowds originally attracted San Diego's surf culture to move north from Pacific Beach. Over time, however, Windansea became just as crowded as the rest of San Diego's favorite breaks. With easy beach access through a small stretch of sand, Windansea is a solid wave rideable with nearly any type of board.

Other Information

Local Surf Shops: South Coast Windansea Surf Shop, 740 Felspar St. #A, San Diego; (619) 483-7660. Pacific Beach Surf Shop, 747 Pacific Beach Dr., San Diego; (619) 488-9575. Rip Curl – Pacific Beach, 4287 Mission Blvd., San Diego; (858) 273-8070.
Places to Stay: La Jolla Beach Travelodge, 6750 La Jolla Blvd., La Jolla; (800) 454-4361.
Places to Eat: Sammy's Woodfired Pizza, 72 Pearl St., La Jolla; (858) 456-5222. Islands Restaurant, 3351 Nobel Dr., La Jolla; (858) 455-9945.

Pacific Beach

Pacific Beach might better be named Party Beach. Marked by a large pier, the surf breaks both left and right along the long, sandy shore.

Best tide: Medium
Best swell direction: Southwest, west, northwest
Best wave size: Waist high to head high
Bottom: Sand
Type of break: Point, right
Skill level: Novice to intermediate
Best board: Longboard
Best season: Winter
Crowds: Crowded
Water quality: Average
Hazards: None
Fees and permits: None

Finding the Break

From San Diego: Take I-5 and exit at Mission Boulevard. Follow Mission all the way to the beach and park. There's parking on many of the side streets, at parking lots, and near the pier. GPS: N32 45.615 / W117 15.140

Surf Description

Pacific Beach represents the past and present of San Diego surfing. Known as PB, Pacific Beach has always attracted the youthful surf culture and lifestyle. Pacific Beach was one of the original surf spots for the San Diego surfers back in the 1940s. Both young and old still surf here today, and if you listen closely while waiting in the lineup, you can eavesdrop on old-school longboarders telling stories that begin with "I remember when . . ."

Pacific Beach is a large offshore point break that attracts crowds year-round. The crowd starts at the beach and works its way into the water. In fact, on a summer weekend it's not unusual to find hundreds of surfers paddling for the same small summer swell from the south. The break is a mushy, easy takeoff that starts off relatively smooth and can slow down in sections to a snail's pace, depending on tide conditions. In larger swells PB can be a fast closeout, though this is more typical in winter.

At Pacific Beach you will find there are really three times of day around which surfing revolves. The first is the early morning. This brings out the locals before the

Enter Sandman: Pacific Beach's Crystal Pier on a blissfully empty morning before the locals have rolled out of bed from a typical party night.   Don Balch

Lucia Griggi

Mission Beach is located just south of Pacific Beach, but it's equally crowded. It's a sandy beach break that works best in knee-high to head-high waves. The wave along the shore tends to be peaky but doesn't spit out perfect A-frames by any means. It also tends to close out, and if there's wind, you might as well sit on the beach and watch the people roll by on the concrete strand.

Anthony Ghiglia

Ocean Beach is the southern sister of Mission Beach, but with a more liberal attitude (if that's possible). Ocean Beach is marked by the harbor jetty at the north end and Ocean Beach Pier to the south. The beach tends to get very crowded in the summer months, and the water isn't as good as other areas of San Diego. The swell varies depending on your spots. Expect a peaky left just off the jetty and softer beach-break mush along the main section of the beach.

winds even have a chance to wake up. Shortly thereafter, at midmorning, the youth of Pacific Beach roll into the water after a long night of hitting the local nightlife scene, which boasts great music and local talent. Finally comes late morning, when most of the early-morning and midmorning crews are hanging out telling stories in the parking lots and breakfast joints around Pacific Beach.

Other Information

Local Surf Shops: Pacific Beach Surf Shop, 4150 Mission Blvd., Suite 161, San Diego; (858) 373-1138. Big Time Surf Shop, 4428 Ingraham, San Diego; (858) 483-2444.
Places to Stay: Crystal Pier Hotel, 4500 Ocean Blvd., San Diego; (858) 483-6983. Catamaran Resort Hotel, 3999 Mission Blvd., San Diego; (858) 488-1081.
Places to Eat: DaKine's, 4120 Mission Blvd., San Diego; (858) 274-8494. Kono's Cafe, 704 Garnet Ave., San Diego; (858) 483-1669. Wave House, 3125 Ocean Front Walk, San Diego; (858) 228-9283.

Sunset Cliffs
Difficult-to-reach Sunset Cliffs is an intermediate to advanced surfer break under most conditions. The current can be strong, and the swell produces fast, hollow waves.

Best tide: Low
Best swell direction: West, northwest
Best wave size: Waist high to head high
Bottom: Rock
Type of break: Point, right
Skill level: Intermediate to advanced
Best boards: Shortboard, longboard
Best seasons: Fall, winter, and spring
Crowds: Crowded
Water quality: Average
Hazards: Locals
Fees and permits: None

Finding the Break

From San Diego: Take I-5 and exit at Sunset Cliffs Drive. Head down Sunset Cliffs Boulevard into Point Loma and park at the top of the Sunset Cliffs Beach parking area. There's limited parking near the top of the access trail. GPS: N32 43.813 / W117 15.392

Surf Description

Sunset Cliffs is located on the shores of Point Loma. This community has a deeply rooted religious background anchored by Point Loma Nazarene University. There are two unusual things you'll notice about surfing Sunset Cliffs. One, not by coincidence, Sunday mornings tend to be less crowded here than at other breaks in San Diego; two, you don't hear a lot of profanity in the water. Currents can be extremely strong, and there's no easy put-in or takeout area for you and your board. Low tides will produce fast, hard-breaking waves, but at mid- to high tide the wave can be slow to washed out. Surf conditions vary a lot here.

Head over to SeaWorld, where the animals go crazy on cue.

The break at Sunset Cliffs stretches over a 3-mile area. Although there are a few beginner spots, the area should be tested only by an experienced paddler. One local who seems to have thorough knowledge of the area and all its breaks is Skip Frye. Devoutly committed to the history and heritage of surfing, Skip Frye has been a vocal advocate of fin design and its effect on board performance. If you do see him in the water, chances are he'll be on a longboard surfing more breaks along Sunset Cliffs than most people can surf in a week.

In the water at Sunset, if you look at the cliff side, you'll see some of the history of both Point Loma and our nation. Several coastal bunker-like defense structures sit along

Sunset Cliffs is like a box of chocolates: a lot of variety, a few surprises, and some of them are sweet. Chris Burkard

the cliff at the Cabrillo National Monument. They were built to protect San Diego from enemies who might approach by sea or air. From the viewpoints high above Sunset Cliffs, you can fully appreciate the various breaks Sunset has to offer. Don't be surprised to see quite a few sportfishing boats cruising along the outer limits of the horizon line. Sunset Cliffs is located near one of the most productive tuna-fishing grounds in California.

Other Information

Local Surf Shops: Point Loma Surf Shop, 4230 Voltaire St., San Diego; (619) 222-2674. South Coast Surf Shop, 5023 Newport Ave., San Diego; (619) 223-7017. Green Room Surf Shop, 1963 Abbott St., San Diego; (619) 226-1311.

Places to Stay: Hostelling International Point Loma, 3790 Udall St., San Diego; (619) 223-4778 or (800) 339-7263.

Places to Eat: Head back to Ocean Beach from Sunset Cliffs. Pizza Nova, 5120 N. Harbor Dr., San Diego; (619) 226-0268. Bali Hai, 2230 Shelter Island Dr., San Diego; (619) 222-1181.

Bryce Johnson

Ralph's is a long right point break that can unleash some of the best tube rides in all San Diego County. Ralph's is not one of the most popular breaks, so the crowd factor here is favorable. The wave works best in low to medium tide and is fairly easy to catch on the takeoff. Located near San Diego Bay, this is a great longboard wave. Although the break is safe, watch out for knucklehead boaters and the occasional sea creature seeking food.

Anthony Ghiglia

Located right in front of the Naval Air Station North Island at the Naval Base Coronado, North Island Beach—like Point Mugu—is pretty much owned and operated by the US government. Access is restricted, but the long stretch of beach at North Island has some surf. The only way to get to this area is to walk up from Coronado Beach. If you're feeling lucky, bring a shortboard for some fast closeout beach break.

Nathan French

Coronado is located just south of Naval Base Coronado. One of San Diego's most popular tourist beaches, Coronado can offer an excellent longboarding wave with mostly hollow-breaking lefts. It can get windy here, and when it does, the surf tends to be mushy and blown out, especially in the afternoons. In a south-to-westerly swell, Coronado can produce some advanced wave conditions that will challenge any ability level.

Silver Strand State Park, a long stretch of sandy shoreline extending down the southernmost tip of San Diego County, is a sand reef and beach break. Wind tends to be the biggest negative about the area, but it offers up some great views of downtown San Diego and the bay from its beaches. If the wave isn't consistently closing out, the best surfing will come from a medium tide with swell from the south. The beach is very family- and camping-friendly.

Imperial Beach

Imperial Beach can be a good beach break with the right conditions. Sandbars run all along the shoreline, creating closeouts and mushy peaks, and allowing for short lefts and rights.

Best tide: Medium
Best swell direction: West, northwest, southwest
Best wave size: Waist high to head high
Bottom: Sand
Type of break: Beach break, left, right
Skill level: Novice
Best board: Shortboard
Best season: Summer
Crowds: Uncrowded
Water quality: Poor
Hazards: Strong currents, polluted water
Fees and permits: None

Finding the Break

From San Diego: Take I-5 and exit at Palm Avenue. Take Palm Avenue toward the beach and turn onto Seacoast Drive. Imperial Beach runs down the coastline from the pier. There's parking near the pier or along any of the side streets that run along the beach. GPS: N32 34.772 / W117 07.957

Surf Description

If you've come this far south for surfing, chances are you're on a Tijuana holiday—intentionally or unintentionally. Imperial Beach sits at the bottom of a peninsula stretching from the coastal northern side of Coronado and the mouth of downtown San Diego on the inner bay side to California's southernmost border. The peninsula and the landscape that make up the coastal section are important to the breaks along its western shore.

The first or last beach in California—depending on whether you're coming or going—Imperial Beach sometimes has wind issues, sometimes has pollution issues, and sometimes is a great place to boost an air.   Chris Burkard

Mostly south- and west-facing, nearly all the coastal breaks in this area—including Imperial Beach—are protected from significant beach erosion. With its giant sandy shoreline, nearly the entire break along Imperial Beach is a gentle, shifting sandbar that remains consistent throughout the year. Imperial Beach, sometimes called IB, is the last decent break in California's southern coastline. It can get very windy and often has blown-out conditions, but when it's breaking, the long, sandy bottom can hold reasonable-size surf from knee to waist high. Any larger and the wave tends to close out.

Imperial Beach is unfortunately susceptible to toxic sewage dumps and other bio-hazards due to its location. Although the United States isn't much better, Mexico's sewage control during rainstorms and runoff into the ocean can be downright deadly. When the rains are heavy or there's a system overload, the sewer systems default to dumping thousands of tons of human waste into the ocean. Any California native surfer will tell you about the eye, ear, nose, or throat infection he or she got back when everyone thought it was no big deal to surf just after a heavy rain.

Other Information

Local Surf Shops: Surf Hut, 710 Seacoast Dr., Imperial Beach; (619) 575-7873. TNT Surfboards, 206 Palm Ave., Imperial Beach; (619) 424-8107. Salt Water Magic, 226 Palm Ave., Imperial Beach; (619) 423-7873.
Places to Stay: Super 8 Hotel, 1788 Palm Ave., San Diego; (619) 575-4421. Sand Castle Inn, 785 Seacoast Dr, Imperial Beach; (619) 429-4796.
Places to Eat: The Tin Fish, 910 Seacoast Dr., end of Imperial Beach Pier, Imperial Beach; (619) 628-8414.

Surf Index

About the Authors

Raul and Jeff are California natives who have been friends since grade school. They've been surfing and playing in the ocean together all their lives and have both traveled extensively for several years. Raul lives in Aptos and Jeff in Carlsbad; they surf their favorite breaks every chance they get. Raul is also the author of *The Art of Surfing: A Training Manual for the Developing and Competitive Surfer*, another FalconGuide published by Globe Pequot Press.

Originally from Santa Cruz, Ben Marcus was an editor at *Surfer* magazine for ten years. He has surfed and traveled extensively and is now unashamedly caught up in the standup-paddleboarding craze.